THE PINK LADY

THE
PINK LADY

The Many Lives of Helen Gahagan Douglas

SALLY DENTON

BLOOMSBURY PRESS

NEW YORK • BERLIN • LONDON • SYDNEY

Published by Bloomsbury Press, New York

All papers used by Bloomsbury Press are natural, recyclable products made from wood grown in well-managed forests. The manufacturing processes conform to the environmental regulations of the country of origin.

LIBRARY OF CONGRESS CATALOGING-IN-PUBLICATION DATA

Denton, Sally.
     The pink lady : the many lives of Helen Gahagan Douglas / Sally Denton.—1st
U.S. ed.
         p. cm.
     Includes bibliographical references and index.
     ISBN-13: 978-1-59691-480-3 (alk. paper hardcover)
     ISBN-10: 1-59691-480-7 (alk. paper hardcover)
     1. Douglas, Helen Gahagan, 1900–1980. 2. Legislators—United States—Biography.
3. United States. Congress. House—Biography. 4. Actors—United States—
Biography. I. Title. II. Title: Many lives of Helen Gahagan Douglas.

     E748.D677D46 2009
     973.9092—dc22
     [B]

                                                                                         2009008148

First published by Bloomsbury Press in 2009
This paperback edition published in 2012

Paperback ISBN: 978-1-60819-100-0

1   3   5   7   9   10   8   6   4   2

Typeset by Westchester Book Group
Printed in the United States of America by Quad/Graphics, Fairfield, Pennsylvania

For Ralph and Sara Denton,
Unreconstructed New Dealers

The liberty of a democracy is not safe if the people tolerate the growth of private power to a point where it becomes stronger than their democratic state itself. That, in its essence, is fascism—ownership of government by an individual, by a group, or any controlling private power.

—Franklin D. Roosevelt

CONTENTS

THE PINK LADY

PROLOGUE

It was a warm Saturday afternoon in September 1938. Recently home from the hospital with her newborn daughter, Helen Gahagan Douglas was resting in her light-filled Hollywood Hills bedroom. She could barely hear the din of conversation taking place outside her open windows. Her husband, Melvyn, had volunteered their spacious poolside terrace for a fund-raiser. Propped up in a sea of pillows, she had a view of the city and the Pacific Ocean.

Suddenly someone burst into the bedroom. "Helen! You really must come and listen to what they are saying. My God, those poor migrant children are suffering from pellagra! They're starving!"

Helen rose from her bed, dressed, and moved toward the back of the gathering to listen. Three years earlier, the biggest dust storm in the history of the U.S. blanketed five states, the Dust Bowl winds lifting millions of acres of topsoil and creating black blizzards that reached as far east as New York. Blamed on rapacious, profit-driven farming, the ecological disaster left untold thousands homeless, depopulated entire communities, and launched the unprecedented influx of migrant families into California. "Tractored out" by landowners switching to modern machinery, or driven out by untillable dirt, they packed their belongings into jalopies and headed west looking for work. An estimated six thousand of these "Okies" were pouring into California every month. "Like a swarm of invading locusts," wrote Mildred Adams, "migrants crept in over all the roads . . . For wings, they had rattletrap automobiles, their fenders tied with string, and curtains flapping in the breeze; loaded with babies, bedding, bundles, a tin tub tied on behind, a bicycle or a baby carriage balanced precariously on the top. Often they came with no funds and no prospects, apparently trusting that heaven would provide for them . . . They camped on the outskirts of town, and their camps became new suburbs."

Confined to filthy camps, thousands of starving families were "herded about like animals," living without toilets or showers, while local officials and growers fought to keep the federal government from supplying the migrants with food and medical supplies, fearing that they would form permanent communities, join unions, and, most significant, interfere with the cheap Mexican laborers they were shuttling across the border and paying slave wages. Importing labor was far cheaper than establishing schools and health-care clinics for American migrant workers, so the growers used every method possible, including force, to get the migrants to move on.

Helen and Melvyn had attended dinner parties at which the subject of the "Okies" was raised and they were frequently appalled at the lack of compassion shown by many of their peers. They "listened in astonishment to people making comfortable statements about how the situation was exaggerated or that the migrants should stop being so lazy and dirty . . . there was an entrenched aversion to recognizing that a problem existed." But nothing had prepared her for the magnitude of suffering she learned about that day in her comfortable Hollywood Hills backyard.

"I could not know it then, and did not realize it until years later, but when I left my bed that afternoon I took my first step into politics."

The thirty-eight-year-old woman who rose from her sickbed that day had led a thoroughly apolitical East Coast life of privilege and fortune. The daughter of a millionaire engineer, wife of one of Hollywood's highest-paid leading men, a successful stage actress and opera singer known on two continents, and an heiress in her own right, Helen now shed her rarefied, insulated past. She would become instead a forceful advocate for America's oppressed and dispossessed, throwing herself into the cause with the same tenacity that had defined her previous two careers, and incurring the ire of powerful enemies and a legion of impassioned followers.

Within days of the patio conclave, Helen agreed to head the John Steinbeck Committee—an organization named for the California author of *The Grapes of Wrath*, a novel about a fictional family of Oklahoma sharecroppers. "I have read a book recently," President Franklin Delano Roosevelt had announced in 1940, referring to Steinbeck's novel. "There were 500,000 Americans living between its covers . . . I would like to see the California Columbia Basin devoted to [their] care." By the following year, the book had sold well beyond five hundred thousand copies. Helen toured the camps and encountered men, women, and children with "faces stamped with poverty and despair."

That *The Grapes of Wrath* was such an enormous bestseller—also garnering the Pulitzer Prize and the National Book Award for its author—was ironic, considering Steinbeck's refusal to write a story on the migrants for *Fortune* magazine. "I'm sorry but I simply can't make money on these people," Steinbeck wrote to his New York literary agent. "The suffering is too great for me to cash in on it . . . the water is a foot deep in the tents and the children are up on the beds and there is no food and no fire . . . It is the most heartbreaking thing in the world . . . so don't get me a job for a slick. I want to put a tag of shame on the greedy bastards who are responsible for this . . ."

She quickly became the national spokesperson for the plight of the migrant workers and began organizing relief for them. In a pattern that would become her future trademark she culled all the information she could find on the subject. Indeed, the thoroughness with which she tackled every issue would be admired by even her most bitter enemies. "When you dig into a problem you will learn what you need to know," she would later instruct her daughter. "You will learn how to solve it, you'll stumble upon authenticity and the people with the answers." Determined to become informed, she studied the migrant-worker crisis as if preparing for her next role. She wrote to the Department of Agriculture requesting statistics and information and inquiring about the part that the Farm Extension Service might play in alleviating the situation. In characteristic fashion, Helen was capable of holding all sides, of seeing clearly the tangled complexities and three-dimensional aspects of a problem that eluded others. Her world was not black and white, but murky shades of gray that she struggled to define with clarity.

She recognized that the migrant disaster was not as simple as the California media was portraying it to be. "The migrants were descended from settlers who had worked single-crop farms, usually cotton or corn, that quickly depleted the soil. Too poor to allow the land to lie fallow, and often illiterate and without any knowledge of crop rotation, they allowed their farms to become less and less productive," she wrote. "Some had never seen running water. Few knew the rudiments of hygiene or nutrition." In fact, Helen had returned home with a case of impetigo after her first visit to one of the camps.

Sixty years before Hillary Clinton announced her intention to run for president, Helen was the first woman in America who had the capacity, the credentials, the ambition, and the political gravity to realistically aspire to the highest office in the land. During her rise as an American female politician, she struggled to define herself in the highly charged climate of Red-scare America. Her trail from Broadway star to California congresswoman to vice-presidential contender to senatorial candidate to nuclear-détente advocate brought her into the spheres of some of the most powerful men in American history. Her relationships with Franklin Roosevelt, Lyndon Johnson, Harry Truman, and Richard Nixon were remarkable, and how each of these men related to her spoke volumes about who they were—and what America was and is as a nation.

It all began at the turn of the twentieth century, in Brooklyn, New York.

1

DIVA 1900–1930

I'm Nobody! Who are you?
Are you—Nobody—Too?
Then there's a pair of us!
Don't tell! They'd advertise—you know!

How dreary—to be—Somebody!
How public—like a Frog—
To tell one's name—the livelong June—
To an admiring Bog!

—Emily Dickinson
(Favorite poem of Helen Gahagan Douglas)

HER LIFE WOULD begin and end in sun-filled rooms—the eighty years between her birth and death shaped by an appreciation of light, a shedding of light, a search for light. "In every house we ever occupied, she wanted the windows to be wider," her husband would write at the end of her life. "She thought no room could have too many windows."

She entered the world at the beginning of a new century, on the eve of what one historian called "the great moral upheaval" that three decades later solidified as the New Deal that would shape her career. Fortunately, in her final years, while battling terminal cancer, she began writing her autobiography. Friends and publishers had implored her to do so for some time, but it was not until after her seventieth birthday that she embarked on the project in earnest. For decades she had refused to discuss her nemesis, Richard Nixon. She worked on the manuscript until the day she died in 1980, her New York hospital room filled with files, clippings, photographs, and stories from her extraordinary life. The book was completed by her assistant and published posthumously by Doubleday. Without her memoir, the real measure of her existence would have been frustratingly elusive.

Born on November 25, 1900, and christened Helen Mary, she was the daughter of an ambitious and brilliant civil engineer and a petite and stylish schoolteacher. "We were raised in acute awareness of our family lines," Helen, as she was called, would write. Her fascination with bloodlines was neither an elite absorption nor boastful obsession with personal lineage. She was descended not from great wealth or American aristocracy, but from solid Midwestern pioneer stock. Prosperous, principled, and genteel, Helen's paternal ancestors served as models for a civic-minded life. The forebears on her mother's side were Wisconsin farmers known for their physical strength and, especially, for their exquisite singing voices.

Walter Hamer Gahagan II was a towering, well-built, handsome man with a fiery Irish temper. He was a native of Troy, Ohio; his great-grandfather had founded the town of Dayton. Raised in comfortable circumstances and instilled with Victorian paternalism, devout Protestantism, and a commitment to education and intellectual rigor, Gahagan was the firstborn son to William Henry Harrison Gahagan and Hannah M. Smith. His father died when Walter was six years old, leaving Hannah a young widow with three small children—Walter and two younger sisters. She quit teaching school in order to manage the large family farm, and when Walter decided to pursue engineering rather than farming, she mortgaged the property to send him to Ohio State Technical School. A man of quick mind and high character, he excelled academically, and by 1887 had graduated from the Massachusetts Institute of Technology and returned to Dayton, where he amassed a small fortune constructing railways across the West. He helped build the Eads Bridge in Saint Louis—the first span across the Mississippi River—and oversaw the construction of seven bridges over the Snake and Red Rivers.

The railroad business took him to Lodi, Wisconsin, where, in 1896, at the age of thirty, he met the beautiful Lillian Mussen. Known for her independent streak and string of suitors, Lillian was working for her hotelier father, James Mussen. Also thirty, Lillian was accustomed to a more liberated lifestyle than her female peers. Her mother had died of pneumonia when Lillian was seven, leaving James with nine children to raise. When he remarried, his new wife wanted little to do with Lillian, forcing the girl to become self-reliant at a young age. By the time Lillian met Walter she had already worked as a schoolteacher and owned a millinery shop, and she was a highly regarded singer in the church choir. Both her beauty and voice set her apart in the thriving community. Her lithe figure and arresting loveliness drew attention, but what most attracted Walter to her was her voice. "She was one of those rare individuals who fell out of bed and hit a high F," Helen would later say of her mother's innate talent. When Walter listened to Lillian sing at the local Methodist church, he fell in love then and there. Though Walter was immediately smitten with her, he would not consider marriage without first seeking his mother's approval of his choice. He courted her for four months while awaiting the arrival of Hannah, who, fortunately for the young couple, pronounced Lillian suitable.

"Unlike many of his generation, he had no contempt for women's intelligence," Helen would recall of her father. "His example was his unusual mother, the formidable Hannah Gahagan, who was sent to Antioch College by her father despite family outrage and intense opposition." Indeed, Hannah had been an indomitable force. After being widowed in the early 1870s, she had become a leading feminist: She had single-handedly integrated libraries in Ohio that had been closed to women under the prevailing belief that women needn't be educated, she had founded the activist Women's Christian Association in Troy, and had become the first female school board member in the state of Ohio.

"Everything his mother did Father found praiseworthy," Helen later recalled. "He picked my mother as his bride only after his mother checked her out. His plan was to raise sons to join him in his Gahagan Company."

If Walter was enthusiastic and fervent, Lillian was decidedly reticent. While she admired her future mother-in-law for her spunky independence, early indications suggested that her fiancé might not have been so progressive. First Walter insisted that she sell her bicycle—a demand that alarmed Lillian, who cherished the freedom it afforded her. Next he insisted that she abandon her dreams of an opera career in order to raise a family. An operatic coach once compared her to Nellie Melba, the legendary Australian bel canto soprano, and she passionately harbored a desire to sing professionally. Still, despite her misgivings, she was charmed by the handsome and dignified man and excited by the prospect of a life in New York, where he had decided to base his engineering firm. They were quickly married by an Episcopal priest.

The couple bought a small but fashionable home in Brooklyn's upper-class Park Slope neighborhood, and by 1898 Lillian had given birth to twin boys, William and Frederick. The following year Lillian was pregnant again, and Walter moved the family to temporary quarters in Boonton, New Jersey, where he was supervising the construction of a dam. It was there that Lillian gave birth to Helen. Two years later Helen would have a little sister, Lillian, and the Gahagans moved their lively brood into an imposing mansion at 231 Lincoln Place in Park Slope.

Designed by Frederick Law Olmsted, the founder of American landscape architecture, and his English colleague, Calvert Vaux, the 585-acre Prospect Park was the backdrop for the Park Slope neighborhood. The Gahagans selected the tranquil locale because of its proximity to the Berkeley Institute, an elite private academy for girls; it was also near an equally highbrow school for boys. The streets were lit by gas lanterns, and horse-drawn carriages conveyed the residents on their daily outings. The area was regularly patrolled by one familiar policeman, providing security to the Gahagan clan in its upper-crust world. Helen later drew a comparison of her Park Slope upbringing to the set of the 1939 Broadway play *Life with Father*, about an upscale nineteenth-century New York suburban couple and their rambunctious red-headed children.

The high-ceilinged, wood-paneled, and book-lined rooms were large and airy. Enormous windows opened onto lush gardens, marble fireplaces warmed nearly every room, and the banister of a massive center hallway staircase provided enjoyment to the children—who numbered five with the birth of Walter Jr. in 1910. Walter kept adding windows, as if there could never be enough. "Noisy, gregarious, affectionate," is how Helen described her family—Walter the stern and pragmatic patriarch, Lillian his fun-loving and creative counterpart.

"Lillian, do you see what the children are doing?" Walter once shouted at his wife. "They're sliding down the banisters."

"Yes, I know. I taught them how," Lillian answered.

"Do you want them to fall and break their necks?" he bellowed.

"No, that's why I showed them how. I've been sliding down myself to set an example."

Helen was a feisty and curious child, strong-willed and theatrical. Irreverent and mischievous, she naturally became the center of attention among the five siblings. A voracious reader, precocious entertainer, and talented singer, she charmed them all—brothers, sisters, parents, relatives, and friends were drawn to her. Her physical attributes—her mane of thick golden hair, sharp blue eyes, alarming height, and robust athleticism—demanded attention as well. She grew so quickly that her mother compared her to a "white potato sprout," and yet, in an era when diminutive features defined feminine beauty, she embraced her unique stature without a hint of self-consciousness. A tomboy determined to keep up with her three brothers, she swam, skied, played golf, rode horses, and took up boxing when President Teddy Roosevelt popularized the sport. When she sneaked away in the family car trying to teach herself how to drive, she slammed it into a tree. Still, she was proud of her accomplishment.

The supporting structure of the woman she would become lay in the character and discipline of the man and woman who raised her. Each parent brought a straightforward approach to life's complexities and the individual's responsibility to society. Behind each parent lay several generations of hardworking, honest, middle- and upper-class American virtues.

Lillian Gahagan imparted to her daughter a devotion to the Episcopal church, a commitment to the value of education, an appreciation of art, music, and culture, and the notion that women, whether single or married, should pursue a career. Despite or perhaps because of the demand that her husband had made that she stop singing, Lillian actively, if covertly, encouraged Helen's obsession with acting and singing.

Stifling her dream of joining the Metropolitan Opera had been the heartbreak of Lillian's life. When an opera coach begged her to sign a contract, Walter had given her an ultimatum. "You must give up this notion of having a singing career or I'll take you back to Wisconsin and leave you there. I love your voice but I didn't marry you to have you become a professional singer. I want you to be my wife and the mother of my children. If you want to live with me, you can't sing opera." Lillian cried all night—racked with a disappointment that she would carry until her death. But she stoically turned her attention to child rearing and never spoke of it again.

Helen watched her easygoing mother manage a household full of energetic children, never losing her temper or imposing her will. It would not be until years later, as she faced her own career decisions, that Helen grasped the full impact of her father's squelching of her mother's artistic talents. For now she marveled at the energy her mother focused upon her family, as if she were running a small country. Lillian trained and supervised a succession of Swedish and German maids and accommodated the erratic schedule of her husband and the comings and goings of her offspring. "At the Gahagans' no two of us ate breakfast or lunch at the same time," Helen recalled. "We usually snatched something from the table and ate on the run, late to school."

An eternal optimist, Lillian created a surprisingly serene environment for her noisy family, and though she seemed unobtrusive, no detail of their childhood escaped her meticulous attention. Helen adopted her mother's laissez-faire attitude toward life, a belief that what is meant to be will be. But despite her mother's calm example, Helen embodied the volatility that her father modeled. "It's good to have a temper, Helen," her mother once told her. "But you'd better get it under control or you'll go through life apologizing."

As gentle and understated as Lillian was, Walter was outsized and boisterous, and perhaps because Helen resembled him in personality and disposition they were often at loggerheads. "He was an impressive man who seemed to use up all the breathable space in a room . . . he was physically big, full of impatient energy, and possessed of a flaming Irish temper," Helen wrote of her father. She adored him and ardently sought his approval, and though she never openly defied him they argued incessantly. He loved the outdoors and would never allow the curtains to be drawn in a room—behavior that Helen would emulate all of her life.

He was alarmed by her consistent and growing love of the theater, and was determined that she would never become an actress. "In his mind, *actress* and *whore* were interchangeable," Helen wrote. His views reflected a common perception of the era that "theatrical folk" possessed notoriously loose morals, combined with his knowledge that some of his friends had mistresses who were stage actresses. He harangued her about the importance of education and demanded that her future include graduation from college. "When I began to read avidly, as he did, he cautioned me to be skeptical. Printing something did not make it true. The written page should be tested." She must learn how to *think*, he insisted. "Did I want to be just a breeding machine?" she remembered him thundering at her one afternoon. He thought uneducated women were broodmares, and he had no patience for useless women in the world—an irony considering the ultimatum he had given his wife. Thinking was Walter's theme in his many instructions to the Gahagan children. "To think was to be in control of oneself, to be less likely to be manipulated, to avoid being a slave to emotion," Helen extrapolated from his lectures. "Thinking, he told us, doesn't come naturally. It requires training. One must gather facts with which to ponder a subject."

Walter took seriously his role as head of the family and demanded that all of his children adhere to a set of unwavering principles rooted in honesty. He taught them never to lie and to make one's word one's bond. He was a dominant force at the dinner table and encouraged each child to explore his or her mind and to converse with confidence.

In spite of their many differences, Walter and Lillian were exceedingly compatible and were united in placing family above all else. Walter wanted nothing to do with domestic logistics, making clear that his life was in the world and Lillian's was in the home. On Sundays the family dined at the nearby Montauk Club—a posh private men's club that allowed women to attend only one day a week. Lillian had season tickets to the Metropolitan Opera and took Helen to every performance from an early age. They routinely visited the Brooklyn Museum and went on cultural outings in Manhattan. All five children were expected to regularly attend the Episcopal church with their mother. Walter eschewed organized religion, claiming he had had enough in Ohio to last a lifetime.

In the summer of 1912, the entire family went abroad. During an extended stay at the spa at Baden-Baden, Helen studied German and attended concerts. Two years later, Walter announced that he did not think it healthy for his children to spend their summers in resort hotels and instructed his wife to find a vacation home in the country. Lillian settled on the Upper Connecticut Valley of Vermont, in a village called Fairlee, near Lake Morey. The family rented a cottage until a Victorian mansion called Cliff Mull finally came on the market. Lillian had desired the property from a distance, enchanted by its setting and expansive veranda. Cliff Mull was a family paradise that offered hiking through dense forests, a private tennis court, lake swimming, canoeing, and camping under the stars, and for the next sixty-five years it would be Helen's favorite place in the world. In her tumultuous future, marked by periods of unrelenting challenges and searing attacks, memories of Cliff Mull centered her. No matter how stressful or precarious life could become, she was always able to close her eyes and transport herself to the quietude of the woods. As a grown woman she would seek solace and renewal there. "It brings me peace. I expand and feel the sweetness and the sadness of this transitory life." Every time she packed her suitcases to leave Vermont and return to her preternaturally busy world, she thought of a line in a play about the tragic Irish heroine Deirdre. "It's a heartbreak to the wise that we have the same things for a short space only."

A natural-born actor, Helen spent her childhood performing for her younger sister, Lilli. After prayers and lights-out, Helen would stand on her bed and whisper lines from various plays. In the daytime the pool table was her stage and she gathered an audience of not only her siblings but the many children in both the Park Slope and Fairlee neighborhoods. Every day she performed eye exercises in front of a mirror, conveying different emotions with each gaze. She practiced flirting with her twin brothers and their friends, once annoying them so much that they carried her down three flights of stairs and threw her, fully clothed, into Lake Morey. From the age of five she had been obsessed with a stage career, and from the age of five she had known of her father's opposition to such an occupation. Undaunted, she spent her childhood and teenage years preparing to be an actress, determined that she would eventually win his capitulation if not endorsement.

"Don't make such a fuss, Helen," her mother wisely told her. "If it is right for you to be an actress, you'll do it."

Though of keen mind and intense curiosity, she had been a poor student from the beginning. The Berkeley Institute for Girls, a high-minded academy named for the Irish philosopher George Berkeley, boasted a curriculum and discipline guaranteed to bring both cultural refinement and a classical education to the daughters of Brooklyn's upper class. She was held back a year because of her ineptness at spelling, and throughout her elementary years she received mostly failing grades. She not only abhorred the same-sex school, she was bored beyond salvation. In the eighth grade alone she was tardy fifty-nine times and absent thirty-eight days. Her aptitude obviously lay in music and drama—areas in which the Institute had no expertise—and she was forced to pursue her passions on her own and without guidance. Still, she was wildly popular, making her early years more fun than expected despite the academic tedium of Berkeley.

The arrival of Elizabeth Grimball at Berkeley shaped the course of Helen's future. The young, enormously talented woman from Charleston, South Carolina, began teaching elocution and drama during Helen's freshman year. "Her arrival dazzled the stagestruck person I was," Helen recalled. "My dreams had a focus, her department. She became my adviser, coach and ally." The attraction was immediate and mutual. Helen was ecstatic to have a venue for her passion, and Grimball recognized the instinctive capacity of her new student. Finally Helen's grade-point average improved due to her high marks in Grimball's classes, though the rest of her performance remained desultory. Grimball was on her way to becoming a renowned Broadway producer, and her Berkeley productions attracted the attention of professional actors and critics. Helen starred in many of Grimball's productions, which brought her her first rave review in the Brooklyn newspaper. Even her father grudgingly tolerated what he considered Helen's obsession with Grimball as long as she continued her other studies as well. But when he thought she had taken it too far, he intervened.

When she was eighteen, the tension between Helen and her father over her dramatic pursuits erupted into one of the most brutal, memorable arguments they ever had. The family had just arrived in Vermont for the summer and Walter Gahagan had received Helen's final high school grades. She had failed every subject. Coldly furious, he interrogated her. "Have you stopped studying?" Candid to a fault, she confessed that indeed she had abandoned her academic studies. She had, she admitted to him, turned her full attention to preparation for the theater. In fact, Helen had become so devoted to Elizabeth Grimball, and so determined to find her way to the New York stage, that she had been cutting classes in order to help Al Jolson and other Broadway stars sell war bonds from the steps of the New York Public Library.

Undaunted, Helen beseeched her father to allow a theatrical career, hoping to sway him with tales of her many successes and laudatory reviews. Such boasting galvanized him, and he berated her for her naïveté, charging that compliments had addled her brain. "Young, attractive girls always were flattered," she later wrote about what her father told her. "If I didn't understand that, I lived in a dream world. I would get no compliments later on unless I was educated." If not for the deep-seated and unexpressed resentment she felt toward his diminishment of her mother's singing, she might have credited his advice. As it was, the more he pushed, the more she resisted.

Her father's tirade lasted an entire day and into the evening, and the distraught and histrionic Helen only agitated him further. She stormed out of the house, determined to climb a nearby mountain and demand direction from God. Family legend held that a rheumatic Welsh great-uncle had made a bargain with the Creator that left him pain-free for life, and Helen determined to find a similar solution. Circling Sawyer Mountain, whose summit eluded her, Helen climbed aimlessly as the brambles scratched her limbs and tore her skirt. Finally she "sank down and sobbed" until her mind cleared and she suddenly saw her rebellion as self-defeating. "If I defied my father I would defeat everything I wanted to accomplish later on," she realized. "I resolved that I would prove to him and to myself that I could concentrate on studies when I wanted to, and that I could sail through college. Father wasn't blocking me. *I* was. After I paid my dues, I could become an actress."

She returned to Cliff Mull and announced her intention to enroll immediately in the Dartmouth summer program, reasoning that if a college education was a prerequisite for a theatrical career, she had no time to lose. Impervious to the fact that Dartmouth was "only for *boys*," as her sister Lilli reminded her, she quipped: "They manage to get know-nothing football players ready for Dartmouth, so they can just go to work on me." She persuaded the school to take her, and while living in a boardinghouse in Hanover she researched college-preparatory boarding schools. By the fall of 1919 she was enrolled in the Capen School in Northampton, Massachusetts, where, in uncharacteristic fashion, she immersed herself in academics. While most of the Capen graduates matriculated at nearby Smith College, Helen set her sights on Barnard—the elite women's college and sister school of Columbia University where women were encouraged to break away from the constraints of early-twentieth-century female roles and to learn, as one historian put it, "the masculine routes of power: how to cooperate, how to compete openly, how to lead."

Before taking her college entrance exams the following summer, she went back to Dartmouth to be tutored in Latin by Harry Edwin Burton, the renowned Daniel Webster scholar. The tutoring succeeded: Helen was accepted by Barnard, much to her father's apparent surprise. She had picked the college because it was close to home and family, and, especially, because it was in New York City, where Elizabeth Grimball had begun running a school and production company near Broadway called Inter-Theater Arts. Helen quickly found her niche in the drama society Wigs and Cues. A professor noticed her preoccupation with all things Irish—from her heritage to Irish independence—and introduced her to a Yeats scholar who would become a lifelong friend. Alis De Sola was Helen's mirror opposite—petite, brunette, reserved, intellectual, and snobbish. Still, the two recognized and appreciated the complementary aspects of their personalities, and soon they were collaborating on a one-act play they called *Shadow of the Moon*, based on an Irish legend and jointly submitted as an English term paper. Helen organized the material while Alis did the writing, and when they showed the play to Grimball she enthusiastically agreed to produce it at Barnard, casting Helen in the lead role of Fand. Grimball's production ultimately "proved to be her ticket out of college and onto the Broadway stage," as one biographer put it. An associate of Grimball's—a playwright named Harry Wagstaff

Gribble—came to see the production out of curiosity and was so taken with Helen's acting talent that he asked her to play the lead role in a satiric comedy he had just written.

Shoot opened off-Broadway, and the twenty-one-year-old Helen created a buzz in New York's theater circles. Her father tolerated her appearance in *Shoot*, thinking it an extension of her Barnard curriculum. But when noted Broadway director John Cromwell saw her performance and offered her a part in *Manhattan*—a play he was producing—Helen's academic career ended. A partner of famed stage producer William A. Brady Jr., Cromwell brought Helen to the attention of Brady's wife, the actress Gladys George.

George attended *Manhattan* at the MacDowell Theater in August 1922 and was riveted by Helen's ability. She raved about Helen to her husband, who was looking for someone to play the role of the ingenue in a new Broadway play he was producing, written by his collaborator, Owen Davis. Brady came to see the next performance and was equally dazzled. He called Helen immediately and "ordered me to stop whatever I was doing and come at once to the Playhouse," she recalled. When she arrived at his office, the "blustering, rough-tongued Irishman" ushered her in, thrust the script for *Dreams for Sale* into her hands, and asked her if she wanted to play the lead. Though she found the play "trivial" and the role "silly," she leapt at the chance.

"I bravely told my parents that I would not be going to Barnard after all."

Walter Gahagan was predictably livid. Brady had demanded that Helen commit to a five-year contract and was threatening to cancel the opening of the play if she refused to sign it. Afraid of the breach it would cause with her father, she refused. At the final dress rehearsal she was distracted and panicked, terrified to sign the contract and openly defy her father, and terrified not to sign it and miss the once-in-a-lifetime opportunity that lay before her.

Her playwright producer friend Harry Gribble empathized with her plight and offered to intervene with her father. Though her instincts told her it was a mistake, she agreed to let Gribble accompany her home to Park Slope and make an appeal to her father. Her father's opposition would melt, Gribble assured her, once Gahagan understood that his daughter had a brilliant career ahead of her. But as Helen suspected, Walter Gahagan could not be swayed. From her upstairs bedroom Helen listened to the two men below.

"Father's bellow, 'NO!' could be heard down the block." His daughter was not going to be an actress, he shouted. There would be no five-year contract. Helen would return to Barnard as a junior to continue her education. Exhausted, Helen drifted off to sleep as the two men argued into the night. When she awakened the following morning—the day the play was scheduled to open—her father had already left the house. Nervous about the opening, even more apprehensive over a confrontation with Brady, she retreated to her dressing room at the playhouse. A drunken Brady burst through the door, knocking over jars of cold cream and rouge. "Sign that, young lady, or the curtain doesn't go up and we don't open," the belligerent producer said, throwing the contract onto her dressing table before stomping out.

She sat paralyzed, unable to make a decision, uncertain if the inebriated Brady was bluffing. At that moment in stage history, women actresses were under the thumb of a patriarchal hierarchy, and Helen's youth and inexperience made her even more susceptible to such bullying. The actress of the early 1920s, while respected and even revered in Great Britain, was an outcast in American society where, as one scholar put it, "her mobility and professional equality did not enable her to fit into a world where a woman's sphere was solely the home and the family." With the enfranchisement of women barely two years old, the self-confidence and self-assurance Helen mustered at this moment was unprecedented. "I felt like one of his prizefighters," she later wrote about how Brady handled her, ". . . about to climb into the ring."

When her friend John Cromwell knocked on the door she faced more male pressure. He drew up a chair and told her calmly and quietly that Brady was serious about canceling the play, that Brady's threat was real rather than mere histrionics. Cromwell urged her to sign, convincing her that her father would become reconciled to her choice once he saw her performance and recognized her potential. While she thought the tactics of both Brady and Cromwell to be disingenuous,

she knew that after demanding independence from her father for so
long, she had no choice but to sign. "If I didn't assert myself now, I
would never be independent of my father," she reasoned. "The play
would have to open in order to show him that I had a talent worthy
of his respect." The difficulty, of course, would be to get her father to
attend.

At twenty-two years old, Helen Gahagan debuted on Broadway in
Dreams for Sale and was an immediate sensation. When the curtain
came down she found her sister and brothers backstage in her dressing room. Lilli told her that her parents had indeed attended and that
they were waiting for her outside. As she left the theater she spotted
her mother and father standing near the family car. Her mother was
obviously jubilant, but Helen saw only sadness and resignation in her
father's face and demeanor. When Brady burst out of the theater and
swaggered over to them, she watched her father stiffen. "Keep her decent," Gahagan barked at Brady. "Good night, sir."

Classically beautiful and staggeringly talented, the "new girl on the
block" was compared to Ethel Barrymore and Helen Hayes. HELEN
GAHAGAN BECOMES STAGE STAR OVERNIGHT, headlined the *Brooklyn Daily
Eagle*. In smaller typeface a sidebar charted her improbable rise under
the caption *Parents Opposed Career*. "The first-nighters had gone to the
Playhouse wondering who this newcomer might be who was entrusted
with the leading role in the new Owen Davis play," the reviewer wrote.
"They left wondering how she could have gained her poise and evi-
dent stage experience without Broadway ever having heard of her."

In the end, despite her father's overbearing insistence, she left college
after two years. "Her father and I have done all we could to hold her
back," Lillian told the press, "but she has so much talent we could not
do it." Eager to pursue her calling to the stage—one of the few professional venues where women could experience financial and personal
equality with men—she saw Barnard as pointless for her grander ambi-
tions. She idolized the famous French actress Sarah Bernhardt and was
ecstatic to be compared to her heroine, the Italian Eleonora Duse,
whom Helen described as "the consummate actress." Given her strait-
laced upbringing and moralizing father, Helen naturally bridled at what
she described to a newspaper reporter as the "promiscuous lovemaking

a few feet behind the footlights." Still, she thought the American stage was on the brink of reaching literary and theatrical heights comparable to Europe's finest theaters, and she intended to be a part of it. She aspired to roles in Henrik Ibsen's prestigious works, and even of owning a theater in which she produced and directed plays that she had written.

"You know," she told her friend De Sola, ". . . anything I really want, anything, I can get. I just have to want it enough."

The brilliant but difficult Brady was roundly praised for discovering Helen—"a real acting genius in the person of the young woman who was never heard of before in all theatredom," as the New York Review described her. It was the beginning of a stellar career at an electrifying and innovative time on Broadway. The New York stage had entered what critics were calling the Golden Age—an era of spectacularly gifted writers, producers, and actors. One of "the most exciting and vibrant decades in the history of American drama," as one historian put it, the 1920s ushered in a period of newly discovered stars, literary geniuses, musical prodigies, and unparalleled commercial successes. Helen found herself at the center of the theatrical universe, with producers vying for her in a ferociously competitive industry. Her peers included such legends as Humphrey Bogart, Katharine Cornell, John Drew Jr., and Ethel, John, and Lionel Barrymore, underscoring the singular position in which she found herself with a five-year contract that assured her of starring roles. "Few, no matter how talented, stepped from any preparatory environment—stock company, drama school, or college theater—to a starring role on Broadway with a leading producer without a long and often discouraging apprenticeship," biographer Ingrid Scobie wrote of the rarity. "And to have this chance at the pinnacle of American theater was the chance of a lifetime."

Throughout the decade she would work not only with Brady but with such greats as George Tyler and David Belasco. She rejected each bad script that came her way, holding out for the best: "I was determined not to appear in any more trashy, poorly written productions." She exuberantly accepted a part in Fashions for Men, written by the Hungarian playwright Ferenc Molnár. That play's opening in Philadelphia brought her to the attention of the famous Philharmonic Hall conductor Leopold Stokowski, who attempted to take the starlet as his mistress. Then at the height of his career, Stokowski had a harem of European and American stage and opera stars.

He was "handsome, tall, slender, sensual, straight as an arrow, with a mane of yellow hair springing from his forehead," as Helen described him. Her encounter with him was innocent, and though she might have pursued a relationship, the "long arm" of her father had reached Philadelphia in the person of a society matron whom Helen barely knew and who demanded that Helen never again be alone with Stokowski. "He . . . admires . . . beautiful women," her father's emissary warned. "He *collects* them . . . it is better for your reputation . . . if you never see him again—*alone*."

Fashions for Men opened in New York before traveling to Chicago, and the night after it ended, she opened with the lead in *Chains*, written by a young playwright named Jules Eckert Goodman. Playing the role of Jean Trowbridge, a young single pregnant woman who refuses to marry the father of the child because she doesn't love him, Helen saw the character as emblematic of the modern woman. There followed a string of plays over the next five years—C.M.S. McLellan's *Leah Kleschna*; Walter Hasenclever's *Beyond*; Laszlo Lakatos's *The Sapphire Ring*; *Enchanted April*, written by an Englishwoman whose pseudonym was Elizabeth; *Young Woodley* by John Van Druten; Sir Arthur Wing Pinero's *Trelawney of the "Wells"*; and Victorien Sardou's *Diplomacy*. Naturally, the plays met with varying degrees of success. But Helen's performances were regularly praised. "Such a combination . . . of beauty, grace, sure technique, and intelligent comprehension of a role is seldom found in the theater," wrote a reviewer of one of her appearances. "This young lady with the timbered, quavering voice, the tragic eyes, and the bitter lips" rose "to the heights of greatness . . . The spectator sat petrified with heart pounding and hands feverishly hot . . . Miss Gahagan is a mystic." One renowned critic compared her to the great Duse, calling Helen "an acting prodigy" who, like Duse, had "a consuming love of art, a worship of individual ideals that transcends everything else."

Helen's entrancing beauty would be a lifelong source of both pride and annoyance to her—"a beauty so compelling it seemed almost to devour her personality," as one scholar put it. Statuesque, fair-skinned, poised, mysterious, patrician, and affable, she had an intoxicating effect on both men and women. With high cheekbones, perfectly straight white teeth, penetrating icy-blue eyes, long, slender fingers, full lips, a wide smile, and thick brown hair, Helen exemplified the traits of a Greek beauty. One audience had gasped so loudly at the sight of her entrance to the stage that her opening lines could not be heard. Still, the public attention to her looks distressed her. When Heywood Braun pronounced her "ten of the twelve most beautiful women in the world," she responded with irritation. "That's irrelevant," she complained. "Looks have nothing to do with acting." She found the attention to her looks boring and shallow and became especially impatient when reporters and critics ignored her substance and dwelled on what she considered the superficial.

Such physical beauty combined with a self-effacing, genuine, innocent personality created a combustible charisma that overwhelmed many observers. "[She] had a very drastic effect on men," recalled her lifelong friend De Sola. "She looked lush and sultry, but she *wasn't* lush. She was really a puritan." While men tended to adore her and place her on a pedestal, women were no less affected by her physical, intellectual, and emotional magnetism. Gregarious and fun-loving, she attracted women friends who were charmed by her joie de vivre.

Longing to be taken seriously as an actor, she sought to mitigate the attention to her physical looks by eschewing makeup and wearing plain clothing and sensible shoes. "Much as she might have resisted the attention focused on her goddess-like form, [she] could do little or nothing to stop it," wrote an observer.

Naturally, her swift rise attracted the attention of the press, and reporters clamored for personal interviews. She would meet them informally—usually in late morning, up in her bedroom where she was propped up in bed, her hair in curlers and her face slathered in face cream—and patiently endure what she considered the most inane questions. "Like most stories about me at that time, the aspect of my parents' opposition to my career played a large part," she later wrote. "I was also asked about marriage, as all adult single women were in that era. I responded by declaring that I was not interested in traditional marriage. I added that if I found myself in the position of becoming an unwed mother, I would on no occasion force the gentleman to marry me." Constantly queried about her beauty secrets, she denied taking champagne or milk baths and attributed her porcelain skin to fresh air and a commercial moisturizer that smelled better than her mother's homemade variety.

Her reputation as an ambitious, driven, hardworking, single-minded actress grew, and reporters became increasingly intimidated by her. "The most intrepid interviewers, male or female, would not think of asking her when she is to marry, her views on romance, and so forth," wrote Anne Randolph of the *Boston Post*, "because they would surmise from the general tone of her conversation that such things are in rather poor taste, which means she has no time for anything but her work."

Still, her lifestyle fascinated her fans and critics. Working on Broadway until late at night, she slept in every morning until ten or eleven. She continued to live with her family in Park Slope and was chauffeured and chaperoned by an employee of her father's. Despite an avowed lack of interest in marriage, she was linked in celebrity and theater gossip with several leading men in her milieu.

In a pattern that would be repeated throughout the rest of her life, she worked herself to the point of exhaustion. The first time she collapsed was in 1924 in Chicago, during the run of *Fashions for Men*. In addition to her performances, she was attending lunches and after-theater dinner parties that continued into the early-morning hours, and she had become "smitten with racing" to such an extent that she went to the racetrack nearly every day. When she couldn't bring down a low-grade fever, a doctor prescribed bed rest and a prohibition of snacks, fried foods, desserts, and starch.

A couple of years later, she once forgot her lines while onstage. Alarmed by her confusion, she visited the family physician, Dr. Leo Stieglitz, in New York. As she sat in an office lined with photographs taken by the doctor's famous brother, Alfred, and the paintings of Alfred's wife, Georgia O'Keeffe, a tranquility returned to her. Stieglitz questioned her closely about her lifestyle and was stunned to learn how many plays she had been in, that she was commuting daily from Brooklyn to Broadway, and that her menstrual periods were coming every fourteen days.

"You should be in bed, Helen," he told her. "You're physically exhausted. You have a remarkable constitution but you have one dangerous weakness. Your body doesn't tell you when you are tired so you never know when you should stop and rest." He prescribed one day a week in bed for the rest of her life—an instruction she would be forced to follow over the next decades.

While such critical acclaim, financial success, and popular fame would have been enough for most twenty-seven-year-old actresses, Helen was finding the stage less and less challenging and fulfilling. In her off-hours she studied music and diction, learned French, German, and Italian, read philosophy and the classics, and began fantasizing about a singing career. All of her life she had loved the opera, influenced as she was by her mother's own passions. While her mother was proud of Helen's theatrical accomplishments, she still nurtured a desire to see Helen pursue the calling that had eluded her in her own life. One day in 1926 the orchestra conductor at the Metropolitan Opera was visiting Helen's mother. Lillian Gahagan asked her longtime friend and admirer, Giuseppe Bamboschek, to listen to Helen sing, convinced that her daughter had an exceptional voice. The request led to an impromptu audition in which Helen belted out her favorite aria from Puccini's *Madama Butterfly*. "We must find you a *teacher*, a good one," the maestro excitedly responded. "You musn't work with just anyone or you'll spoil your voice."

Several months later, toward the end of Helen's run in *Young Woodley*, Bamboschek called to say he had found just the person. Madame Sophia Cehanovska, a Russian émigré who had fled the Bolshevik Revolution, was considered one of the finest voice teachers in New York City. Her son George was a baritone at the Met, and they lived together in a brownstone at 1 West Eighty-sixth Street, near Central Park. Short and broad with expressive brown eyes, "Madame," as Helen called her, wore simple handmade smocks crafted from a large piece of cloth with a hole cut for the head and crudely basted side seams.

"Maestro Bamboschek tells me you are an actress," Madame said to Helen on the day they met. The two were standing in Cehanovska's study—a sparse room furnished with a grand piano and absolutely nothing else on the floors or walls. Helen replied that she was indeed an actress, but that now she wanted to learn to sing as well. "Why? Do you want to be a singer?"

"No," Helen answered, explaining that she was interested in study-ing. "But I would like to study for the pleasure of singing."

Helen explained that she had always loved singing, but that when she took lessons as a child she was told she was a mezzo, which deeply disappointed her, for she wanted to sing contralto. Madame took her place at the piano and began playing scales, ordering Helen to sing single notes up and down two octaves. "I trusted the authority of this small, sixtyish woman," Helen wrote of the encounter. "I would have obeyed instantly if she had asked me to stand on my head."

Madame stopped as abruptly as she had started. "You are not a mezzo," she declared. "You are not a contralto. There is nothing you can do of contralto. You are a soprano. When do you want to begin?"

So began a thirty-year relationship marked by both grand success and deep disappointment. Cehanovska thought she had found in her pupil an operatic diva whose vocal size and range could rival the best singers in the world. Helen threw herself headlong into the lessons, meeting with Cehanovska three times a week while also traveling and appearing first in *Young Woodley* and then *Trelawney*. She practiced until her di-aphragm ached as she learned to expand her rib cage rather than strain her throat. Madame had her "sing single tones on one breath," teach-ing her to "feel the physical relationship between breathing and tone production." Only after she mastered that did they move to the scales, and within three months Madame's prodigy could reach and sustain high C—a necessity for a lyric dramatic soprano. "My intensity led me to the edge of exhaustion," Helen recalled of the experience. "Once I sank down beside my mother and rested my head on her knee, com-plaining, 'Why do I drive myself so?'"

Even her mother worried about the concentration with which Helen approached her new enthusiasm. What began as a leisure pursuit would evolve into the defining passion of Helen's life as she steadily lost interest in the theater while being drawn further into the world of music. When the *Trelawney* tour ended in the spring of 1927, she asked Madame if she could work with her throughout the summer. But her teacher had plans for spending the summer at a health spa in the Black Forest of Germany. Helen was welcome to join her, but it would mean an intensive immersion in voice lessons. That June, Helen, accompanied by her mother and brother Walter, set sail with Madame and George Cehanovska, ultimately bound for Bad Reichenhall.

Walter stayed in Paris and Lillian and Helen rented a large room with a piano in a modest pension near Madame. For six weeks Helen worked all day, every day, taking only a break for lunch, on the score of *Cavalleria Rusticana*. With a one-act Italian libretto by Pietro Mascagni and known for its forty curtain calls when it premiered in Rome in 1890, the opera was both a delight and challenge for Helen. Studying the role of Santuzza, a pregnant, unmarried peasant girl, Helen was so absorbed that even her mother lectured her about moderation. Bringing her an armful of Agatha Christie novels, Lillian Gahagan insisted that her daughter read every night to clear her mind of music. But she was obsessed with the music, adding the Ethiopian slave girl, Aida, to her repertoire.

When the summer sojourn came to an end, Helen made the rash decision to leave the theater altogether in favor of a singing career. Helen found Madame surprisingly lukewarm to the idea. Worried that it would be foolhardy for her pupil to abandon a successful profession for something highly competitive and notoriously precarious, Madame attempted to dissuade her.

Helen had four more years on a contract she had signed with the producer George Tyler, who had cabled her saying he had acquired the rights to her next play and that he expected her to begin rehearsals the day after her ship arrived back in New York. Tyler was "thunderstruck" when she begged him to release her from the contract, and for two solid hours implored her to change her mind. Finally, she promised to come back and work for him without a salary if he ever needed her in the future.

Her press release shocked both her colleagues and the press. Announcing that she planned to "devote herself to grand opera exclusively," she left the door open for a return to the stage. "Of course, the Metropolitan Opera Company is my aim, but I have only a hope and no assurance that I will attain it. If I fail—well, you'll see me back on the stage fast enough."

Perhaps Tyler expected that she would fail and return to him, for he well knew that to become a successful opera singer was an overarching, even grandiose ambition that would require fluency in Italian, French, and German in addition to musical perfection. When it became clear that her decision was unchangeable, he gave in. "Go then," he told her with disappointment. "Leave the theater to kitchen mechanics."

Determined to quickly master her new vocation in order to begin performing, she embarked on a rigorous schedule. She decided that the daily commute on a drafty subway from Brooklyn to Madame's new apartment at 49 West Eighty-ninth Street jeopardized her voice. Still, it was only after much deliberation that she decided to move into the city. She had lived at the Gahagan family home in Park Slope her entire life and had blithely assumed that she always would. But at twenty-eight years old, she finally moved into her own apartment on the third floor of Madame's brownstone. The tiny dwelling had two rooms and a wash closet with a sink and bathtub; the toilet was down the hall. She brought her upright Steinway from Brooklyn and only the most necessary furnishings. It was a spartan existence, for her absorption in her study was complete.

She began practicing at seven A.M. every day, had a two-hour lesson with Madame at midmorning, and continued working well into the night. Both Madame and her mother became worried about her, as she neglected to eat and rarely slept. She finally installed a telephone at the insistence of her family, but only after demanding that all calls be initiated by her. Her only outings were to the Metropolitan Opera to hear particular pieces that she hoped to master.

After less than a year of study she was approached by a Met singer who wanted to hear her *Tosca*. Pavel Ludikar, a Czech bass whose father was a conductor at the Prague National Opera, had recently made his debut at the Met. He was intrigued by Helen's audacious shift from acting to singing. When she felt she was ready, she sang for him, and his enthusiasm was so palpable she could actually envision her future. He told her he wanted to play Baron Scarpia to her Floria Tosca when she made her debut in the Puccini opera, urging her to sing with him in Prague. "I was enchanted," Helen recalled. "Pavel's Scarpia was so magnificent it often was compared to that of Antonio Scotti." Now, with a fixed goal in sight—to debut in a major role at an opera house in Czechoslovakia—Helen became even more single-minded in her pursuit.

Though her father was skeptical that she would succeed in singing—ironically complaining that her voice was not as fine as her mother's—he supported her financially if not emotionally. Madame tried to convince Walter Gahagan that Helen's voice was very different from, but not inferior to, Mrs. Gahagan's. Lillian was a lyric soprano, she explained to Walter, while Helen was a lyric *dramatic* soprano whose voice "must be placed." When that occurred, she assured him, he would be quite satisfied.

Her former theater associates were also dubious. Her onetime mentor Elizabeth Grimball echoed the doubts of Harry Gribble and George Tyler, letting no opportunity escape in urging her to stop wasting her time and return to the stage. But such naysaying only strengthened Helen's resolve. "If I made a mess of things, well, I could live with it," she believed. "I owned my life." Willful, indomitable, and motivated, Helen Gahagan had an ambition and confidence unusual for a woman of her time and place. The one person who never wavered in supporting her, and who believed unconditionally in her capacity to accomplish anything, was her mother.

As it happened, Tyler called in his marker in early 1928, imploring Helen to join the star-studded cast in Victorien Sardou's *Diplomacy*. Tyler had had a string of failures since Helen had canceled her contract, and he begged her to play the part of Countess Zika. After meeting with great success in New York, *Diplomacy* toured the U.S. and Canada. In the various cities she rented a room with a piano so that she could continue to practice her singing. When the play finally closed, she was ecstatic to be able to focus once again on *Tosca*, though she had thoroughly enjoyed the hiatus that included a romance with Tyrone Power Sr.

The Irish stage and screen idol had been recently widowed and was smitten with Helen, who was thirty years his younger. "Dear Helen. You are covered with flowers—covered with all of beauty," he wrote her in a note than accompanied a bouquet. "Alas, the days are ending 'Diplomacy' but I shall never forget the happiness that has been [mine]."

Helen concurred that the time spent together had been lovely, adding that "if it weren't that I have to get back to my lessons I would be more than sorry that it is over."

In the spring of 1929 she and Madame sailed for Paris to buy costumes for her performance in *Tosca*. As luck would have it, Otto Kahn—the fabulously wealthy New York investment banker and legendary benefactor of the Metropolitan Opera—was on the same ship. Called "America's foremost patron of the arts," Kahn had poured more than two million dollars into the Met and was responsible for bringing the renowned Arturo Toscanini in as the principal conductor. Like most men, the sixty-two-year-old Kahn was instantly taken with Helen. Whether the two had a romantic fling is unclear, but subsequent correspondence suggests that they rendezvoused in Vienna. "Don't be surprised to hear your name called very loudly from the mountain some morning," she wrote to him from Paris. "At just this time last week I was having a beautiful ride with you through Vienna . . . I write you on Sunday so that you will have to think of me . . . and in this hour I put a spell upon you, that hereafter forevermore Sunday is my day— and on this one day . . . you must think of me."

"I have the pleasantest recollection of the Sunday near Vienna, of the meadows," Kahn responded. "[I do] not need your Irish spell to direct my thoughts on Sundays and to wish you well, both personally and professionally. I hope to have the pleasure of meeting you in Paris, where I expect to arrive on June 3."

Her debut at the opera house in the Czech mining town of Ostrava was everything she had hoped for and worked toward. Initially unnerved to learn that the company had planned only one rehearsal— and further dismayed that the company would sing in Czech while she and Pavel sang in Italian—she managed to compose herself. "Despite the pain of the preceding twenty hours, I suddenly felt marvelous in the middle of a second-act duet with Pavel," she wrote of the experience. "Pure ecstasy swept over me. I felt sublimely at ease. The orchestra seemed an extension of me, of my voice. I felt weightless; a sense of elation swept over me. This was what I had been searching for, this *unity*. I had never found it in the theater, never found it anywhere."

The summer and fall of 1929 found her touring Europe, thanks to a booking agent who recognized a growing demand "for the American

soprano who spoke and sang in German and could do Italian opera."
She sang several concerts in Bad Reichenhall, performed the complete
Tosca and *Aida* in Augsburg, *Cavalleria Rusticana* in Pressburg, and ended
with *Tosca* at the prominent music and drama fall festival at Salzburg.

She was particularly delighted by the Salzburg reviews, as the critics
were considered among the most sophisticated in Europe. "An extraordinary artist," the *Salzburger Chronik* gushed. "Her well-trained
soprano possesses equal sureness in all registers, is of exquisite sweetness and inspiring warmth, and thrills especially in the high tones . . .
accomplished, natural acting, noble gestures, and convincing mimicry;
in a word, acting and singing show as noble a style and line as her
stage appearance."

Ecstatic at the success of her tour, she was optimistic about her future and eager to return to New York to audition with Maestro Gen-
naro Papi of the Met. She traveled from Salzburg to Paris, where she
planned to board the *Mauretania* for home. She walked into the lobby
of the Paris National City Bank, where she maintained an account,
and picked up a copy of the Paris *Tribune* to check the stock quota-
tions for her numerous investments. As one of the highest-paid Broadway actors, with few living expenses, she had amassed a small fortune
that she had used to buy stocks on margin. "Stock prices have reached
what looks like a permanently high plateau," a renowned American
economist had pronounced just weeks earlier—a commonly held notion that only deepened her shock at the figures she saw in the French
newspaper. Dumbfounded, she asked a teller if she was reading an old
edition of the paper.

"Miss Gahagan," the banker replied, "the stock market has crashed."

2

ACTIVIST 1931–1944

Peace time can be as exhilarating to the daredevil as wartime.
There is nothing so exciting as creating a new social order.

—Eleanor Roosevelt

THE CRASH OF October 29, 1929, marked a critical moment
in American history and the beginning of an international economic downturn that resulted in the nation's Great Depression. Helen
Gahagan lost a hundred thousand dollars in stocks, as well as all of her
savings from months of singing in Europe, and was further indebted
by the margin calls on her investments. She had also lent five thousand dollars to her former employer, George Tyler, from what she referred to as her "fast-shrinking" resources to help her old friend
cover "frightful losses in an ill-fated production of *Macbeth*." Still, she
felt more fortunate than most, as she came from a family of means
and she assumed she would be hired by the Met. But the audition
with the maestro that had been arranged by Otto Kahn was disap-
pointing. The Met's management had decided to shorten its season
and could not afford to keep its current singers employed, much less
hire an unknown.

Initially undaunted, she turned her attention to the New York Philharmonic, and Toscanini granted her an audition in Carnegie Hall. "I
awaited his verdict in an agony of suspense," she recalled of her trepidation. "The great maestro nodded and smiled. He thought my voice
was good. However, there was no opening for a newcomer. 'Keep on
working,' he consoled me."

Now becoming desperate, and realizing there was no work for her in New York, she had no choice but to turn her attention back to Europe. But even Europe held little real promise for a novice, and when she set sail with Madame in the spring of 1930 it was with melancholy and uncertainty. Her booking agent had not been able to secure any performances and seemed increasingly pessimistic about the future. From the moment she left New York, she was homesick and could not quell an unease about her father's health. In fact, she was gone only a short time when she received a cable from her twin brothers: "If you want to see Father alive, come home at once."

As fortune would have it, the celebrated producer David Belasco was begging Helen to appear in a new play he was producing. Known as the "Bishop of Broadway" for his black, priestlike garb, Belasco had written, directed, or produced more than a hundred Broadway plays. Considered the most powerful producer of the New York stage, he attracted a legion of actors seeking to work with him.

Determined to hire Helen to play the lead role of Nella in *Tonight or Never*, written by the Hungarian playwright Lili Hatvany, Belasco was unrelenting in his pursuit of her. He had come to every one of her New York openings and had long coveted the talented actress as an addition to his legendary stable of stars. Though she had rejected his offers numerous times, she was now as eager to find employment as to return home to New York. When she cabled Belasco to inquire if the part was still available, he answered enthusiastically: "I have been waiting for you." He offered her $1,000 per week for the first season and $1,200 per week for the second—an exceedingly generous salary for a stage actor, especially when much of Broadway was going dark from the financial impact of the Depression. New York ushered in the new decade with uncertainty and panic, and the theater was emblematic of all that was to come. Broadway productions dropped in record numbers, affecting everyone in the industry from producers to actors. Indeed, the coming year would see a 35 percent drop in the number of stage productions. To make matters worse, an estimated three quarters of the industry's best actors had fled to Hollywood, where the nascent movie industry seemed unaffected in comparison to the stage.

Aware of the dire circumstances and feeling fortunate to have such an offer in the economic and political climate of the moment, Helen sailed at once. When she met the white-haired Belasco in the private apartment at the top of his Belasco Theater, he was seated behind an ornate antique desk. Though she looked forward to working with him, she thought the play "monumentally silly" and intended to tell him so. Helen's character, Nella, was a virginal prima donna whose sole ambition was to sing at the Metropolitan. That goal continually eluded her, however, because her voice lacked the mature timbre of a true diva—which accompanied sexual virtuosity. To remedy the situation, a talent scout for the Met disguised himself and seduced her. Only after losing her virginity was she able to put her heart and soul into singing *Tosca* and secure a bright future with the Met.

Helen thought the premise contrived, shallow, and improbable. "Mr. Belasco, the plot of *Tonight or Never* is preposterous," she told him. "Audiences will never accept that an opera singer can be changed by having an affair. It's going to take all of your genius to make anyone sit through this nonsense. The only way it can work is if the actor who plays the man, the talent scout from the Met, is wildly attractive. Who is going to play that part?"

"I make it a rule to bring together my future hero and heroine before I make my selection," Belasco had told a reporter for the *New York Herald Tribune*. "I listen to their voices. I see how they talk to each other. I can't explain it, but I can sense how they will play together, in each other's arms, or kiss each other." This was especially important for this particular play, in which, according to Belasco, everything hinged on Helen's believability as a virginal singer who, "when she is deflowered . . . becomes the full woman whose voice comes alive."

Helen was unimpressed with the various actors that Belasco suggested, and when he showed her a photograph of a callow, handsome man, she scoffed. Not only did he seem too young for the part, but she was not attracted to blond men. "He's a juvenile," she declared. "I'll never fall in love with him! No one would believe it. *I'm thirty years old!*"

Belasco asked that she at least meet the twenty-nine-year-old man the following day. "If you still object, I'll not insist."

The next morning, Melvyn Douglas entered Belasco's office and found Helen Gahagan standing in front of the massive desk: "one hand poised on her hip as if she was about to push past me out the door," as Melvyn recalled their first meeting. "I heard the rat-a-tat-tat of her nails, drumming impatiently on the desktop." When Belasco introduced them, "Helen half-turned and peered over the top of her white fur collar. The light from the lamp caught a gold earring and lit her eyes. She stopped, stared openly at me and abruptly, her hand slid from her waist to her side . . . After a few minutes of forced conversation I was dismissed—and ran down the stairs for dear life."

"He will do," Helen managed to utter to Belasco after Douglas had left.

By all accounts, their first meeting was fatefully charged. It was the beginning of a fifty-year bicoastal and dual-career partnership that would be marked by politics, intrigue, war, celebrity, wealth, betrayal, and loss. He would be her first of several intellectual mentors, she his lifelong touchstone of courage and integrity.

"That's the handsomest back I've ever seen," she had thought, trying to maintain her composure. "Here was a mature man, only half a year younger than I—tall, broad-shouldered, slender, and exceedingly handsome. His speech was cultivated, his bearing aristocratic, and his personality magnetic." No other man had ever affected her "at first sight" as Melvyn did that day.

Helen had fiercely protected her independence, enjoying romantic liaisons with costars, fellow singers, and other dynamic men in her circle. Keenly aware of how marriage and family life, however gratifying, had stymied her mother's professional pursuits, she was determined not to repeat the pattern. Despite her love for her father, she harbored a deep resentment of her mother's artistic suppression by him and had held firm to a commitment not to let any man ever control her in the same way. But then here was Melvyn, and her life became suddenly and irrevocably complicated. "I was obsessed with thoughts of him. My longing to be alone with him became a consuming desire . . . I don't know what happened to me. Call it intuition. Call it love at first sight. I'm Irish, so I'll call it fate."

Apart from their onstage chemistry, the two seemed to have little in common. Melvyn's father was a Russian émigré, a concert pianist and composer who had been pronounced a musical prodigy in Riga, Latvia, at the age of seven. Born Kurljandsky Graoidanin Edouard Emal Hesselberg, the short and dapper musician had been trained at the Moscow Conservatory of Music, where the famed Rachmaninoff was his classmate. His family had smuggled him out of Russia so that he could avoid military service under the Czarist regime, and he landed in Philadelphia under the sponsorship of department store magnate John Wanamaker. After a Carnegie Hall debut, Hesselberg made his way to Denver, where, as a piano teacher, he met Melvyn's mother— a divorcée who had fled her native Kentucky for a kindergarten teaching position in Colorado. Lena Shackelford was the daughter of a Civil War general on the Union side, and had been raised in relative affluence in Mount Sterling. The buxom blonde held firm Victorian beliefs and was alternately "fascinated and repelled" by her talented and passionate Eastern European husband. The couple moved from Denver to Macon, Georgia, where Hesselberg headed the Wesleyan Conservatory, and where Melvyn was born on April 5, 1901.

Despite their differences in background and temperament, Helen and Melvyn were irresistibly drawn to each other when cast as lovers in *Tonight or Never.* "Am I not the best caster in the whole world, Miss Helen?" Belasco had asked her. Helen had moved into a new apartment on Central Park South, and she and Melvyn often met there to practice their love scenes in privacy. For her it was a magical time as she fell ever deeper in love while getting to know her leading man.

His father was a Jew, he told her. "I'm a Jew," he said, as if that would scare her away. Most of his life, Melvyn had been unaware of his Jewish roots. His mother and her family were deeply anti-Semitic, referring to Edouard simply as a "foreigner." Lena had joined various evangelical cults before finally becoming a Christian Scientist, and had raised Melvyn with Bible stories from the New Testament. It was not until he was a teenager that he became close to an aunt on the Hesselberg side of the family and learned that he was descended from a long line of Russian Jews and that his grandparents had survived two pogroms. This aunt—a pathologist with Washington University in Saint Louis—encouraged him to read Tolstoy and Dostoevsky, to study the Bolshevik Revolution, and to develop a social conscience about the plight of the oppressed in the world. Eager to leave home and experience the adventures "implied in popular tunes like . . . 'Hinky, Dinky, Parley-Voo,'" as he later wrote of his wanderlust, he joined the army during World War I.

Melvyn returned to Chicago, where his financially struggling parents had moved, and found himself at what he considered a crossroads in his life. Unable to attend college because of the family's economics, he took a job selling hats at Marshall Field's department store. He found the city "a yeasty place" that was the current backdrop to the muckraking exposés of the day, and he immersed himself in the bohemian environment of artists, writers, and musicians. He read the works of the authors who were based there—socialist and progressive writers such as Frank Norris, Theodore Dreiser, and Upton Sinclair— and he heard labor leader Eugene V. Debs and flamboyant populist lawyer Clarence Darrow speak. It was in Chicago at the beginning of the roaring twenties that he "got a first inkling of the sexual revolution started by Havelock Ellis, and of that other revolution initiated by a man named Lenin."

He enrolled in evening classes in elocution and befriended a young theater director named William Owen, who was studying drama at the Cosmopolitan School of Music. A "Shakespearean star in the Midwest," as Melvyn described him, Owen hired Melvyn as his assistant and soon Melvyn was an apprenticing actor who was touring with Owen's theatrical company. Appearing in the play *Pollyanna, the Glad Girl* at the 1921 Lake Chautauqua season, Melvyn joined a troupe of performers that included Wheelock's Indian Orchestra, who were described as "genuine native Americans." That summer at the adult-education camp he also attended lectures by Stanley Krebs, who promised to "make plain what is obscure and render easy what is difficult," and J. P. Morgan, who had "Christianized a community of barbarians." By the time the tour was over, Melvyn had decided to become a professional performer.

After a couple of years with Owen, Melvyn took a job as a leading man with a Sioux City, Iowa, theater company. His fifty-dollar weekly salary supported his parents as well as himself, as his father was finding it increasingly difficult to get work. When the company traveled to Madison, Wisconsin, Melvyn was immediately drawn to the cerebral character of the thriving college town. He quit his job and founded his own acting company. Though he couldn't afford to enroll at the university—in fact, with all of his parents' moves he had never even graduated from high school—he threw himself into the academic setting, reading voraciously and socializing with avid thinkers and scholars. An autodidact, Melvyn had a fine mind, a photographic memory, a craving for knowledge, and an insatiable curiosity. He was fascinated by political theory and social justice, and Madison provided him with his first intellectual "home." He frequently went to Chicago to see the top-flight plays that toured there from New York, and it was while he was in the audience of Molnár's *Fashions for Men* that he first laid eyes on Helen Gahagan. Besotted by her beauty, he wondered then "if she could possibly be as dazzling up close as she looked on the stage." The possibility that he would ever find out seemed as likely to him then as setting foot on the moon.

In Madison he met the "romantic and statuesque" Rosalind Hightower, whose flowing strawberry-blonde hair and pale skin made her seem a real-life Lady Godiva. She had "everything," he recalled of his infatuation. "She was exceedingly comely, she was talented—and so I loved her." They were quickly married and almost as quickly divorced. Melvyn described the young nuptials with a characteristically sardonic quip. We "were ecstatically happy. I was busy, she was bored. We had a baby boy, we were ecstatically happy once more. I was busy, she was bored, I was cruel, she was angry, we were done—all within a period of what seems in memory no more than a few moments."

Their son, Gregory Hesselberg, would be "shunted from relative to relative throughout his dependent years." Melvyn abandoned Rosalind and Gregory and set his sights on Europe. "This is obviously not a record of which I am proud," he would write sixty years later. He gave Rosalind and his parents all of his savings and left for France, where he hoped to travel extensively, learn the language, read French literature, and improve his acting. Captivated by Paris, he attended the theater that showcased some of the most extraordinary performers of the era. He found the city "utterly fascinating. These were the days of Ezra Pound and Gertrude Stein, when Ernest Hemingway was first in Paris."

When he returned to the U.S. in 1925, he moved to New York and joined the legion of unemployed stage actors seeking parts. Youthful and determined, he came to the attention of Jessie Bonstelle—a Detroit-based director who was visiting New York with the hopes of finding actors to join her company. As director of the Harlem Opera House in 1923, she had served as mentor and coach for several promising young actors including Katharine Cornell and William Powell. Known in theater circles as the "Maker of Stars," Bonstelle saw a depth and promise in the young Melvyn Douglas—but only if he changed his name from Hesselberg, which she claimed would not fit on a marquee. "I searched for something that would retain at least a shred of family identity," Douglas recalled of how he settled on his maternal grandmother's maiden name. Only later did he suspect that Bonstelle's insistence on the name change was based on anti-Semitism. Still, Bonstelle's selection of Melvyn would signal a turning point in his life. Highly regarded by Broadway producers, she often tried out plays in her Detroit theater to test the market, and her reputation for picking talented performers resulted in lucrative contracts for her protégés.

By the time he met Helen Gahagan in Belasco's office in the fall of 1930, Melvyn had made his Broadway debut the previous year as the gambler Ace Wilfong in *A Free Soul*. That play had been produced by the belligerent William Brady, who had also "discovered" Helen. When Melvyn appeared in his next play, *Reception*, a scout for Belasco thought him perfect to play the suave seducer in *Tonight or Never*.

It would be Melvyn who informed and nurtured Helen's nascent political awakening, for his progressive views were already deeply rooted, inspired by such social observers as H. L. Mencken and Sinclair Lewis and novelists F. Scott Fitzgerald and Ernest Hemingway.

One morning, soon after they met, Melvyn knocked on her door. When she opened it, "he thrust an armful of books" at her. "We can't go through life just making love," he told her. "We have to study too." He had given Helen dozens of books to read on subjects ranging from literature to political science to philosophy to history.

Steeped in the journalism of the moment, Melvyn was an informed observer of the events leading up to Black Thursday, as the first day of the stock market crash was dubbed, and the economic, political, and social complexities that ensued. "It was 1929 in the United States of America," as one account depicted the era. "The people, as could be seen in the advertisements, were all white, and although they occasionally worried about halitosis, falling hair, and common mistakes in English, they were an optimistic lot and spent much of their time showing their new cars, their toasters, and their refrigerators to envious visitors."

The previous decade had seen a great concentration of wealth and industry, with banks, railroads, manufacturers, and retailers merging into massive unregulated combines. Rampant speculators had driven up stock prices. A consolidated, free-enterprise, monopolistic system—unrestrained by government interference—was the clarion cry of the era. But it was all a fragile façade.

By midsummer 1929, warning signs could be seen in the slackening residential-construction and industry-production markets, in pervasive bank failures, and in rising unemployment and plummeting commodity prices. But newly inaugurated President Herbert C. Hoover—described by historian Richard Hofstadter as a "wild-eyed Utopian capitalist"—ignored all indices, remaining optimistic and strangely, if not disingenuously, reassuring. Despite the frenetic plunge in trading on October 23, which ushered in widespread panic throughout the nation and triggered rampant selling of shares by fearful investors, Hoover issued a sanguine statement the following day. "The fundamental business of the country, that is, production and distribution of commodities, is on a sound and prosperous basis." The losses on that day alone, October 24, were estimated in the billions of dollars. Such bastions of American enterprise as Westinghouse and DuPont lost more than half of their value. More than thirteen million shares traded hands at record low prices, fueling further panic in foreign markets and rumors of speculators committing suicide. "You want a room for sleeping or jumping?" hotel clerks sarcastically asked their clientele.

"Surely your administration could assemble the banking and financial leaders of the nation and insist that they cooperate with the government in reviving confidence and restoring normal prices," newspaper magnate William Randolph Hearst wrote to Hoover. The following month, privately fearing national economic collapse and alarmed by the growing unemployment rate, the president called together a group of business and banking titans and asked them to increase production and unite with organized labor to keep wages on an even keel. He then appealed to all forty-eight governors to initiate public works programs. By the end of the year he had asked Congress for $175 million for federal construction projects.

"If the crash of '29 was high drama," wrote T. H. Watkins, "the Depression that followed was a threnody—muted, constant, stupefying in its persistence." Indeed, the Wall Street collapse had been only the beginning.

The human toll has become embedded in American iconography, from the literature of Studs Terkel and the photographs of Walker Evans to numerous histories, films, and documentaries. The sharecropper shacks and soup kitchens, unemployment lines and bank runs, migrant mothers and homeless fathers, boxcar hoboes and barefoot children. "Still," as Watkins put it, "the dry horror of statistics is inadequate to the story. It was about terror, not numbers, the terror of uncertainty, helplessness, inchoate frustration, despair; it was an anomie of spirit that left millions constricted by guilt and hopelessness."

The figures were staggering: unemployment rising from two million to thirteen million in a two-year period; nearly a half million farm foreclosures; more than thirteen hundred bank closures; untold millions wandering the country in search of work. And yet the U.S. government had no safety nets in place, none of what historian Arthur M. Schlesinger Jr. later called the "built-in economic stabilizers" of unemployment compensation, social security, minimum wage, and federal bank-deposit insurance.

President Hoover, who was increasingly inaccessible to the press and was being derided for championing what Republicans had called their "party of prosperity," seemed uncharacteristically ineffectual. As if to underscore his failure to grasp the significance of the crisis, he summoned Christopher Morley to the White House. "What this country needs is a great poem," he told the renowned author. "Something to lift people out of fear and selfishness. Every once in a while someone catches words out of the air and gives a nation an inspiration . . . I'd like to see something simple enough for a child to spout in school on Fridays."

It was this nightmare through which they were living, relatively unscathed and immune, that consumed Melvyn's thoughts. Like other progressives of the time, he saw an opportunity to right the wrongs of the previous decade of personal greed and institutional piracy. He became convinced that the solutions to end poverty and eliminate the grotesque concentration of wealth in the hands of the few lay with upcoming leaders of the Democratic Party. Helen, a lifelong Republican descended from generations of Republican roots, found it all foreign to her innate sensibility. Still, she embarked on a journey of self-education that would eventually culminate in a political career of her own.

Tonight or Never opened in November 1930, a week before Helen's thirtieth birthday. Critics were dazzled by the chemistry between the two. Helen was pronounced one of the top five actresses of the season. While she drew the most attention from the press—the role catapulting her into stardom—Melvyn received positive reviews that suggested that the relative unknown was also destined for celebrity.

Though her father was mostly bedridden, battling terminal throat cancer, he came to a matinee a few days before Christmas. In her role as Nella, the ingenue prima donna, Helen had the opportunity to sing *Tosca*. It would be the first time that Walter Gahagan heard his daughter sing in public. After the performance, the frail and emotional invalid came backstage and hugged her. "It was beautiful, Helen," he said. "Now I know what you wanted." Finally, she had gotten his approval and blessing. That evening, he died quietly while dining alone in his bedroom.

Helen's grief was mitigated by her deepening relationship with Melvyn. By February 1931 they had decided to marry. Giddy in love, they each also harbored grave feelings of ambivalence. Helen had had several engagements—a state she had previously considered perfect. "Being single and occasionally engaged—I was engaged to someone when I met Melvyn—had seemed to me an ideal arrangement." Melvyn, too, was a bit gun-shy, having already endured one failed marriage.

Her mother responded indifferently to Helen's declaration of marriage. "To whom?" Lillian asked.

"I told you. To Melvyn Douglas."

"Your leading man?" Lillian responded with incredulity. "But you don't know him!"

"I do know him, Mother, and I love him. We're going to be married, or, if you prefer, we'll live together. I must tell you, though, that we'll live together openly."

"Live with him," she snapped.

Lillian soon acquiesced, though, and the couple set a wedding date of April 5, 1931—Melvyn's thirtieth birthday. In the weeks leading up to their marriage, Helen became acquainted with Melvyn's family, visiting his parents at Sneden's Landing on the Hudson River. Melvyn got to know Helen's mother and siblings as well, and even though he seemed quiet and remote compared to their intrinsic rambunctiousness, he won them over with what Helen described as his "infinite capacity for kindness."

Helen was reluctant to announce their engagement and had second thoughts up until the moment they were wed. For so many years she had dreamed of becoming an actress, and then of becoming a singer, that she had never thought of becoming a wife. "The way you two play the love scene in the second act, getting married is the only decent thing you could do," an actress friend responded on hearing the news. "It was love at first sight," Belasco had told the press. "I've seen so many romances in the theater but none so fine, so old-fashioned, so honest."

The press asked her if she intended to take her husband's name. "Of course I'll be a good wife," she responded, "in the sense of what wifehood means, but I'll always be Helen Gahagan. I'll keep the good old Irish name. I was born Helen Gahagan and I'll die Helen Gahagan." Mostly she insisted that she had no intention of becoming a housewife, and declared that she would never give up the theater until she was ninety-five years old.

They were married on Easter Sunday in the Park Slope home under a canopy of sweet peas, gardenias, and lilies of the valley. "I love you both and hope that your ship will sail serenely and successfully in pleasant waters with just enough rough weather to weld you closer together," cabled Jessie Bonstelle.

Shortly before their wedding, Hollywood film producer Samuel Goldwyn purchased the movie rights to *Tonight or Never*. The son of Hasidic Jews, Schmuel Gelbfisz was born in Poland, immigrated to New York in 1899, and eventually changed his name to Samuel Goldwyn.

Goldwyn had gotten in on the ground floor of the fledgling film industry. By 1931 he was a partner in United Artists and had won his
first Academy Award for a film directed by John Ford. Known as a
business genius, Goldwyn was famous for discovering talented actors,
directors, and writers, while also lining up crucial investors.

Goldwyn bought *Tonight or Never* as a vehicle for Gloria Swanson,
one of United Artists' silent-film stars who wanted the role for her
transition into the talkies. Romantically involved with Joseph P.
Kennedy—the father of the future president—Swanson was the
highest-paid and most powerful film actress of the day. Goldwyn hired
the entire Broadway cast—except for Helen—and offered Melvyn a
lucrative five-year contract to play the leading man with Swanson.
Melvyn, who was supporting his parents, his son, and now a wife, immediately accepted the offer, causing the first rift between the couple.
Helen vehemently opposed the contract for numerous reasons: She
thought Hollywood beneath them as stage actors; she thought that to
accept an acting role purely for money was "madness"; she feared that
Melvyn would break his ties with the New York theater; she worried
that they would either live apart or that she would be forced to abandon her own stage career and move to California; and she saw the contract as exploitative and constricting. Melvyn would owe his life to
Samuel Goldwyn and "might wind up playing in trash," she reasoned.

But all of those objections were Helen's rationalizations, serving
to exonerate Melvyn from the real transgression and making palat-
able what was a devastating emotional blow. What apparently went
unspoken—at least in the written recollections of both Helen and
Melvyn—was the sorrow and anger, if not fury, that she certainly felt.
She, after all, was the most celebrated, talented, and experienced of all
the actors in the play. To be so publicly and blatantly undermined and
purged from the cast, to endure her husband's complicity in her ex-
clusion, would have elicited outrage in a woman of Helen's temperament. But the record is silent on the matter.

Melvyn was resolute. Unlike Helen, he had been raised in precar-
iousness and poverty, and he refused to pass up five years of steady
income—especially during the thickening Depression. "The studio
agents talked of astronomical sums and audiences of unimaginable
size," Melvyn recalled of Hollywood's allure. "They described ideal

working conditions collaborating with the outstanding directors of the day, palm trees and swimming pools, a life of satisfaction and ease."

Though doubtlessly jealous that her role had been usurped by a rival and angry that her husband had colluded in her snubbing, Helen gamely determined to make it work, even if it meant commuting between California and New York in order to pursue her own career. "I was helplessly in love with him. We would *have* to work it out."

"I think that Helen was always, from the beginning, rather sad," about the move to California, Melvyn wrote with both understatement and an uncharacteristic lack of compassion for her circumstances. At thirty-one years old, she had actually spent very little time away from home and family. Their train trip west was wretched, with summer temperatures creeping into the hundreds. On the night of their arrival they dined at the Musso and Frank Grill—the oldest eatery in Los Angeles and a favorite hangout of screenwriters and actors. When they finished dinner, they walked out onto Hollywood Boulevard. Helen looked up and down the street and then buried her head in Melvyn's chest. "I had tried to prepare myself for Hollywood's tawdriness," she wrote, "but a wave of desolation swept over me." She suspected that Melvyn felt the same way, for he "faced five years in this celebration of bad taste."

Goldwyn had arranged for them to stay at the Roosevelt Hotel in Hollywood—a tacky little joint that seemed a caricature of Hollywood garishness—and Helen set about immediately to find a home. "Where does one live out here?" she beseeched Barney Glazer, her scriptwriter friend.

"There are only two places one *can* live," he answered. "Beverly Hills or Malibu."

Helen and Melvyn thought both places hideous and settled on an isolated tract in the San Fernando Valley. The spacious house in Van Nuys had a swimming pool, a tennis court, a small green lawn, and dozens of pink rosebushes that seemed an oasis amid the surrounding brown foothills. "I expected camels to loom over the horizon," she wrote. With her father's death she had inherited a considerable fortune—by Depression standards—and that, combined with her own stage earnings and now Melvyn's film contract, provided the newlyweds a more lavish lifestyle than that of their acting colleagues. Melvyn bought her a Pierce-Arrow limousine to remind her of her chauffeured trips from Brooklyn to Broadway, and when her driver took her on the twenty-minute trip to Hollywood to visit Melvyn on the movie set, she often drew the shades in the backseat, hoping to forget she was in California.

Though rough and rustic, Southern California was on the verge of a population explosion that could not be imagined by this displaced New York couple.

Settling into life in the San Fernando Valley, Helen purchased a Steinway piano and continued to work on her voice. She generally drove Melvyn to work and then practiced her singing. She accepted a few performing engagements—*The Cat and the Fiddle* in San Francisco, *Aida* in New York—and began negotiations with RKO for a possible film contract. While the negotiations were under way, she rejected offers from Universal and Fox Studios, but when neither she nor RKO representatives could agree on terms she became discouraged. For the first time in her life she felt scattered and indecisive, unsure whether she wanted to pursue stage, opera, or screen.

Meanwhile, Melvyn made several films on loan from Goldwyn to other studios. But he was bored and dissatisfied, thought the films were formulaic trash and the business a racket, and felt guilty that Helen's career was foundering while his was flourishing. They valued their time together, which was usually only on Sundays. They played tennis and occasionally socialized with a handful of friends—mostly actors from Melvyn's movies. They hated to be apart, and when it was unavoidable, they spoke several times a day on the telephone. They wrote love letters and cables to each other, all filled with ineffable longing.

One weekend they decided to take a drive through Southern California. Crossing Death Valley, they were caught in a violent windstorm. Their car was blown off the road and they choked and coughed as the fine dust found its way through cracks in the doors and windows. For Helen, the daughter of an engineer, the moment brought a realization. She had come to the desert from "a part of the country where the earth was moist, rich, and embracing." So began her first glimmer of interest in a California political issue: water. "I wondered if any effort was being made to establish reclamation projects to bring California's dry soil to life."

Alone for many hours of every day, Helen spent a good deal of time listening to the radio and reading the newspapers. Chandler's *Los Angeles Times* was predictably full of "angry stories about jobless people pouring into the state looking for handouts," which Helen thought a one-dimensional and callous viewpoint. Traveling across the country from New York to California, she had witnessed the stark human toll of the Great Depression crowding the roadsides. Though she did not know it at the time, the experience would serve as inspiration later for her move into national politics. It was now clear throughout the country that the prosperity of the 1920s had been unevenly distributed throughout American society, giving way to the severe economic crisis of the 1930s. At the height of the Depression, nearly one quarter of all Americans were out of work, and many of those who had jobs were working long hours for low pay. Not since the Civil War had there been such financial upheaval, resulting in personal devastation and unemployment for millions upon millions of Americans. There were "thousands of them," as she remembered the migrant workers making their way from the dust bowls of Oklahoma, Arkansas, and Missouri to California, "living in boxcars and in caves dug out of the sides of hills."

A man widely perceived as a dangerous radical was challenging the incumbent Hoover. The only son of wealthy, aristocratic New York Dutch parents, Franklin Delano Roosevelt was considered a traitor to his class—a perception held by the Gahagan family. But as poverty and unemployment swept the nation, even the solid Gahagan family engineering firm, now in the hands of Helen's brothers, was struggling for survival.

"I looked for signs in the political speeches that someone knew how to put the country together," Helen recalled of those desperate years. "I'd always believed that problems could be solved, but what was happening in America was so appalling I wondered if anyone could do it."

Still, she planned to vote Republican like the previous four generations of Gahagans. But the more she listened to the candidates, the further alienated she became from her party. Roosevelt was hardly more convincing, in her opinion, with his arrogance, erudition, and elitism. She decided to sit out the election without voting.

Later, after Roosevelt had won, she became so appalled during a conversation at a Pasadena dinner party at which Roosevelt was gratuitously lambasted and lampooned that she registered as a Democrat. The dinner guests—all Republican—spoke of their hatred of Roosevelt and made ad hominem remarks about him and his wife. Helen found herself taking Roosevelt's side, arguing in favor of job creation rather than the "toughly administered dole" the Republicans were advocating. "People need dignity and a feeling of self-worth," she argued. "Except for those unable to work, a handout is no substitute for a job." Her mother and brothers were shocked by her defection, associating Democrats with the corruption of the Tammany Hall political machine that dominated New York for more than a century.

Gradually, Helen was finding her political bearings, and it would be Franklin and Eleanor Roosevelt who would ultimately guide her. When she heard the new president's inaugural address—the "nothing to fear but fear itself" speech—she deeply regretted not voting for him. From that point forward she would be a lifelong devoted Roosevelt New Deal Democrat.

In January 1933, Melvyn somehow convinced Goldwyn to release him from his contract and came to San Francisco to see Helen near the end of the run of *The Cat and the Fiddle*. Helen had been disappointed to learn that touring plans for the play had fallen through, and she had nothing else lined up for the immediate future. As they lay in bed in their hotel room, Melvyn could not sleep. He worried about Helen's unhappiness in California, about her homesickness for the New York stage, the lack of fulfillment in her professional life. Listening to the foghorns in the San Francisco Bay, he had an epiphany: "It came to me that we should get on a ship and sail away." The next day he spontaneously bought two tickets for a round-the-world tour.

Helen was delighted, both to see the world and to spend time with her beloved husband. Within two weeks they left Los Angeles, bound for France, their passage booked under the names "Helen and Melvyn Hesselberg." They boarded a small cargo boat headed down the Pacific coast to Panama, and over the next nine months they rode elephants in Ceylon, visited the Wailing Wall in Jerusalem, saw a play in Tel Aviv,

went to a healer in Bali, took a train to Peking, and made some lifelong friends in Shanghai and Kyoto. "Never have two people complemented each other so well as these two," a columnist for the *China
Critic* gushed after interviewing the celebrity couple. "She will argue
for half an hour about a book the name of which she can't remember
but what does that matter . . . He tells you the facts about everything.
She even forgets the composers whose music she sings and loves." Their
trip would have continued even longer had Melvyn not contracted
malaria and Helen become so nauseated with an illness that turned out
to be pregnancy.

In the event, the trip was a life-changing experience for Helen and
would serve as a primer on world affairs. While they toured the globe
in marital bliss, buoyed by substantial earnings and yet vaguely aware
of the deepening crisis at home—even unaware that banks in thirty-
eight states had closed their doors—this "honeymoon cruise" was the
last time they would be removed from the pressing domestic and foreign issues of the day. The trip solidified their relationship and focused their future. Helen had never been happier in her life. "Melvyn
sensitized Helen to worldly issues," as one biographer put it, "took
her outside of her narrowly defined world and encouraged her in a
gentle, persuasive way to care about how people lived in other cultural, political, and economic circumstances, and to gain 'intellectual
clarity.' "

They decided to return early to have the baby on American soil,
and they determined to move back to New York in order for them
both to pursue their stage careers.

They arrived back in San Francisco in early October 1933 and traveled immediately to Los Angeles. Melvyn had been offered a role in a
new film called *Counsellor-at-Law*. As a supporting actor to John Barrymore, Melvyn thought it a quick way to make back the money they
had just spent on the trip and reasoned it would give Helen time to have
the baby and make preparations for their return to New York. They
checked into the Château Elysée—an upscale Hollywood chateau at
5930 Franklin Avenue that was home to such stars as Errol Flynn, Clark
Gable, George Burns, Gracie Allen, and Spencer Tracy, who was then
having an affair with Loretta Young.

On the evening of October 7, Helen and Melvyn were entertaining friends for dinner and a rubber of bridge when they heard a rumble and saw the chandelier swinging above them. The earthquake tremors continued throughout the night and into the following morning. When they stopped near dawn, Helen realized that she was in labor. "This is taking too long," she told the nurses at the Pasadena Hospital before passing out from the anesthesia. Almost twenty-four hours later, on the morning of October 9, she opened her eyes. Melvyn was kissing her on her cheek and whispering. "We have a beautiful seven-and-a-half-pound baby boy, Helen."

The couple could not decide on a name for the infant—we "were waiting for inspiration for his first name"—so they temporarily christened him Gahagan Douglas and called him Baby. Melvyn left immediately for New York to look for work while Helen convalesced for several weeks in Hollywood, reading scripts sent to her by Broadway producers. She thought the plays "awful" until Dan Totheroh sent her *Moor Born*—the story of the Brontë family.

When Helen arrived in New York she was surprised at the fascination her baby—finally named Peter—held for the press. Reporters acted as if it was bizarre for an actress to have a baby. "[It] worries me," she wrote, "the way people think having a baby is going to change everything. Isn't having a baby the most natural thing in the world?" She adored being a mother, displaying photographs of Peter throughout her dressing room and talking endlessly about him. She acted as though she had been the first to discover the pleasure of babies. "I'd have twenty of them—they're so nice—if I only had the time."

Moor Born, in which Helen played Emily Brontë, was Melvyn's directing debut, and opened in April 1934 to lukewarm reviews. The couple had invested thousands of dollars in the production, and when it flopped they began looking for a play in which they could appear together. Deeply in love and wildly happy, they hoped to repeat the onstage chemistry and critical success of *Tonight or Never.* When they could find nothing that appealed to both of them, they turned their attention back to California. Helen had been offered the lead in Maxwell Anderson's play *Mary of Scotland*, scheduled to run in San Francisco and Los Angeles, and Melvyn was offered roles in four films. When those ventures turned into financial successes, they invested all of their earnings and savings in another play called *Mother Lode*, which Totheroh had written specifically with them in mind. Melvyn directed and starred in it with Helen, but the play was so roundly panned that it closed in two weeks and they lost all of their investment.

At their lowest moment, Helen received a most unexpected offer: a lucrative contract to play the lead in an RKO film called *She*. A bizarre action-adventure fantasy, made by the producer of *King Kong*, that immortalized the line "She who must be obeyed," *She* had been a favorite of Helen's when she read the book—by H. Rider Haggard— as a teen. Desperate for money, Helen accepted the offer without reading the script. When she finally read it, not only did she find it "appalling" and "atrocious," as she put it, but she learned that no fewer than a dozen writers had tried to doctor it. "I knew on the first day that motion pictures were not for me." She could not relax in front of the camera and "detested having a makeup artist constantly at my side, fussing with my face and hair. The rhythms of film-making distracted my concentration. I fumed at the long, debilitating waits for lights and cameras to be adjusted, and then the suddenness of turning on the required intense emotion."

Though nominated for an Academy Award, the film was a commercial bust. "It fell in the indeterminate category somewhere between flop and success," Helen wrote. Clearly unsuited for the medium— she found film acting stilted and contrived after her experience on the stage—she neither sought nor landed another Hollywood part.

The year 1935, it would seem, marked the turning point in the Gahagan-Douglas marriage. Melvyn initially stayed in New York, directing a Sean O'Casey play, while Helen was filming *She* in Los Angeles. He followed that with a role in Louis Bromfield's *Deluxe*, but he was lonely and increasingly depressed without his little family. Helen, too, was overcome with loneliness, and in order to maintain a connection between them she arranged for a single flower to be delivered to Melvyn every night. "Each evening when the flower arrives," he wrote her, "I am suffused with a warm weakness and a few tears. So write me often and keep me warm."

They wrote to each other regularly, but the long-distance relationship was inevitably strained. As the absence grew longer, Melvyn experienced the first real pangs of mental depression that would haunt him for decades to come. "God, how I miss you two," he wrote. "Everything else is pointless."

While Melvyn was despairing in New York, Helen was basking in the celebrity limelight, receiving a steady stream of fan mail and granting interviews to the suddenly ubiquitous Hollywood writers. She usually met with reporters in her bedroom, baby Peter on her lap, her face smeared with Pond's. She gratefully accepted theater roles and advertising jobs—"a balm" to her "damaged self-esteem" after *She*—appearing in an ad for milk and in "The Smiles of Lady Lux" soap campaign. She wrote fashion columns in which she advocated feminine dresses rather than trousers for women, and her own stylish elegance made her a fashion icon. One writer described her standard wardrobe as a "white wool cape that she used for sailing; a navy sailor-style coat made of the Latin American fur vicuña, which she wore to the Santa Anita race track; and an imported gray and red tweed suit complemented with a red, broad-brimmed hat for various business purposes."

After the terrible experience with *She*, Helen retired permanently from the movie business. At the same time she was thinking of turning her full attention back to the New York stage, Melvyn decided to return to California. He missed Helen and Peter desperately, once even asking Helen not to take the child to the beach because he wanted to be with them for the boy's first ocean experience. When *Deluxe* closed, he made a half hearted attempt to find work, and when nothing significant materialized, he left New York.

While Melvyn had had an impressive start in the movies—beginning with the box-office hit *Tonight or Never* followed by *As You Desire Me* with Greta Garbo—Samuel Goldwyn had apparently decided the role of the sophisticated leading man was better played by William Powell. Just as Helen had feared, Goldwyn had stuck Melvyn in B-grade movies until Melvyn finally finagled his way out of his contract. So it came as a great surprise to Melvyn that he was treated by Hollywood producers as the returning prodigal son. Courted and feted, he now had his choice of parts as RKO, Paramount, and Columbia all vied for him.

Now, just as Helen's film-star power fell, Melvyn's rose. "Melvyn, a more deliberate actor who could find something worthwhile in almost any part, was to have great success in film," Helen later wrote. "That year he did *She Married Her Boss* with Claudette Colbert and his career took off." Indeed, the part led to a seven-year contract for Melvyn, and his film future would be secure until his death forty-five years later. It also led to a distance between him and Helen, as his whirlwind career throughout the rest of the decade left little room for domestic closeness. The suave leading man was now one of the highest-paid actors in Hollywood and a regular escort for Hollywood's glamorous actresses. Costarring with such luminaries as Garbo, Colbert, Joan Crawford, and Barbara Stanwyck, he was the subject of rumor and innuendo. The credibility of the rumors was never addressed by either Helen or Melvyn in their memoirs, though she would later write to him about his unfaithfulness. Society columnist Louella Parsons and others linked him in romantic liaisons with various women. "His enigmatic grin, arched eyebrow and delicately shaded vocal inflection were sufficient to romance a bored Marlene Dietrich in *Angel* (1937), repel the post-pubescent advances of Deanna Durbin in *That Certain Age* (1939) and unfreeze Garbo in *Ninotchka*, her delicious Ernst Lubitsch comedy," one piece said of the magic of Melvyn Douglas between 1935 and 1940. Helen kept private her feelings about these hints of philandering, later referring to what appeared to be a single transgression.

How Helen felt about this period of her marriage remains unknown, for as public a person as she was and would continue to be, she was intensely protective of her private life. She continued to shuttle back and forth between Los Angeles and New York, performing in both plays and operas, and was preoccupied with motherhood as well. Whether she recognized it or not, the pressures on her marriage to Melvyn were building as their personal and professional lives began to diverge.

In April 1936, the Douglases moved into a spacious seventeen-room house near the exclusive Wilshire Country Club. The Spanish-style mansion surrounded by lawns and palm trees was the quintessential Beverly Hills home. Its signature red tile roof and stucco walls were reminiscent of the mission-style ranchos of early California. On Melvyn's thirty-fifth birthday, they threw a combination house-warming, birthday, and anniversary party that Helen had catered by a local Mexican restaurant. They were only in the home for five months before Helen moved to New York to appear in *And Stars*

Remain and Melvyn and three-year-old Peter moved into an apart-ment. Though the play was critically acclaimed, Helen thought it "the poorest Guild comedy production in an otherwise long and distinguished chain of hits" by radical writers Julius and Philip Ep-stein. Julius Epstein would later win the Academy Award for his script *Casablanca*.

When the play closed, she decided that neither film nor stage acting brought her much joy or held much promise for her, and she set her sights once again on opera. Her singing had been well received in Los Angeles and San Francisco, and Walter Hofstötter, her European agent, planned a six-week summer tour for her. But when she cabled him that she intended to bring her accompanist, Sanford Schlussel, Hofstötter frostily rejected the American pianist. She and Melyvn had been following reports of rising anti-Semitism in Germany and sus-pected that it lay behind Hofstötter's reasoning. She wired back that if Jews were not welcome, she would not sing in Germany, and asked that he book her performances in Paris, Prague, Budapest, and Salzburg. She had been studying intensively for the past few years and now spoke proficient German; she had added sixteen Schumann songs and several more from Austrian composers.

She booked passage on the *Queen Mary*—the world's fastest, grand-est ocean liner—and prepared to sail in March 1937. Melvyn decided to join her, figuring he could travel both ways, spend a day and a half in Paris with Helen, and still return to California in time to begin shooting *That Certain Age* with Deanna Durbin. "It was an expensive, romantic plan," Helen remembered. "We sailed together on what I calculated was my twenty-ninth Atlantic crossing and had a rapturous few hours in Paris, after which he caught the boat train to Cherbourg and I caught another train for Salzburg."

Helen's tour was a great success—a rarity for an American singer. So great, in fact, that she enthusiastically signed a contract to sing *Tosca* in the 1938 season of the Vienna Opera Company. But all of the geniality and excitement disappeared in an instant. "Helen Gahagan Douglas . . . had not the slightest interest in politics until the late 1930s," First Lady Eleanor Roosevelt would later write. "Her conversion was as dramatic as a first-act curtain in the theater." While sitting in a Viennese coffee-house with an English music critic who was a friend of several colleagues, the two discussed her new contract. Suddenly, the man leaned in conspiratorially and whispered, "Of course, Miss Gahagan, you are pure Aryan?"

Helen felt sick to her stomach as the man attempted to recruit her to the Nazi cause. "Aryans such as we," he told her, "[have] a duty to defend the superior race against Jews." At first she couldn't speak. Until that moment the persecution of Jews in the world was a purely abstract notion. Now, as the Englishman spouted the familiar rantings of Hitler and Goebbels while asking her to enlist the support of fellow Nazi sympathizers in America, she felt forever changed. Her "Irish blood at the boiling point," she tore up her contract and left for home.

She took a taxi from the Los Angeles airport to the Metro-Goldwyn-Mayer set where Melvyn was filming and found him in his dressing room. She stood at the door, her face brimming with emotion. "I'm not going back. I'm not going to sing *Tosca* in Vienna." She then burst into tears, no doubt sensing an end to her life as an operatic artist, a premature and unanticipated conclusion to the dream that had driven her ardently for most of her adult life. Her career cut short, she would never know for sure if she had had the talent and capacity to attain international stardom in that realm—if the Floria Tosca that she sought to make her own would ever have immortalized her.

Had she fulfilled her contract, she would have been singing in Vienna when Hitler's storm troopers marched into Austria, where he was welcomed by flowers and cheers in the spring of 1938. As it was, she had returned to California with a newfound passion for anti-Nazism and a decision to put both acting and singing on the back burner in her life.

Melvyn had decided it made better sense for them to buy a home than rent, so they set about building their dream house. They purchased a three-acre lot in the Hollywood Hills and commissioned the noted architect Roland Coates to design a spacious, open, modern one-story home that was filled with windows and light. At thirty-eight years old, Helen discovered that she was pregnant again. Delighted with the news and finally reconciled to making California her permanent home, she took great pleasure in helping to create their perfect domestic space. She attended to the details—hand-carved doors, pegged plank floors, prime wood paneling and stairs. While Melvyn initially objected to the spacious quarters, disdainfully calling the living room "big enough for a camp of gypsies," he well knew Helen's passion for space and sunshine and quickly acquiesced. She decorated the nursery and bought a wardrobe of doll-sized dresses, hoping for a little girl. She hired a young, dark-eyed college student to act as her personal assistant and babysitter. Evelyn Chavoor's Syrian father was a produce merchant with whom the Douglases had a standing order for fresh fruit and vegetables to be delivered every Saturday morning. His attractive daughter, "Evie," was only a teenager but sensible and sophisticated beyond her years and background. "She could do anything," Helen wrote of Evie, who would become her lifelong aide, friend, and confidant. "Good natured, bright and possessed of dignified authority, she was the first stranger to come into the Douglas household since our marriage who didn't seem a stranger."

On August 14, 1938, Helen went into labor and Melvyn drove her to the Pasadena hospital. As with her first childbirth experience, she went under general anesthesia to awaken several hours later with a grinning Melvyn leaning over her. "Helen, we have a beautiful little girl with a head of blonde hair," he said when she awakened. They named her Mary Helen—Helen's name in reverse—and brought her home to the new house. It was there, plumped up in pillows in the lavish master bedroom, that she overheard the discussion about the "Okies" that ignited her social consciousness.

During that fall of 1938, home with a baby, recuperating from the Vienna ordeal and enlivened by a newfound cause, she began cultivating friends outside the movie community. To her surprise and satisfaction, she found that Los Angeles was home to a varied and interesting circle of artists, scholars, and scientists. She became especially close to Remsen Bird, the president of Occidental College, and his wife, Helen. She was in awe of their political and cultural sophistication and touched by their devotion to each other. "The Birds were registered Republicans but strong supporters of Franklin Roosevelt. Such was their urbanity and grace that they numbered staunch Republicans and Democrats among their closest friends"—a feat Helen saw as "quite a trick" during any era.

Helen's exposure to Nazis, anti-Semitism, and the burgeoning German militarism had been pivotal in galvanizing her embryonic political sentiments. Melvyn joined Hollywood's Anti-Nazi League—the only organization in California speaking out against Hitler—and Helen reluctantly participated in the movement as well, agonizing over her decision, for she loved Germany. "I spoke the language and sang the songs . . . people had been kind to me . . . but neither could I passively accept the monstrous activities of Adolf Hitler." But joining the league was not enough for Melvyn, and he soon became one of California's most outspoken supporters of FDR's interventionist foreign policy. Melvyn was one of the first Hollywood movie stars to take an active role in politics, and he traveled the state speaking out against Hitler and alerting audiences to the dangerous developments in Germany. "In a period that was profoundly isolationist," as Helen recalled the moment, "it was unusual for anyone to claim that events in Europe had any importance for Americans." The country was becoming polarized between Left and Right, interventionists and isolationists, Nazi sympathizers and Communists, and Hollywood was increasingly becoming a microcosm of the extremes. Appeasement was in the air—England's prime minister Neville Chamberlain had placated Hitler and fascist Italian dictator Benito Mussolini—and even the U.S. ambassador to Great Britain, Joseph P. Kennedy, was urging the British to make a deal with Hitler.

Melvyn and Helen both became particularly interested in efforts to circumvent the U.S. Neutrality Act of 1935, which banned the shipment of American arms to aid Britain and other targets of Nazi Germany. When William Allen White, the famous Kansas journalist, formed what would become known as the William Allen White Committee as a vehicle for aiding U.S. allies, Melvyn was active in forming a California branch.

Republicans had controlled California for forty-five years, but when the mild-mannered socialist Upton Sinclair captured the Democratic nomination for governor in a landslide victory and ran on a platform of raising taxes for big business in general—and the movie industry in particular—studio moguls became alarmed. "Previous to 1934 Hollywood had been so indifferent to governmental matters that Dorothy

Parker had observed that the only 'ism' to which anyone subscribed was 'plagiarism,'" Melvyn wrote of the political apathy of the early movie industry. But that year, with millions of Americans out of work, Californians rallied support behind the muckraking author of *The Jungle* and his End Poverty in California (EPIC) campaign. Horrified by the prospect of a Socialist governing the state, Sinclair's Republican adversaries responded with a level of viciousness never before seen in American politics. "They churned out the crudest kind of propaganda," Melvyn noted; he and his family would later become tragically ensnared in the same kind of politics. "The anti-Sinclair crusade in 1934 introduced publicity and advertising techniques that shaped the modern political campaign," wrote political journalist Greg Mitchell of the anti-Communist themes, the sophisticated trickery, the use of political consultants, and the dawning of the electronic media age.

The *New York Times* called Sinclair's campaign "the first serious movement against the profit system in the United States," and historian Arthur M. Schlesinger Jr. observed that the Republican response marked the beginning of an era "in which advertising men now believed they could sell or destroy political candidates as they sold one brand of soap and defamed its competitor."

Sinclair's candidacy posed a problem for Roosevelt, who was being pressured by the progressive wing of his party to support the Democratic nominee while his conservative advisers warned him not to be seen as coddling socialism. Since the Douglases' allegiance was first and foremost to the Roosevelts, they were ambivalent if not opposed to Sinclair, and in any case were not disappointed when he was defeated.

Louis B. Mayer led the Hollywood effort to raise anti-Sinclair money from studio executives and to produce and disseminate propaganda films. For the first time, actors and writers were plunged into politics. Neither Melvyn nor Helen had been involved with Hollywood's politically liberal writers, directors, and actors, and at first they remained outside the fray. But in the run-up to Roosevelt's 1936 re-election, Melvyn's efforts on behalf of FDR "stirred up the moribund Democratic party on the West Coast," as Helen put it. He also continued to work tirelessly for the Anti-Nazi League and the White Committee. He enlisted the support of many of his colleagues, organizing a gathering of fifty-six directors, producers, writers, and actors to sign a petition calling for the economic boycott of Germany. Included in this elite cadre of early Hollywood activists, which held its first meeting at the home of Edward G. Robinson, were Claude Rains, James Cagney, Groucho Marx, Henry Fonda, and Myrna Loy.

"What do you care about Hitler?" Mayer asked Melvyn. "If they want you to say, 'Heil Hitler,' say 'Heil Hitler.' What's the difference?" Like many in America, Jews and non-Jews alike, Mayer did not realize where Hitler's anti-Semitism was heading.

When the Democrats finally had a strong gubernatorial candidate in 1938—a liberal state legislator named Culbert L. Olson—Melvyn threw himself into the campaign. Melvyn was active in anti-fascist organizations, raising money to aid Spanish loyalists, and participated in efforts to unionize motion picture artists. In all of his political affiliations with what were considered leftist organizations, Melvyn found himself repeatedly at odds with the avowed Communists within them. He considered Russia as totalitarian a state as Germany and Italy and saw no place in American politics for the Communist Party. Still, his efforts on behalf of the victorious Olson incurred the wrath of Mayer. A staunch Republican and member of the Los Angeles power elite, Mayer had a long history of strong-arming contract employees to support Republican candidates. He saw Melvyn's political antics as those of an upstart threatening Hollywood's status quo, and Mayer would seek his retribution later.

While Melvyn was immersed in the Olson campaign, Helen began her transition from actress, singer, and mother to politician. Having risen from her sickbed that early fall morning in 1938, she joined a social movement to bring both relief and publicity to the human ravages of the Great Depression. Given her knowledge, passion, beauty, and oratory skills, she inevitably became a much sought-after speaker on the subject, and her efforts quickly brought her to the attention of several high-level Roosevelt administration officials.

One of the first speeches she gave was at Mills College in Oakland, where she met the nationally renowned economist Paul Schuster Taylor. The Berkeley professor, commissioned by the federal government to study agricultural labor in the states where the migrants had originated, was considered the leading academic authority on the matter. He and his wife, Dorothea Lange, had completed a thousand-mile fact-finding tour "of ditchbank settlements, pea-pickers' tents and sheds on the edges of cotton fields"—a project supported by the government's Farm Security Administration. Lange's photographs, along with Taylor's essays—published as *An American Exodus*—would become one of the preeminent collaborations between a photographer and a sociologist. Lange would be called "without doubt our greatest documentary photographer" by Edward Steichen, and her photograph of an emaciated mother holding two scrawny children would soon help stir Congress to approve Roosevelt's Farm Security Camps to provide food, hygiene, and shelter to migrant workers.

Taylor and Lange would become Helen's dear and lasting friends along with several others who had been in the audience that day at Mills College. This group from California's Bay Area would be instrumental in her intellectual enlightenment as she moved with astonishing ease into the realm of politics. Her new world comprised academics and social workers, journalists and civil libertarians. Among them were Dr. Alexander Meiklejohn, the former president of Amherst College, and his economist wife, Helen Everett; Myer Cohen, who was an authority on the U.S. Supreme Court; philosophy professor Charles Hogan, who was active with the American Civil Liberties Union; and many faculty members from various California campuses.

When Roosevelt had come to power in 1932 he used a football meta-phor, comparing himself to a quarterback who had to make quick de-cisions based upon the results of his team's first move. In one of his early press conferences, he said that "future plays will depend on how the next one works." Indeed, the evolution of what would become known as Roosevelt's New Deal was an exercise in continuous restruc-turing. "The New Deal will never be understood by anyone who looks for a single thread of policy, a far-reaching, far-seeing plan," wrote Richard Hofstadter, the distinguished historian of American Progres-sivism. "It was a series of improvisations, many adopted very suddenly, many contradictory." Others saw more method in the seeming chaos, as Roosevelt gathered "around him in his cabinet and throughout his administration one of the most remarkable collections of minds and skills ever to assemble in Washington," as author T. H. Watkins put it.

"None of these individuals knew precisely what they were going to do to remove fear and restore hope. But they considered themselves innovative pragmatists, and were willing to try any likely avenue."

Inheriting a deep economic depression, Roosevelt had initiated a series of emergency relief programs to stimulate the economy and get Americans back to work. He drew on ideas contained in thousands of books, the advice of academics who would become known as the "brain trust," and the experience of dozens of economists, populists, labor leaders, and social reformers. At the heart of the reforms was a massive redistribution of wealth, which alarmed Wall Street and America's elite.

The program was "a radical departure from American life," as his onetime closest adviser, Columbia professor Raymond Moley, described it. "It put more power in the central Government. At the time, it was necessary." This revolutionary experiment for the federal government to shore up the nation's institutions came at a moment of such utter despair that millions of Americans threw their support behind the president with the fervor of a religious cult. Helen counted herself among the most passionate of devotees.

The first real contact she had with the Roosevelt administration was through Aubrey Williams, head of the National Youth Authority—a favorite program of Mrs. Roosevelt's that sought unemployed youth for public service projects. Williams contacted Helen and told her that he acted as a sort of talent scout for Mrs. Roosevelt. The First Lady had heard of Helen's work on behalf of the migrants, as well as Melvyn's work with California's Democratic Party, and wanted to invite the couple to Washington. Stricken by polio in 1921 and confined to a wheelchair, President Roosevelt had come to rely upon his wife as a fact gatherer. Because it was difficult for FDR to move around the country, Eleanor Roosevelt had taken on "the responsibility of collecting people who possessed the grass-roots information he needed," as Helen put it. Mrs. Roosevelt, as it turned out, had further delegated that mission to Williams and others who moved out into the nation and found the community activists and issues that they thought Roosevelt should embrace.

In November 1939, Helen and Melvyn had their first visit to the White House. Shortly after they checked into a Washington hotel,

they received a handwritten note from Mrs. Roosevelt inviting them
to tea with her the following day and asking that they spend the night
after dining with her and the president. A White House driver re-
trieved them, and so began a deep and abiding friendship between the
Douglases and the Roosevelts.

It was near the end of his second term, and the president was preoccupied with Germany's invasion of Poland and the possibility of
a foreign war; Mrs. Roosevelt was consumed with domestic policy.
"Unless democracy were renewed at home," Mrs. Roosevelt continually argued, according to historian Doris Kearns Goodwin, "there
was little merit in fighting for democracy abroad."

With that in mind, Eleanor Roosevelt threw her full support behind
Helen and her work for the migrants, and, for that matter, behind any
issue that Helen deemed important for as long as Eleanor was alive to
support her.

Helen met several high-level New Dealers during this first trip to
Washington—men and women who would help her in her efforts in
California while also guiding her toward a political career of her
own. Secretary of the Interior Harold L. Ickes and Labor Secretary
Frances Perkins—the first woman cabinet secretary—would become
particularly close to Helen, as their interests were inextricably en-
meshed. All who met her were enchanted by her persona. "We all remember the first time we saw the Grand Canyon, Niagara, or other
great wonders of nature. Similarly, people always seem to remember
their first meeting with Helen Gahagan Douglas," wrote Assistant
Secretary of the Interior Arthur Goldschmidt about meeting Helen
during this period. Goldschmidt "came away from that meeting enchanted and with a sense of wonder at Helen's display of energy—at
the physical, emotional and mental drive of this beautiful and glamorous person." Years later, Goldschmidt would say of her: "Why did
people like us respond so readily to Helen? Her charm, her warmth,
her beauty, her glamour might well have been enough. But there was
always something more . . . an elegance of style, a brilliance of performance, and a commitment so passionate that it has rarely, if ever,
been equaled. It was thrilling and deeply satisfying to play even a
small part in her battles."

Upon her return to California, things began to move quickly for Helen. What few knew was that while Helen's star was rising on the national political stage, her marriage was in crisis. Melvyn was involved in an extramarital affair during this period—reportedly with one of his famous costars. Though Helen was devastated, she soldiered forth with characteristic stoicism.

Typical for her era, Helen had refused to divorce Melvyn despite the terminal rupture in their marriage, and for the next forty years their marriage was platonic. Though they would stay married, they essentially would never live together again as husband and wife. It would not be until many years later, near the end of her life, that she documented her refusal to divorce. "1. I loved you. 2. the family, brought up as I was the thought of breaking up the family was like considering murder. 3. I could not believe what had happened so I just suffered dumbly."

Whatever the context and complexities of their union in the 1940s, they remained devoted friends and dedicated coparents until their deaths—apparently forging an arrangement that served them both, perhaps not unlike that of the Roosevelts, whom she idolized. "There was an understanding, a closeness, a bond between Eleanor and Franklin Roosevelt that I found beautiful," Helen would later write of the couple, whose traditional marriage had been irrevocably broken following Franklin's longtime affair with Eleanor's social secretary, Lucy Mercer. She described Eleanor's manner with her husband as "at once intimate, informal, natural and deeply respectful"—a comportment that Helen would emulate with Melvyn in years to come. Near the end of his life, Melvyn too would compare their marriage to that of the Roosevelts. "I suppose it is commonplace that most long-lived couples divide areas of emotional response, even as they share responsibilities and material goods. Certainly our friends, the Roosevelts, had done something like that . . . But this was a private problem involving Helen's and my inner lives."

While most in their social circle were naturally unaware of the reasons and depth of the breach between them, the changed dynamic was clear. From the wreck of her sorrow and humiliation she turned away from the marriage. The couple went their separate ways, Melvyn back toward Hollywood and Helen ever deeper into national politics.

FDR appointed her to the presidential advisory committee for the

Works Progress Administration (WPA), and, after writing an article about migrants for the magazine *Democratic Digest*, she moved up the ranks of the National Democratic Party's Women's Division. In addition to the Steinbeck Committee, Helen also became director of the National Youth Authority and the state Democratic Party's Women's Division. The national job creation programs of the WPA would become famous, with Helen at the center of its historic California projects. The First Lady mentored Helen and guided her entrance onto the national stage, and she was soon in demand throughout the nation as a writer and speaker. Perhaps no one was more appalled at Helen's move into politics than Madame Sophia Cehanovska, who blamed Eleanor Roosevelt for her prodigy's distraction. "If it hadn't been for *that woman*, you'd have gone back to your music and had a great career!" the Russian coach later admonished her.

Helen and Melvyn—separately and together—were active in Roosevelt's 1940 campaign for an unprecedented third term. The Democratic Party was deeply divided over Roosevelt's decision to run. But FDR was unbending, certain that war was imminent and that he was the best person to lead America through the impending crisis. At the end of the summer, FDR had announced the trade of fifty destroyers to Great Britain in exchange for long-term leases on British bases— a bold interventionist move that circumvented Congress's Neutrality Act.

Melvyn had been the first movie actor to become a delegate to the National Democratic Convention in Chicago, and Helen was named an alternate delegate. At the convention, Helen sang "The Star Spangled Banner" at the opening session, and when she was elected Democratic National Committeewoman for California, she was suddenly thrust into the limelight of national politics.

As committeewoman, she discovered that she was expected to play a part in what she called the pork-barrel "patronage system which has oiled the wheels of politics since human history began"—a role that she resisted. She discovered as well the deep-seated sexism intrinsic to the party politics of the era. Dozens of women appealed to her, all conveying the "same story," as she put it. The male politicians used them for manual labor—stuffing envelopes and making coffee—but never consulted them on their views or appointed them to influential positions. Helen encouraged the women to educate themselves in domestic and foreign affairs. "I was raised in a household of dominating males," she told them, "and I learned early that men guard their authority over women jealously. As for politics, they sincerely believe public life to be a male bailiwick. They reason that men have been running the country for the past two hundred years and are meant to continue to do so for centuries to come. In short, men never would share power with women willingly. If we wanted it, we would have to take it."

Helen worked indefatigably for Roosevelt and his running mate, Henry A. Wallace, crisscrossing the country at her own expense and making more than 250 speeches for the ticket. She organized an event for Wallace that drew eighteen thousand to the Hollywood Bowl and arranged for a gathering of fifteen hundred women to meet Eleanor Roosevelt in Los Angeles.

The Douglases' immersion in national politics drew press attention throughout the country: It signaled the first powerful convergence of the Hollywood film industry and Washington public policy, with the couple credited for the unprecedented campaign efforts on FDR's behalf by Hollywood Democrats. The ticket swept the state, and the conspicuous power couple led an influx of film stars into the process, including Mickey Rooney, Charlie Chaplin, Ethel Barrymore, Myrna Loy, Douglas Fairbanks Jr., and Edward G. Robinson. Along the way, Helen developed an ever closer friendship with the First Lady and was a frequent overnight guest at the Roosevelt White House.

In April 1940, Helen ushered the First Lady onto a private plane she had chartered. Eleanor had come to California to see firsthand the conditions of the workers. Landing in Bakersfield, the two women drove through the Tehachapi Mountains north to the San Joaquin Valley. Passing one of the ubiquitous ditch-bank communities and spotting a cluster of shacks constructed out of tar paper and flattened tin cans, Eleanor asked the driver to stop the car. The two women walked briskly across a field toward some workers bent over in their labor. "Oh, Mrs. Roosevelt, you've come to see us," said a man as he stretched out his hand. "He seemed to accept as a natural event of American life that the wife of the President of the United States would be standing in a mucky field chatting with him," Helen recalled of the moment.

When the First Lady headed for one of the makeshift lean-tos, the man said: "Please, don't go in there. My wife and children are sick with the raisins"—the colloquialism for chicken pox. Undaunted, Eleanor entered the cabin.

Photographers swarmed their car. A reporter asked the First Lady if she was now convinced that *The Grapes of Wrath* was an exaggeration, which Republican critics of the president's New Deal were roundly claiming. A wealthy local grower had recently presided over a much publicized book-burning, claiming "the Communist Party wrote the outline and Steinbeck filled in the rest of the crap."

The unflappable Eleanor replied evenly: "I have never believed that *The Grapes of Wrath* was an exaggeration."

3

Congresswoman 1944–1950

Great spirits have often encountered violent
opposition from mediocre minds.

—Albert Einstein

I *DECIDED* I WANTED to be an actress; I *decided* I wanted to
be a singer; I *didn't* decide I wanted to get into public affairs . . . The
current of the times . . . carried me," Helen mused of her destiny. As
one observer saw it, just as Helen had considered singing an extension
of acting, she would now "consider politics merely an extension of
being a good citizen." Her rise would be momentous—yet another of
her overnight sensations.

By the beginning of the 1940s, Helen was the most powerful
woman in the state of California. In addition to holding the position
of national committeewoman for the Democratic Party, she had been
appointed vice-chair of the state party and head of its Women's Division. Her "fervent commitment to Franklin Roosevelt's domestic and
foreign policies, [and] Eleanor Roosevelt as her political 'fairy god-
mother,'" as scholar Ingrid Scobie saw it, gave her a "good start up
the political ladder."

Her path from involvement in various antifascist fronts to becoming
a political powerhouse in two short years was rare for mid-twentieth-
century America. As a member of the first post-suffragist generation—
it had been a short twenty years since women had been allowed to
vote in all fifty states—Helen was charting new territory for herself

and her gender. All the while, she had unique access to the highest political powers in the land.

On the fateful day of May 10, 1940—the day that Nazi Germany's tanks rolled into Belgium and the Netherlands—Helen was a guest at the White House. It was a grave moment for the president and for the country. Addressing his cabinet that afternoon, Roosevelt asked his secretary of state to provide the latest news from abroad. With the only hint of good news in an otherwise somber meeting, Treasury Secretary Henry Morgenthau reported that the Belgian and Dutch gold reserves had been safely evacuated. Secretary of Commerce Harry Hopkins, chain-smoking and world-weary, was the messenger of despair. The United States had "only a five-, six-months supply of both rubber and tin, both of which are absolutely essential for purposes of defense," he told his colleagues. Then, in the midst of that solemn meeting, an aide brought word that British Prime Minister Chamberlain had resigned under pressure from Parliament, opening the way for Winston Churchill. Finally, some welcome news for the president, who, according to Harold Ickes, believed "Churchill was the best man that England had."

Despite the drama of the day, Roosevelt retired to his study for his favorite time: cocktail hour. There, Helen and Harry Hopkins waited for him. Eleanor was in Connecticut addressing the student body at the Choate School and the president's longtime secretary, Missy LeHand, was acting as hostess. In keeping with routine, the cocktail conversation turned away from the gloomy discussion of war and politics and to light banter. Roosevelt had a wickedly incisive sense of humor and loved gossip of all kinds—especially the titillating sort that Helen Gahagan was privy to in Hollywood. After dinner that evening, as he left to give a speech to several thousand scientists and academics at Constitution Hall, he stopped by Helen's room. He asked if she would meet him privately upon his return, saying that he had a very important question to ask her. Of course she would, she assured him, wondering what the president might have on his mind.

When Roosevelt returned that night, he found Helen in his study. As they both started to relax, he received a telephone call from Churchill. Helen waited patiently while the new prime minister of Great Britain and the president of the United States had their first conversation on the eve of a world war, all the while preparing herself for what she assumed would be a question about California politics.

"OK, Helen," Roosevelt said to her when he had concluded his affairs of state. "Now, I want you to tell me exactly what happened under the table at Ciro's between Paulette Goddard and Anatole Litvak." The wildly juicy tale that Roosevelt wanted to hear involved the beautiful actress married to Charlie Chaplin, who had recently starred in Clare Boothe Luce's *The Women*. Helen had heard about the Ciro's scandal and told the president that Goddard and the Oscar-nominated Russian film director had been overtaken with passion and slid under the table to make love. In order to provide the couple with privacy, the waiters in the exclusive restaurant hurriedly brought extra tablecloths to drape the table.

"I love it, I love it!" Roosevelt responded.

The president would relish these lighthearted moods in the upcoming months, as the "phony war" came to an end the following day with Hitler's invasion of France. The false calm had been in effect since Britain agreed to Hitler's annexation of Czechoslovakia, but now the future was ominous. The remainder of Helen's visit with the Roosevelts was "very subdued." She dined quietly the next evening with Franklin and Eleanor and the three then watched a film together.

When the film ended, Mrs. Roosevelt excused herself and Helen was left alone with the president. She thought him tired and depressed and was reluctant to add to his burdens. Still, she had come to Washington seeking help for the migrant children, and felt compelled to press her cause. "Surely, Mr. President, we can't abandon those children?" she implored.

His eyes filled with tears and his voice broke. "Don't tell me any more, Helen. You and Eleanor, you must stop ganging up on me. There are some things we can't do now . . . we just *can't*."

Helen knew it was true. She saw evidence everywhere of the New Deal social programs rolling back as the country focused its attention on the crisis in Europe. That very day, Nazi Germany's tanks "were in France, sweeping around the concrete bunkers of the Maginot Line that we had been promised were impregnable," she later wrote of the deepening conflict. "By the end of the month British troops were evacuated from the port of Dunkirk by pleasure boats able to shuttle across a miraculously calm English Channel. A few weeks later we saw newsreel footage of Hitler dancing a jig as France signed the surrender . . . Mussolini . . . picked that moment to exercise his function as Hitler's ally. Italy declared war on Britain."

Helen returned to California and threw herself as wholeheartedly into Roosevelt's interventionist agenda as she had his New Deal domestic program, giving speeches on America's moral responsibility to help Britain. Aiding America's allies was in the nation's self-interest, she argued. Her impassioned support incurred the wrath of the isolationist, antiwar America Firsters. The most prominent public spokesman of that movement, aviator Charles Lindbergh, was the dashing hero who had completed the world's first transatlantic flight and enjoyed wide public sympathy from the earlier kidnapping and murder of his baby. But Lindbergh's support and credibility began to wane when his deepseated anti-Semitism spewed forth. Warning the country of Jewish ownership and influence in the press, in the movie industry, and in the federal government, Lindbergh became an increasingly polarizing figure, prompting Roosevelt to dismiss him as a Nazi.

On December 7, 1941, Helen's life—like everyone else's in America—changed instantly when the U.S. entered the war. After the Japanese bombed Pearl Harbor, the Roosevelt administration began to prepare for a Japanese invasion of the West Coast. The president appointed Helen cochairman of civilian defense for Southern California. Her job was to train women to respond with food distribution and medical supplies in the event of an enemy attack. Hysteria surrounded the Nisei—the second-generation Californians of Japanese origin— who were accused of being spies, and calls came for their internment. Within two hours of Pearl Harbor, Los Angeles police were rounding up everyone in the Little Tokyo neighborhood. Within days, the U.S. Treasury had seized all Japanese banks and businesses and frozen all bank accounts, but even those actions did not quell the paranoia in the country. "The Japanese in California should be under armed guard to the last man and woman right now—and to hell with habeas corpus," proclaimed the nationally syndicated columnist Westbrook Pegler.

Helen was genuinely ambivalent about the subject and discussed it frequently with Harold Ickes. The interior secretary was "distressed at the tide of sentiment against Japanese-Americans and felt it did loyal citizens a grave disservice," as Helen remembered his views. While she disagreed with Pegler and his ilk about the Nisei being spies and traitors who were sympathetic to Japan, she also feared for their safety if they remained in the community as mob violence against them escalated. "Herd 'em up, pack 'em off and give them the inside room in the badlands," brayed one columnist who embodied the anti-Japanese sentiment set loose in the country. "Let 'em be pinched, hurt, hungry and dead up against it . . . Personally, I hate the Japanese. And that goes for all of them."

Japanese immigrants had first poured into California's goldfields in the 1860s and were initially a welcome source of labor on cattle ranches and fruit farms as well. Through a combination of industriousness and astuteness, they invested in farmland and commercial real estate—especially small hotels and warehouses—and by 1941 wielded significant economic influence in the state. Though Japanese-owned farms constituted less than 1 percent of the land, they produced 40 percent of the food. The Japanese attack on Pearl Harbor unleashed a vicious xenophobic resentment that had merely been dormant beneath the surface for many decades, and many Californians were all too eager to put the Japanese in their place.

California Attorney General Earl Warren, who had his sights set on a challenge to Governor Culbert Olson, testified before Congress in support of the incarceration of 120,000 West Coast Japanese and the seizure of their property. "There is more potential danger among the group of Japanese who are born in this country than from the alien Japanese who were born in Japan," Warren opined. As it turned out, Roosevelt's decision was based on a false assessment by the U.S. military about the Nisei's threat to national security, prompting the ACLU many years later to label it "the worst single wholesale violation of civil rights of American citizens in our history," according to presidential biographer James MacGregor Burns.

In characteristic fashion, Helen insisted on touring the internment camps to see conditions for herself. Once she was convinced that the housing arrangements were humane, she supported Roosevelt's

Executive Order 9066, signed on February 19, 1942, which gave the secretary of war the power to place the Nisei in "relocation centers"— a euphemism for concentration camps—hastily constructed throughout the American West.

"The issue of the [N]isei's abandoned property was dealt with in the same harsh manner as the prisoners themselves," investigative journalist Gus Russo reported in 2006. "Suddenly without employment, they could not afford mortgage payments or indefinite storage for their possessions. Given mere days to sell their homes, businesses, and all the belongings they could not carry, their plight defined a 'buyer's market' . . . for speculators with deep pockets, the real bargains were in houses, undeveloped [N]isei land, and commercial property such as stores, warehouses, and hotels." They were virtually powerless to resist. The Issei, or first-generation Japanese-born parents of the Nisei, had been denied the right to vote and to establish citizenship, so they were easily victimized.

A month later Roosevelt would sign Executive Order 9095, establishing the Office of Alien Property within the Department of Justice and ushering in a real estate grab unlike anything seen in California since the gold rush of the 1840s. Property seized by the government included 535,000 acres of the state's most fertile farmland as well as downtown Los Angeles real estate worth hundreds of millions of dollars. Though she could not yet have foreseen it, the unprecedented land grab would have a far-reaching impact on Helen's future.

While Helen focused on the war effort at home, Melvyn volunteered to work in the arts division of the Office of Civilian Defense in Washington. Now one of the highest-paid actors in America—his salary topping $200,000 after the box office hit *Ninotchka*—he envisioned a way in which actors, directors, producers, and writers could make films in support of America and its allies. By January 1942 he had been appointed to the OCD upon the personal recommendation of Eleanor Roosevelt. The appointment brought what historian Goodwin described as "a withering attack" against "Hymie Hesselberg," as Douglas was called during his confirmation hearings before Congress. "I want the members to take into consideration today the fact that we are paying Melvyn Douglas $8,000 a year—as much as we are paying that matchless and heroic soldier, General MacArthur, when he is battling in the Philippines every day," thundered Representative Charles I. Faddis of Pennsylvania. California Republican congressmen used the opportunity to imply Douglas was a Communist sympathizer—particularly ironic since the Communist Party had boycotted *Ninotchka* because of its anti-Communist caricatures. Leland Ford from California's Sixteenth Congressional District tactlessly and repeatedly brought up the specter of the "movie Jews," making sure that his colleagues knew that Melvyn was one of them. "Do we always have to have men who have changed their names . . . in high places in Government?"

Helen was livid, focusing her anger on the Red-baiting Ford, and decided to make Ford's defeat a priority. "[I]f we don't clean some of the people out of Congress, this program for a better world is never going to take place," she wrote to her friend Norman Littell, an assistant attorney general in Washington who had witnessed Ford's week-long assault against Melvyn. She considered running against Ford herself, worried as she was about the Democrats losing congressional seats in the 1942 midterm elections. In the end, at the urging of Eleanor Roosevelt, she decided she could be more helpful to the administration by continuing to mobilize Democratic women.

On December 7, 1942—the first anniversary of Pearl Harbor—Melvyn joined fellow movie stars Henry Fonda and Tyrone Power in enlisting in the army. He was sworn in "at a special ceremony set up to beat an automatic exemption from service for men over forty," as he put it. Sensitive to the problems he felt his activist past brought to the Roosevelts, and indignant at the suggestion that his OCD position came via favoritism, he refused a commission and enlisted as a private.

Characteristically gracious, Eleanor assuaged his concerns. "I do not mind any kind of nastiness and I hope you and Helen do not mind either," she wrote to Melvyn. "Evidently any friend of mine has to go through [such criticism], and I hope the effect will be strengthening of our friendship rather than the lessening of any bond that may exist."

Melvyn became a first lieutenant and was assigned to the India-Burma-China theater as director of the Entertainment Production Unit. The night before he sailed for India, Helen and nine-year-old

Peter had dinner with him at a restaurant near the naval base. Stoic and dry-eyed, Peter held Melvyn's hand tightly throughout the meal. But the minute Melvyn was out of sight, the young boy dissolved into a sea of tears. While Peter "flung himself on the floor of the car and sobbed his heart out," Helen found herself in "a state of agony and loss—and fear," she wrote of her feelings. She had left three-year-old Mary Helen at home, thinking the toddler too young to experience the sad parting. Suddenly Helen felt utterly alone.

With Melvyn's enlistment, the family income vanished. Helen had never before had to worry about money. For years she had received dividends from her stock in her father's company as well as income from his numerous investments, but Walter Gahagan's fortune disappeared with the stock market crash: He had personally lost more than two million dollars. By 1943, the Gahagan Construction Corporation was barely viable despite contracts for dredging what would eventually be John F. Kennedy Airport on Long Island and Logan Airport in Boston, as well as a renovation of the Panama Canal.

Melvyn "left me with his savings, some $18,000, which we knew would not stretch very far," Helen recalled. "I determined not to touch them at all. I still had some money of my own. But it would take major economizing to get through." On the day after he sailed, Helen gave two weeks' notice to all of her household help, and she learned to cook and clean. She considered selling their home, even thought about moving back to New York following rumors that Los Angeles might be bombed, but ultimately decided it was important to keep the children in a stable environment amid the turmoil of circumstances. Evie Chavoor had taken a job elsewhere, and while Helen found herself surprisingly competent at the domestic duties that absorbed the lives of most women, she was nonplussed by raising young children. She placed them both in boarding school, seeing them only on weekends, which allowed her to pursue her political interests and professional commitments.

She kept her office in downtown Los Angeles, where she coordinated her efforts for the Women's Division, working at the grassroots level while maintaining her contacts with Washington. She socialized with her dear friends, Orson Welles and his wife, Rita Hayworth, and spent a good deal of time with Lillian Ford—"a tiny dynamo" married to

Congressman Thomas F. Ford, who represented the city's Fourteenth District. She took a long trip to Washington in 1943, intending to see for herself just how Congress operated, and, as had become customary, stayed in the Roosevelt White House. Eleanor hosted several events in order to introduce her to various congressmen, and Helen spent many hours watching Congress in session. "There is no leadership in the House or Senate," she wrote to Melvyn. [John] McCormack and [Sam] Rayburn just lack what it takes . . . We are certainly paying a heavy price for the loss of our good men in Congress, but then we get what we deserve in a Democracy."

One day in 1943, Lillian Ford asked Helen when she intended to return to the theater, and she casually responded that once she finished her terms as national committeewoman and state vice-chairman, she would consider it. "You're hooked," Lillian told her, unconvinced. "You might as well do something really important and run for Congress."

"Never," Helen answered quickly.

A few days later, Tom Ford approached her and told her he wanted to retire after serving twelve years. "If you'll run in my place, I can retire with a clear conscience," he told her.

"I've sat in the gallery of the House of Representatives and listened to the discussions," she replied. "They're *boring*."

Ford was tenacious, making a strong argument for the necessity of a New Dealer in the district to support the Roosevelt doctrine. When she firmly declined to run, Ford mentioned it to the president, who wrote a letter to Helen urging her to change her mind so that Ford could retire knowing a New Deal Democrat would take the seat. Eleanor also weighed in. Visiting Helen in California, the First Lady recommended that she run only if she was certain of being elected. "Helen, don't you run, no matter how you are urged to do so, unless you are sure you can win," Eleanor told her. "I think Franklin would just like to have you in Washington."

Given the time and place in American history, it was a bold and extraordinary concept, and no one grasped the pioneering aspect of a woman's run for Congress more than Helen. At the "forefront of a new generation of postsuffrage women who entered the political arena," as journalist Greg Mitchell wrote of Helen and the moment, she found few examples of leaders of her gender. Women had only had the vote in all states for less than twenty-five years, and Helen—if she ran and won—would become only the thirty-second woman ever to serve in the House of Representatives out of a body of 435. Most of them had ascended to the august legislative body to fill the seats of their retired or deceased husbands rather than by election on their own merits. Even so, the U.S. Senate remained off-limits to women, as if the old boys' network of national politics grudgingly abided a handful of women in the House but observed a tacit but ironclad rule that the Senate was for men only. To add insult to injury for the progressives, Republicans had six women in Congress to one for the Democrats.

Helen firmly believed that women must be "willing to compete on an equal basis with men and expect no favors," as she would later contend in a speech imploring women to enter politics. "They must neither ask nor give quarter. They must have principles, based on knowledge and understanding of their own, and not be the mere shadows of someone else."

While her gender presented a complex set of obstacles, her celebrity status posed an additional ingredient that was impossible to quantify. To be the first Hollywood personality making a foray into national politics was daring. To be the first female movie star to do so was audacious. No one seemed more aware of that than Helen herself, and no one was less intimidated by it than she. Her hesitation was purely pragmatic.

She wrote a letter to Melvyn in which she weighed the pros and cons of running for office. "Certain people will heave bricks and throw mud," she had written him, "but I think there is enough Irish in me to handle that. Pray for me to be able to fulfill the grave responsibilities which election to Congress would place upon me." She never received a response from him.

"Helen, this is a call to duty," Ford wrote to her. "You have unusual gifts and at this time you cannot conscientiously refuse the urgent request to use them where they will benefit the people of the 14th District and of the entire nation."

As pressure mounted on her to file for the seat, Helen was consumed with mixed feelings. She worried that it would take her away from her two young children—then ten and five years old—and she knew it would signify a final break with her career as an actress and singer. In the end, she could not stand by and watch while the Fourteenth District seat was taken by a Republican or right-wing Democrat who would not support Roosevelt. She walked into City Hall in late spring 1944 and filed for the congressional seat of the urban Los Angeles district that encompassed a small enclave of wealthy estates as well as one of the largest black ghettos in the country. Despite her involvement in community affairs, Helen was woefully unaware of the many layers that constituted the Fourteenth.

Those who envisioned where Los Angeles was headed—those directing the fount of money that would shape Helen's political life—wielded their power from behind the scenes. "Every city has its boom," wrote California's most noted social historian, Carey McWilliams. "Actually, the growth of Southern California since 1870 should be regarded as one continuous boom punctuated at intervals by major explosions." Helen had joined the boom in the decade of the city's most pivotal transcendence. Harry Chandler, publisher of the Los Angeles Times and the town's biggest booster, promoted Los Angeles as "the White Spot of America"—a city with "no crime, no corruption, no Commies." Chandler's claim lured hundreds of thousands to this new sun-drenched mecca, and would have been impressive if not for its patent absurdity. Like the rest of America, "L.A.'s moral fiber marinated in bathtub gin during the 1920s," as Chandler biographer Dennis McDougal put it.

Los Angeles had been populated by American immigrants since the mid-nineteenth century, for three hundred years before that by Spanish, British, and Russian explorers, and for thousands of years before that by dozens of Native American tribes. Spain had been the most significant colonizing power until 1821, when the Republic of Mexico successfully revolted against it. But to both Spain and Mexico, California was nothing more than a faraway, barren outpost. The Mexican Colonization Act of 1824 allowed influential citizens to acquire massive land grants consisting of thousands of acres of lush vineyards, orange groves, and irrigated farmland that supported herds of horses, sheep, and cattle. The vast ranchos were supervised by what became known as the Californios, who used Native Americans as slave labor. "In the hands of an enterprising people, what a country this might be!" the author Richard Henry Dana wrote enthusiastically in 1840. Until Dana's book, California was considered a no-man's-land, but the Harvard student's *Two Years Before the Mast* brought national attention to the golden land of opportunity.

In 1844 Los Angeles reportedly boasted a total of 250 inhabitants. After the U.S. declared war on Mexico in 1846—in pursuit of its "manifest destiny" to control North America and with its eye on California as the real prize—the American military ran the California government until Congress granted statehood in 1850. That same year, Los Angeles incorporated as a city, and over the next fifty years its population would swell to one hundred thousand. And that was only the beginning.

"Januslike, southern California faced both the ocean and the filling continent behind, vaguely promising the fortunes of yet another inexhaustible frontier, beckoning to the East as the final El Dorado of climate and opportunity," wrote historian Roger Morris. "Knowing a sure thing, a legion of professional boosters and real estate hustlers, their persuasive skills honed in land bubbles in Chicago or the plains, came to tout and entice."

By the 1920s, more than 1.2 million people had moved into Los Angeles—the largest internal migration in American history and the first mass movement of the automobile age. They came for two reasons: oil and movies. Both industries offered dramatic opportunities for entrepreneurs and charlatans, businessmen and gangsters. Los Angeles would become the prototypical marriage between the upper world and the underworld, and Helen would unwittingly be caught in the cross fire between them.

In the early twentieth century, a band of Jewish businessmen from Chicago—a tightly knit group of Ashkenazic Russians who had emigrated to the U.S. within ten years of one another—moved en masse to Los Angeles.

Though she had no way of knowing it, Helen's professional and personal life would be fatefully, and inextricably, entwined with this gang, dubbed the Supermob by a U.S. Senate's organized crime investigator. Defined as "a group of men from the Midwest, often of Russian Jewish heritage, who made fortunes in the 20th century American West in collusion with notorious members of organized crime," this "Kosher Nostra," as it would eventually be called by federal law enforcement, seized control of the movies.

These movie titans, whose roots could be traced to a hundred-square-mile region in Russia, would become not only some of the highest-paid men in the nation but personal friends of several American presidents. They included Louis B. Mayer, David O. Selznick, Adolph Zukor, and the Warner, Schenck, Balaban, and Cohn brothers. "Hollywood was largely the invention of Eastern European Jewish immigrants and their sons," wrote cultural historian Nick Tosches. "Twentieth-century organized crime in America was a primarily Jewish-Italian coalition that shared the sensibilities but lacked the ethnic purity of the true Sicilian Mafia pioneers in the business of the new land, each in his own way."

Like an earlier manifest destiny, the golden promise of California beckoned everyone—the scrupulous and unscrupulous alike. "The Chicago group took over," mused an investigator with the California attorney general's office. "We used to sit around and wonder how they all got here."

Helen would be oblivious to this axis of power that was assembling in her midst, swirling in the very milieu that would ultimately demolish her. But that would be years in the future.

The inner-city borough that comprised the Fourteenth District stretched from Sunset Boulevard to South Los Angeles, and was once described as a politician's "horror." The largely Democratic district was a hodgepodge of nonhomogeneous, ethnic neighborhoods and was home to the second-largest urban concentration of Mexican nationals after Mexico City. A "combustible mixture of different races and nationalities" populated the Fourteenth, as one scholar put it, with blacks, Hispanics, Japanese, Jews, Italians, Romanians, Filipinos, and Chinese living in extremes of wealth and poverty. Out of a total population of 346,000, more than 86,000 were blacks who had migrated to the district, first with the railroad and then with World War II defense contractors; most of them lived far below the national median. The district also saw a migration of nearly 10,000 new residents every year while battling such primitive epidemics as bubonic and pneumonic plague and diphtheria. Entire families lived in squalor. Shacks and garages sometimes housed as many as fifty people, and alleys were filled with the homeless and skid-row derelicts.

Of the eleven identifiable neighborhoods, over 70 percent of them were considered segregated, according to a study by journalist McWilliams, and included Central, Chavez-Ravine, Wholesale-Industry, Downtown, Bunker Hill, Little Tokyo, Elysian Park, Westlake, Echo Park, Temple Street, and Figueroa-Adams.

Though identified as a carpetbagger—her house was in the tony Fifteenth District, where blacks could live only as servants—she had rented an apartment in the Fourteenth. And though her lifestyle was far different from most of the constituents she sought to represent, she worked hard to convince voters that she had the determination to help them. She had filed under the name Helen Gahagan, her stage and opera name, but she soon began using her married name, calling herself Helen Gahagan Douglas—which she would be known by for the rest of her life.

She hired the now-twenty-five-year-old Evie Chavoor—the children's babysitter who had worked for the Douglas family while attending UCLA several years earlier—and she inherited Ed and Ruth Lybeck from Ford's campaign team. Ed was a salty New Yorker, a former newspaperman and mystery writer who had moved with his wife, Ruth, to Los Angeles in the early 1930s. He was a veteran political operative who had helped Al Smith become governor of New York in 1926. Though she had lived in the city for nearly fifteen years, Helen was thoroughly unfamiliar with the Fourteenth, having spent most of her time in the affluent neighborhoods of the movie people. In contrast, the Lybecks knew the district inside out.

It was an uphill battle from the beginning, with the powerful *Los Angeles Times* accusing her of being a radical leftist. Her support of Vice President Henry Wallace brought further slurs, and she was accused of being a "pinko," "commie," "Red," "fellow traveler," and "confidential agent of Stalin." The Daughters of the Confederacy called her a "nigger lover," and Catholics thought her the "anti-Christ."

She was an indefatigable campaigner and "literally ran her campaign on pennies," according to one account. With singular energy and enthusiasm, she swept into the neighborhoods, unafraid and unintimidated, her theatrical skills and supreme self-confidence carrying her through. She began riding the local streetcars—once someone showed her how to embark and disembark—and she was fearless in even the worst neighborhoods, picking up hitchhikers and shaking hands in dark alleys. No place was off-limits to her, as she went to soda fountains and tenements. She gave a one-hour speech about the Tennessee Valley Authority in a rundown theater that she thought resembled a flophouse. "I saw before me a ragged collection of bruised and lethargic old men dressed in castoffs. I was the only woman present." Many of her Hollywood friends supported her, including television star Ronald Reagan, who had been on the board of the Screen Actors Guild. Eddie Cantor and Rita Hayworth also joined her on the campaign trail, causing much excitement, and movie moguls Sam Goldwyn, Otto Preminger, and David O. Selznik provided much-needed funds.

She survived an embarrassing gaffe when her enthusiastic proclamation at a black church—"I just love the Negro people!"—was met with stony silence. She quickly recognized the condescension in the remark and determined to show her commitment to their cause. "I knew from the cold silence that fell on the crowd that I had made a frightful mistake. I kept talking and eventually they warmed to me again." She solidified her platform, advocating the abolition of the poll tax, job training, affordable housing, veterans' benefits, civil rights, and protection for small farmers and small-business owners.

"The sleeper in the campaign," as Helen saw it, "was the issue of Tidelands Oil. Who was to have control of the oil reserves off the coast of California, Louisiana, and Texas." As the daughter of an engineer, she felt she had a unique understanding of reclamation. She had been an early student of water issues in the West and supported efforts to save the redwoods in California, but her real introduction came from Eleanor Roosevelt, who was concerned about the coming world population explosion. "I believed that the conservation of land, water, energy is vital to the well-being of life on this globe."

Thanks to the California tradition of cross-filing—a mechanism by which congressional candidates could simultaneously place their names on the ballots for both political parties—Helen gained widespread support from both the Republicans and Democrats in her district. In June 1944 she won an impressive primary victory with 14,000 votes to 5,200 from her closest rival. Still, she faced an uphill battle in November's general election.

"You are going to be a real Congressman, not just a beautiful cloak model," President Roosevelt told her, referring to the Republicans' glamorous femme fatale, Congresswoman Clare Boothe Luce.

Helen astonished her audience from the podium of the July 1944 Democratic National Convention in Chicago. Her speaking ability, her grasp of the issues, her demeanor and intellect, her passion and conviction, caused a stir. Fans unfurled a banner across the platform that read OUR HELEN, and behind-the-scenes discussions took place about her viability as a future presidential candidate. The trepidation she inspired in her opponents was palpable, their criticism swift and biting. Her national convention speech was virtually ignored by the establishment press for its substance, while reporters focused instead upon her high-pitched feminine delivery and coiffed hairstyle. The *Los Angeles Examiner* correspondent referred to her "shrewish voice," and she tolerated numerous inane interviews in which reporters questioned her about her weight, height, nail polish, and shampoo. One crusty male political rival called her a "self-seeking, highly perfumed, smelly old girl."

The press portrayed women in politics as aberrant freaks— "sufficiently odd to warrant a place in a zoo or museum," Helen wrote. When this new generation of political women audaciously sought public office, they became objects of ridicule. She was called a sexpot, a glamour puss, an uppity woman, and a fluttering satellite, and was accused of pussyfooting and flitting about, of relying upon emotional histrionics and the female prerogative of changing one's mind. Despite her attempts to downplay her legendary beauty—avoiding makeup and manicures—her womanhood became the subject of scrutiny, with much attention paid to her blushing complexion and long legs. As she rose in stature and her political power expanded, the barbs became less subtle. A male congressman called her "the bitch from California."

She had been invited to the Chicago convention to give a prominent keynote speech. The Democrats had decided to showcase Douglas as a counterpart to the reactionary playwright, Luce, who had been prominently featured at the Republicans' nominating convention. The press eagerly seized the glamour-girl rivalry, creating a "cat fight" while ignoring the substance of both women's speeches. HELEN VS. CLARE: TORCH VS. ICICLE, headlined the *Chicago Sun-Times*. "How about a nation-wide cat fight—pardon, how about a nation-wide debating tour by Mrs. Luce for the Republicans and Mrs. Douglas for the New Dealers and Communists?" wrote a journalist for the *Washington Times Herald*.

To their credit, both women refused to take the bait. "I'm not going to get into any hair-pulling contest with any woman—regardless of what side of the fence she's on," Luce told the *New York Daily News*. Helen was equally adamant, telling a reporter from the *New York Post* that she had "great respect for Mrs. Luce. I am not a fencer. I am not a wit," and she had no intention of sparring with Luce or anyone else. "I'm in politics because there's a world upheaval and I just hope that I can be of some help."

For her part, Helen was preoccupied with the convention machinations around retaining Vice President Wallace as Roosevelt's running mate for the president's campaign for an unparalleled fourth term. Wallace, a liberal Republican who had switched to the Democratic Party in 1933 to join the Roosevelt cabinet as secretary of agriculture, became Roosevelt's vice president in 1940. But by 1944 there was "a strong wind of conservatism blowing," Helen wrote of the moment; "the mood of the country was swinging away from the New Deal." The Republicans had nominated New York Governor Thomas E. Dewey, and though the Democrats would overwhelmingly choose Roosevelt, there was a movement afoot to replace Wallace with a more moderate candidate.

The "dump Wallace" campaign, as it became known, appalled Helen. She had been a longtime supporter of Wallace and saw him as the symbol of continuing progressivism in America and in the Democratic Party. As a floor manager for Wallace, Helen fervently lobbied the deeply divided California delegation. She even threatened to move back to Brooklyn if California didn't support Wallace on the first ballot. Appealing to Democrats not to cede the "conservative" label to the Republicans and not to waver from Roosevelt's New

Deal, she gave a highly emotional speech that would be often quoted in the future—a speech that she wrote while visiting the First Lady at the Roosevelts' Hyde Park, New York, home.

> The Democratic party is the true conservative party. We have conserved hope and ambition in the hearts of our people. *We* are the conservative party. We have conserved the skills of their hands. We have husbanded our natural resources. We have saved millions of homes and farms from foreclosure and conserved the family stake in democracy. We have rescued banks and trust companies, insured crops and people's savings. We have built schools. We have checked the flooding rivers and turned them into power. We have begun a program to free men and women from the constant nagging fear of unemployment, sickness, accident—and the dread of an insecure old age. We have turned a once isolated, flood-ravished, poverty-stricken valley, the home of four and a half million people, into what is now a productive, happy place to live—the Tennessee River Valley. We have replanted the forest, refertilized the soil. Ours is the conservative party.

As it turned out, Roosevelt had opened the way for the vice-presidential fight when he notified party bosses that he intended to leave the choice up to the delegates. Though it is not clear whether Roosevelt sensed his imminent death, White House insiders were "alarmed by his deterioration," as author Michael Janeway wrote about his physical frailty in the summer of 1944, and so the fight for the vice-presidential nomination became a "ferocious struggle for the Roosevelt inheritance." DNC leaders had decided that Wallace was too liberal and too intellectual, and although they discussed several possible candidates, including Alben Barkley, William O. Douglas, James A. Farley, and Jimmy Byrnes, the unanimous compromise choice was Harry Truman—then a little-known Missouri senator. Helen particularly opposed Truman, whom she thought a machine politician abysmally beholden to California oil magnate Edwin Pauley.

Roosevelt seemed strangely apathetic about the choice, which baffled his advisers. "He just doesn't give a damn," aide Edwin "Pa" Watson remarked. What virtually no one knew at the time was that Roosevelt was preoccupied with a much larger vision that summer—of joining forces with Republican Wendell Willkie to create a new party comprising liberals from both sides of the aisle. In his view, the reactionary elements of the Democratic Party in the South should have joined the conservative wing of the Republican Party, while the liberal factions in both parties should have coalesced. Clandestine dispatches between the two men indicated they shared the same vision. "You tell the President that I'm ready to devote almost full time attention to this," Willkie responded to Roosevelt's discreet overture. "A sound liberal government in the U.S. is absolutely essential to continued co-operation with the other nations of the world." But the dream both men shared died with Willkie's fatal heart attack a few months later.

At the convention, Wallace led in the first-round floor vote, but by the second ballot Truman was the unmistakable winner. When a delegate made a motion from the floor to accept Truman's nomination, Helen refused to cast a vote for him, thinking it all a grand betrayal of Wallace. She stood on her chair, tears streaming down her face, in what a later scholar called a "rare loss of composure." Such open defiance of the man who would be president would come back to haunt her.

"Campaigning with the determination and aplomb of a ward boss, not a blue blood," as one observer put it, Helen was unflagging. The general election would be tougher, its outcome remaining in doubt until the day after the polls closed. When the dramatic ballot counting was over, Helen had narrowly defeated her opponent by less than four thousand votes.

It was not until Helen had already moved with the children to Washington that Melvyn read in the *Stars and Stripes* that she had been elected to Congress. Her letters to him in India had not arrived until after the military newspaper had reported the news.

"My God, how out of touch I had become with my own life," was Melvyn's reaction.

She entered the male-dominated sphere of the Seventy-ninth U.S. Congress as one of only nine women—an austere body where most female members were congressional widows merely holding their husbands' seats while awaiting a suitable male replacement.

Immediately after the election, the national press once again head-lined the battle of the glamour queens. Douglas and Luce had both been associated with the Broadway stage, both had famous husbands (Luce was married to Time Inc.'s Henry Luce), and both were per-ceived as glitzier and more sophisticated than their female colleagues. Still, the superficial attention became increasingly annoying to them. "The implication was that we were frivolous, vacuous women rather than serious, committed politicians," Helen later wrote. "I was deter-mined to clear the air of such insulting innuendo as soon as I possibly could."

"Pretty Helen Gahagan . . . was deep in political discussion with a group of 'big wigs,' " the *New York Times-Herald* once reported. "In-cidentally, she wore one of the best looking tailored costumes—a narrow maroon hiplength striped jacket of black over a black skirt and a severely tailored blouse."

Driving cross-country with her secretary Evie Chavoor, and a friend, Jarmila Marton, having decided to make the move to Wash-ington by automobile, the women tuned the radio to a morning news broadcast. They listened with amusement to the announcement that Helen had defeated Luce as one of the ten best-dressed women in public life. The rookie congresswoman had broken a cap on her front tooth, leaving a gap and stump when she opened her mouth to smile. Evie "turned around and looked at Helen, and there she was in the back seat with terrible sloppy pants on . . . huddled in a blanket, her hair all streaming down." The women howled with laughter, wishing a photographer could see her in such a state.

Humor aside, the constant comparisons to Luce aggravated her. "Congresswomen's ideas should rate above their clothes and their looks. Why all this emphasis on the sexes anyway, in a serious thing like government?" Luce was also annoyed, once saying that she hated "the gender in which she felt imprisoned." A libertine who had had affairs with many powerful men, including Bernard Baruch—financier and presidential adviser to Woodrow Wilson—the conservative Luce had supported a new national party in 1932 to counter the "arch-liberal" Roosevelt. When Helen first arrived in Washington, she re-ceived word that Congresswoman Luce wanted to see her. "I wanted to make an agreement [that] we would never discuss the same subject on the same day," Luce said, and Helen readily concurred. More than two decades later Luce still believed that women must tread lightly in the national political arena. "The time has not yet come when two women can safely debate politics (or any other subject) in public," Luce wrote in 1963. "Differences of opinion between women are always treated by the press as inspired by personal dislike and are used as evidence that every woman, at bottom, fears and hates every other woman for reasons of sexual jealousy."

Helen attended the swearing-in ceremony and listened as House Speaker Sam Rayburn made the pro forma resolution stipulating that the rules of the previous Congress would remain in effect. Such resolutions routinely passed without comment, but on this second Tuesday in January 1945, Mississippi Democrat "Lightnin'" John Rankin rose and proposed an additional standing committee to the Seventy-ninth Congress—the House Un-American Activities Committee. A professional anti-Semite famous for defending the Ku Klux Klan as a venerable American institution and referring to Jews as "communist kikes," Rankin surprised everyone with his proposal. The HUAC committee had been essentially inactive since the beginning of the war, and when its "splenetic chairman," as one historian described Martin Dies, decided not to seek reelection in 1944, the committee was considered virtually defunct. Members could only speculate about the motives of the bigoted Rankin. "An embarrassment even to his most benighted southern colleagues," as historian Roger Morris wrote of him, Rankin thought communism was a Jewish conspiracy dating back to the crucifixion of Jesus, and would paw "through a scurrilous volume called *Who's Who in American Jewry* to see if witnesses were hiding their incriminating ancestry."

Helen sensed at this opening salvo that she would tangle with Rankin and HUAC. Indeed, not long afterward, Helen would hiss Rankin on the floor of the House when he blamed World War II casualties on the ineptitude of black soldiers at the front. She had been one of the few House members to vote against permanent HUAC status—a tragic irony, considering it would be Rankin and HUAC that would help destroy her political career in a few short years. But for now, at the opening session of the Seventy-ninth Congress, the future of this freshman congresswoman seemed bright and promising, just as the future of America finally seemed to be heading toward peace.

From the beginning she sought to influence foreign policy and set her sights on the Foreign Affairs Committee—a committee newly energized as World War II was coming to an end and world peace moved to the forefront of national policy. She thought it a pivotal moment in American history, a moment of monumental international challenges surrounding atomic energy and postwar European recovery. With the help of Roosevelt and the powerful House Speaker Sam Rayburn, she maneuvered her way onto the committee. Luce also coveted the same assignment, but apparently possessed less clout within her own party than Helen did with the Democrats.

Shortly after her arrival in the capital, the Washington press corps invited her, Luce, and their fellow congresswomen to a welcoming party. She and Luce were seated on opposite sides of their hostess, and Helen was asked to speak first. Eager to use the opportunity to put an end once and for all to rumors of their feud, she rose and addressed the subject. "We're in a war. My husband is overseas. I will be in Washington with our two small children. I came here to support our country's war effort and to do what I can in Congress to help bring the fighting to a successful end as soon as possible. I'm not here for petty quarrels or a competition with anyone, and certainly not with Clare Boothe Luce."

Luce rose quickly to her feet, smiling and nodding her head in agreement. The camera bulbs flashed as the two brainy beauties shook hands, putting an end to the confected rivalry.

Helen was assigned a two-room, ground-floor office in the Cannon Building with a pleasant view of the Library of Congress. On one of her very first days on the Hill, a lanky Texas congressman stopped in to welcome her. The flirtatious and charming Lyndon Johnson congratulated her on her appointment to the prestigious committee and draped "his long frame in one of my easy chairs." From that day forward, for several years to come, the two were inseparable—fellow progressives who savored each other's company, their laughter and uninhibited physical affection much remarked upon by their colleagues.

The Douglases were still married, although their relationship was irreparably strained by Melvyn's infidelity. He was stationed in India when Helen decided to run for Congress and then moved to Washington to take office in January 1945. "She kind of took over," Melvyn told the *Los Angeles Times*, referring to Helen's co-option of his political role in California. "By the time I got back from the Army she was already a national figure."

Though Johnson was married to Lady Bird, he was just ending a decade-long affair with the Texas beauty Alice Glass—an affair that illustrated "how power and sex were joined in Johnson's mind," according to Mrs. Johnson's biographer. As Helen replaced Glass in Johnson's intimate life, Johnson replaced Melvyn as Helen's intellectual and emotional partner, and the two fervent New Dealers served as each other's political guiding light. "We were cut from the same piece of cloth—the Roosevelt cloth," Helen wrote. Johnson relished the conspicuousness of his affair with the brilliant and seductive Helen. Their relationship was described as an "open scandal" that would continue for twenty years, and both were seemingly comfortable with the semipublic nature of the liaison. Horace Busby Jr., a longtime aide and associate of Johnson's, claimed to have been told about the affair by other staff members and then to have become personally aware of it when Helen and Lyndon spent so much time alone together in Johnson's private office. Busby's intuition was confirmed when he came upon the couple lounging by a pool, their hands entwined and their conversation revealing a sexual familiarity that Busby thought unmistakable.

After Johnson's affair with Glass ended following Glass's marriage to newspaper publisher Charles Marsh, Johnson "began arriving on Capitol Hill in the morning in the company of another tall, beautiful woman—one who was famous as well," according to Johnson biographer Robert Caro, who described the couple walking to the congressional offices "openly holding hands." Soon they were arriving on the Hill together in the same car, either his or hers, and often left together for the evening, dining at her home, where his car would be seen parked "night after night," according to a neighbor. "Whatever the considerations that had deterred Lyndon Johnson from advertising his relationship with Alice Glass they evidently didn't apply to Helen Douglas," wrote Caro. "He made sure that people believed he was having a physical relationship with her," prompting at least one observer to pronounce them "a handsome couple," and was said to have personally confessed the affair to several people.

Eliot Janeway, Roosevelt's economic adviser, was alarmed when Johnson boasted of an affair with Clare Boothe Luce at the same time. "I told Lyndon if he thought that was the way to get publicity in *Time* he'd better lay off," Janeway later recalled. Johnson responded to Janeway that Luce "wasn't so hot and you had to listen to her."

Douglas rented a house in Chevy Chase for herself, her children, and her longtime aide, Evie, who served as nanny, secretary, hostess, and office manager. She described a typical day to a reporter for *Redbook* magazine. Most mornings began at four thirty A.M., when her two children crawled into bed with her. She then cooked them breakfast and got them off to school before she and Evie made their way to Capitol Hill. Helen always drove so that she could dictate correspondence and memoranda. At ten every morning she rushed through the underground tunnel to the Foreign Affairs Committee, which she thought was composed of the most seasoned and intelligent legislators from both parties. By noon she was on the House floor for roll call, and in the afternoon she researched upcoming legislation and oversaw her correspondence with her Los Angeles constituents. She took stacks of files home with her every evening and fell exhausted into bed at night.

"At home, the untrammeled Miss Gahagan is the kind of woman who leaves the cooking to somebody else and lets the broom fall where it may," a magazine portrait observed.

Serious, hardworking, dignified, and confident, she was a quick study on the functioning of Congress. Her patrician breeding, theatrical training, and didactic enthusiasm combined to make her far more influential than her freshman rank would normally dictate. The Gal from Cal, as she was called, fought hard for the issues that mattered to her—"an unabashed New Deal liberal at a moment when the old ardor was fading elsewhere in Congress," as a historian described her.

Johnson showed her how to organize her office and guided her through the more confusing aspects of governing. He had been one of the youngest members ever elected to Congress when, at twenty-eight years old in 1937, he won a seat in a special election. He had risen quickly to power through his loyalty to Roosevelt, whom he idolized, and, "above all else," as Helen put it, "his friendship with the Speaker," his fellow Texan Sam Rayburn.

"As in all congregations of human beings, there was an elite within the elite of Congress. Lyndon Johnson effortlessly belonged to it," Helen wrote of the behind-the-scenes power he wielded despite his lack of seniority. "Everyone knew that he knew what was going to happen and what would make it happen."

He bragged about the efficiency with which he ran his office. Helen thought him an operator who saw Congress as his personal operation. Johnson and his staff had perfected the old-style patriarchal political system that other legislators sought to duplicate. Every birth, high school graduation, marriage, and death in his Texas district was acknowledged with a handwritten note from the congressman. Johnson boasted of the love he engendered in his constituents, proudly showing Helen photographs of the dozens of babies who had been named Lyndon, Baines, Johnson, or all three out of admiration for him. She was struck by the dichotomy of his paternalistic sense of noblesse oblige and his seemingly insatiable need for approval and affection, and thought his overbearing self-confidence masked a surprisingly frail ego.

Even though he rarely spoke or listened to others on the floor of the House, he insisted on being present when every bill came to a vote. "His style was to vote and leave, loping off the floor with great long strides," she remembered with amusement. "If he did remain he looked the picture of boredom, slumped in his seat, eyes half closed. Then, suddenly, restlessness would seize him and he would leap to his feet all energy, stride to whisper something to a colleague here and a colleague there, and leave—taking something out of the room with him."

The better Helen got to know Johnson, the more his explosive temperament both fascinated and repelled her. Sometimes he would react with such unexpected violence to what she thought was a minor irritation that his response actually frightened her. She eventually came to believe that his anger was related to exhaustion and frustration, and realized that he truly seemed to have no control over it. His volatility was completely different from the even-tempered, emotionally suppressed Melvyn, and more reminiscent of her hotheaded father. Like anyone who came to know Johnson intimately, Helen was alternately spellbound, attracted, startled, and overwhelmed. The man's sheer power—ruthless and manipulative—was disarming, while his affection—deep and outsized—was compelling. She thought his speeches "often overblown, sentimental, even grandiose . . . exaggerated," and was frequently perturbed by his moody withdrawals. "There was always a kind of disparaging humorous jibing in dialogue with him," which she saw as intentional so that he could later dismiss any offensive remarks as jest. Still, just as she had learned how to navigate her father's emotional storms, she became skilled at deflecting Johnson's random fury, and their friendship evolved and strengthened.

In early spring 1945, President Roosevelt addressed both houses of Congress to report on his secret meeting at Yalta on the Black Sea. What would become known as the Big Three meeting between Roosevelt, British Prime Minister Winston Churchill, and Soviet Premier Joseph Stalin dictated the strategy for the unconditional surrender of Nazi Germany and the redrawing of the map of Europe. Each of the three allies had various additional agendas as well. America wanted immediate Soviet support against Japan; Great Britain wanted the establishment of a democratic government in Poland; and Stalin wanted Soviet influence in Eastern Europe and the Far East. In the end, all three leaders had been relatively satisfied with the agreements reached.

Though initially applauded, Roosevelt's concessions to Stalin at Yalta would later be seen as a foreign policy failure—what critics considered "a series of surrenders to Russia that led inexorably to the Cold War and the loss of Eastern Europe to the communists." Much of the later condemnation would fall on Roosevelt, who was physically impaired and possibly not up to the task at hand. "It must be agreed at the outset that Roosevelt *was* a sick man at Yalta," historian Doris Kearns Goodwin observed, while concluding that the degree to which his ill health affected his judgment cannot be definitively assessed.

But when Helen watched the president address the joint session of Congress on March 1, she was shocked by his appearance. "For the first time he had not been able to tolerate the iron harness that kept him on his feet for such public occasions, but was brought into the chamber in his wheelchair. I learned that he was in agony from the long plane trip during which he was strapped into an Air Force bucket seat."

Helen had a strong premonition that she would never see him again, and as the solid double doors closed behind him after his address, she rushed to a back staircase where she knew his entourage would exit. When he came into view she called out to him: "Good-bye, Mr. President!"

Roosevelt looked up, recognizing his dear friend. He nodded and waved to her. Six weeks later he was dead.

Shortly before three thirty P.M. on April 12, 1945, the man who had been president for an extraordinary thirteen years suffered a fatal cerebral hemorrhage at his Little White House in Warm Springs, Georgia. His death marked the end of one era and the beginning of another in American history, and was met with shock and grief throughout the world. "As word spread from city to town within the United States, ordinary people, politicians and reporters struggled to come to terms with Roosevelt's death," Goodwin wrote. "For the millions who adored him and for those who despised him, an America without Roosevelt seemed almost inconceivable."

Helen was crushed. She and fellow Democrats "huddled together in mutual grief. We felt rudderless in a storm. Who was Harry Truman anyway? None of us knew much about him."

An inconsolable Helen Douglas spent the day of the funeral with Lyndon Johnson in his most secret of several secret hideaways. "He had them scattered all over the capital, but this was his most private one," she remembered. She felt lost, perhaps realizing for the first time just how much she had depended upon Roosevelt as her guide. Those closest to her became increasingly worried about her, as the usually stoic Douglas seemed extremely depressed and unable to handle her grief. She was truly bereft at the loss, unsure how to proceed as a public official without Roosevelt's example. With his death she lost her own confidence, so reliant had she been on his leadership, and the jolt brought her abruptly to a political maturity. Eventually she would turn to Eleanor as a mentor replacement, but not before a mourning period that seemed excessive to her staff. "The shock is terrific but she seems to have taken hold now and is feeling much better," Evie Chavoor wrote to the Lybecks. "I tried to get her out as much as I could. We went visiting to the [California Congressman George] Outlands, then to Lyndon Johnson's home . . . She saw Eleanor Roosevelt before she left for Hyde Park."

Others thought she had reacted to the president's death as if part of her had died as well. Helen had absolutely idolized Roosevelt, her personal friend and political ally: "She dined at his table and smoked his cigarettes." Lorena Hickok, the First Lady's closest friend and confidant who, decades later, would be identified as Eleanor's lover, wrote Helen an empathetic note in response to Helen's grief. "I can only say that last night my heart ached when I looked at you. And I wished Melvyn was here. It seemed to me that, in spite of the fact that you are surrounded by people who admire and love you—you are so alone."

Helen thought Roosevelt personally responsible for bringing the country from economic depression to the brink of prosperity, and she was unsure that Truman had the necessary courage and character to guide the nation forward. Indeed, Truman faced the future with trepidation and uncertainty, confessing to an old friend shortly after the 1944 campaign his fear that Roosevelt would not survive a full term. "The prospect, the friend recalled, seemed to scare the very devil out of Truman," according to biographer Alonzo L. Hamby. The challenge must have been daunting to a vice president who had met only once or twice with his president and who admitted that Roosevelt and his men did not tell him "anything about what was going on here." Truman knew nothing of what had transpired at Yalta and had only a vague notion of the atom bomb. All "he had as background was his storybook view of history and a rousing Fourth of July patriotism," wrote historian Daniel Yergin.

Just weeks after Roosevelt's death, the war in Europe came to an end with Hitler's suicide and Germany's unconditional surrender. On May 8, President Truman, Churchill, and Stalin made the announcement across international radio waves. While the moment brought great elation throughout the country, Truman was deeply distrustful of Stalin. "Russia will emerge from the present conflict as by far the strongest nation in Europe and Asia," the wartime intelligence service, the Office of Strategic Services, had reported in a top secret report to Roosevelt just days before his death.

Secretary of War Henry L. Stimson sent word to Truman that he needed to speak with him "as soon as possible on a highly secret matter." On April 25—twelve days after Truman took office—Stimson arrived at the White House and handed the president a letter. "Within four months we shall in all probability have completed the most terrible weapon ever known in human history, one bomb of which could destroy a whole city."

The Manhattan Project, as the crash program to develop an atomic weapon was called, was officially instituted in late 1942 in response to reports from scientist Albert Einstein to FDR nearly a decade earlier that Nazi Germany was building one. The largest, most complex scientific undertaking in the history of the world, the two-billion-dollar Allied project was dispersed among numerous laboratories and involved more than two hundred thousand people. The actual design of the bomb was under the direction of J. Robert Oppenheimer at Los Alamos Scientific Laboratory in New Mexico. It had been initiated under Roosevelt, who had left behind no written policy for Truman to follow other than an amorphous reference to the bomb's possible use against Japan. "The politicians do not appreciate the possibilities and consequently do not know the extent of the menace," a concerned Einstein would write during this crucial moment of the bomb's development.

In July, Truman went to Potsdam to meet with British and Russian leaders. While discussing the political future of Europe and strategizing the defeat of the Japanese, he received a top secret telegram hand-delivered by Secretary Stimson confirming that the weapon had been successfully tested.

On Monday, July 16, 1945, the first nuclear explosion in world history—an implosion plutonium bomb—took place in an area of the New Mexico desert the Spanish had called the Journey of Death. Oppenheimer named the site Trinity after a John Donne poem. Marking the beginning of the atomic age, the test forever changed the very character of war. The U.S. now had a weapon capable not only of obliterating its enemies, but of ending all of civilization—of wiping out the two billion people then living on earth.

"We knew the world would not be the same," Oppenheimer recalled of his immediate reaction to the indescribable mushroom cloud. "A few people laughed. A few people cried. Most people were silent. I remembered the line from the Hindu scripture . . . 'Now I am become death, the destroyer of worlds.'"

"I casually mentioned to Stalin that we had a new weapon of unusual destructive force," President Truman wrote in his memoirs on July 24. "The Russian premier showed no special interest. All he said was that he was glad to hear it and hoped we would make 'good use of it against the Japanese.'" In fact, Oppenheimer and his scientific colleagues had recommended to Truman that, in addition to Russia, he inform Britain, France, and China of the existence of the new weapon. Thinking secrecy more dangerous than transparency, the scientists recommended seeking suggestions from each country as to how best use the technology to further peaceful international relations.

On August 6, 1945, under orders from Truman, a B-29 aircraft called the *Enola Gay* dropped the untested "Little Boy" atomic bomb on the Japanese city of Hiroshima. Within minutes of learning about the successful detonation, the White House released the president's message to the world:

Sixteen hours ago an American airplane dropped one bomb on Hiroshima . . . It is an atomic bomb. It is a harnessing of the basic power of the universe . . . We are now prepared to obliterate more rapidly and completely every productive enterprise the Japanese have above ground in any city. We shall destroy their docks, their factories, and their communications. Let there be no mistake; we shall completely destroy Japan's power to make war . . . If they do not now accept our terms they may expect a rain of ruin from the air, the like of which has never been seen on this earth.

Two days after Hiroshima, in keeping with Stalin's promise to Roosevelt at Yalta, the Soviet Union declared war on Japan, beginning with the invasion of Manchuria. But it was not until August 9, after the U.S. detonated the nuclear bomb code-named "Fat Man" over Nagasaki, that Japan finally surrendered, bringing an official end to World War II. The U.S. government estimated more than 225,000 mostly civilian fatalities from the two bombings in Japan, while some 50 million people had died in the European theater—with Soviets accounting for a staggering 20 million.

Melvyn had returned to the U.S. on leave in preparation for reassignment to the Pacific and was with Helen in New York when news of the Japanese surrender hit the airwaves. Celebrating in Times Square, Helen was overjoyed that the war had ended. "Few of the celebrants cared that victory had been achieved as the result of a terrible new weapon," she recalled, though her Hollywood friend Lolita Leighter, who was with the couple, kept saying, "We shouldn't have dropped those bombs."

It was only after the bombing of Hiroshima and Nagasaki that the enlightened intelligentsia of the United States began to ask: *What should the country do with the capability of destroying the human race, and who should control the weapon?* Helen had been a congresswoman a mere eight months when suddenly, and without any preparation or even prior knowledge, the Seventy-ninth Congress was expected to figure out how to regulate and control a new weapon that had the capability of bringing about global annihilation. She did not initially oppose Truman's decision to bomb Japan, thinking it justifiable if it brought an end to the war and further Allied casualties. But as details of the mass destruction—the vast scale and unspeakable suffering—began to surface, she became obsessed with the possibility of mankind destroying the entire human race. "The scientific community remained at a loss to quantify the unquantifiable or imagine the unimaginable," one scholar wrote of the dilemma. "That they expected the members of Congress to do so seemed unreasonable."

Within two days of Nagasaki, Oppenheimer and several other Los Alamos scientists fell to arguing among themselves about the proper course of development and control of the newly unleashed power. In a devastating final report to Secretary Stimson and President Truman, Oppenheimer conveyed the scientists' doomsday assessment. "We are not only unable to outline a program that would assure to this nation for the next decades hegemony in the field of atomic weapons; we are equally unable to insure that such hegemony, if achieved, could protect us from the most terrible destruction . . . We believe that the safety of this nation . . . can be based only on making future wars impossible."

The "culmination of three centuries of physics," as one physicist described the Manhattan Project, went not toward the creation of something positive and beneficial to the world but toward absolute ruination. The debate over how to control atomic power in a postwar world began immediately. Stimson—the aging ethical pragmatist who as secretary of state in 1929 had disbanded an intelligence unit because "gentlemen don't read each other's mail"—favored sharing atomic secrets with America's ally, the Soviet Union. But he was in the distinct minority within the Truman administration, the military, and the national security establishment, and on Capitol Hill.

Indeed, increasingly annoyed by Oppenheimer's celebrity status, gloomy apocalyptic warnings, and attempts to influence government officials, Truman sought to muzzle him and his outspoken fellow scientists. The president issued a gag order prohibiting further public discussion about atomic warfare. On September 9, Oppenheimer sent to the War Department what became known as "the Document." Circulated to three hundred scientists and signed by all but three, it was a "strongly worded statement on the dangers of an arms race, the impossibility of any defense against the atomic bomb in future wars, and the need for international control."

Helen Douglas came down firmly on the side of the scientists. The issue would become the single most defining passion for the rest of her life and bring her once again into conflict with Truman. The president had little patience with what he saw as conveniently pacifist scientists whom he thought ill equipped to grasp the political consequences of atomic power. Still, Truman was eager to meet the brilliant and charismatic Oppenheimer. Not surprisingly, the two took an instant dislike to each other. Escorted into the Oval Office, Oppenheimer made a fateful and unfortunate remark that would come back to haunt him.

"Mr. President, I feel I have blood on my hands."

The statement infuriated Truman, who abruptly ended the meeting and had Oppenheimer ushered out. "Blood on his hands, dammit, he hasn't half as much blood on his hands as I have. You just don't go around bellyaching about it," he said after Oppenheimer had left. Truman reported the meeting to Undersecretary of State Dean Acheson, writing that he didn't "want to see that son-of-a-bitch in this office ever again" and calling him a "cry-baby scientist."

In fact, 72 percent of the Manhattan Project scientists, led by the genius Hungarian physicist Leo Szilard, had been opposed to the bomb's use on civilian targets in Japan and had signed a petition in support of demonstrating the bomb to a Japanese delegation. Had Szilard and his colleagues been aware that Truman had decided to drop the bomb while knowing that Japan was negotiating a peaceful solution, the scientists would doubtless have been outraged. As it was, their entreaties fell on deaf ears.

Instead, shaping the course of events for the rest of the century and ushering in the cold war, the Truman administration moved quickly to classify "the Document," took steps to place atomic energy under military control, and put Oppenheimer under surveillance. In the fall of 1945, Truman's FBI director, J. Edgar Hoover, began investigating Oppenheimer's ties to Communists and leaking derogatory information about the scientist to Congress, the White House, and the State Department. The nation's second Red Scare was beginning: Anyone favoring an international atomic energy policy would be labeled a "traitor"; anyone recommending civilian rather than military control of nuclear power would be called a "communist sympathizer"; and anyone suggesting sharing atomic secrets with the Soviet Union was a "communist" or "Red."

Outspoken and zealous on the subject of an international peacekeeping force, Helen Douglas was an immediate and favorite target of Hoover. In fact, Hoover relished the opportunity to label her a Communist, for he had long been suspicious of her support of blacks and had actually opened a dossier on her as early as 1939. According to Colleen M. O'Connor, a California scholar, "Long before Douglas came to Washington, D.C., Hoover had linked, in his mind, Negro unrest in the U.S. with an international communist conspiracy." Hoover thought Russian Communists were actively fomenting instability in America's ghettos, and saw the civil rights movement—which Helen Douglas ardently advocated—as a Russian-sponsored race revolt. "This Black American–Red Russian connection served as a kind of

credo for Hoover throughout his career," wrote O'Connor. Hoover's
own political ties were with the ultra-patriotic conservative and na-
tivist groups such as the Daughters of the American Revolution, the
Freedom Foundation, veterans' organizations, and the fringe anti-
Communist Christian Crusades that were just beginning to flourish in
Texas and Oklahoma. In his mind, liberals, Communists, civil rights
activists, and now atomic arms control advocates were one and the
same—all treasonous, foreign-inspired agitators. In fact, Hoover was
building a shamefully mediocre political police force focused entirely
on repressing dissent while allowing political and white-collar corruption to thrive. It would be decades before his own personal compro-
mises would be revealed—his ties to the organized crime figures his
agency protected, his blackmailing of enemies who were homosexuals,
and his active pursuit of homosexuals in federal government when he
himself was a closet homosexual. The full extent of his corruption
would not come to light for many years. For now, he was the arbiter
of patriotism.

At the heart of subversive activity, in the minds of Hoover and
right-wing Republicans, were the Roosevelt New Dealers who had
allowed Communists to infiltrate the national security establishment.
As one scholar depicted their thinking, "liberalism equaled socialism;
socialism equaled communism; therefore liberalism was only two precarious steps away from a treasonous embrace of the Communist menace." Most emblematic of this treasonous atmosphere, the person most
reviled by the Right, was Eleanor Roosevelt. That she was one of
Helen's closest friends and advisers further fueled Helen's vilification
by Hoover.

She didn't see it coming—the breadth and depth, the power and
fury of the smear. Only later would she realize what had happened.
"I was standing in the path of tanks."

Harry Truman and the Seventy-ninth Congress were faced with
pressing domestic issues as they segued from managing a wartime economy to planning for postwar prosperity. On September 6, 1945, the
president sent a sixteen-thousand-word message to Congress detail-
ing his twenty-one-point domestic program. Transitioning from the

New Deal to what was called the Fair Deal, Truman articulated what biographer David McCullough described as an "all-out, comprehensive statement of progressive philosophy and a sweeping liberal program of action." He called for an increase in unemployment compensation and the minimum wage, crop insurance for farmers, an extension of Social Security, job creation, and government housing assistance for a million new homes a year.

Preempting his own State of the Union address the following January, he sought to send a strong and urgent message from the start. He spent a full ten days writing his platform, eager to set "his domestic program on a liberal path at the very start."

Helen Douglas greeted Truman's "Twenty-one Points" speech with great enthusiasm, proud of the president for addressing the domestic postwar problems as well as what she agreed was America's obligation to its European allies. Even though she saw him as a "shaky and inadequate man who gave us no sense of security," she was willing to give Truman the benefit of the doubt. While she had made civil rights a priority—more because her congressional constituency was 25 percent black than because of a deeply felt commitment to racial equality—she was among very few in Congress to do so. Indeed, her blue-blood Republican upbringing had instilled in her a racial prejudice to which she had been oblivious for much of her adult life. It was not until she had become involved with Eleanor Roosevelt—through whom she met several national black leaders—that she became genuinely sensitized to the racial bigotry endemic in American society.

She was the first to hire a black congressional aide—a young woman named Juanita Terry, who was the daughter of a constituent and whose two-hundred-dollar monthly salary Helen paid out of her personal funds. She forced the desegregation of the House cafeteria, nominated a black man to West Point, and introduced legislation rescinding the tax-exempt status of the Daughters of the Revolution, who had refused to allow black singer Marian Anderson to perform in Constitution Hall. Still, though her efforts on behalf of blacks were tireless and sincere, she shared the patronizing attitude of the contemporary civil rights advocates—white activists who believed that blacks should wait patiently for reform, should devotedly and unquestioningly support the

Democratic Party, and should entrust socially enlightened whites with
their cause. In an article she wrote for the magazine *Negro Digest* entitled "If I Were a Negro," she admonished blacks to "quiet the righteous wrath of [their] indignation." There was "no Negro problem,"
she assured them. "Only a white problem which, in the final analysis,
must be solved by whites." That J. Edgar Hoover considered her a wild-
eyed radical on this issue was but one of the many ironies that came
to define Helen's public life and legacy. In fact, in the mid-1940s she
was a mainstream Democrat, ardent anti-Communist, passionate supporter of Jewish immigration into Palestine, opponent of the equal
rights amendment, and avid proponent of the United Nations who
embraced few, if any, radical notions. None of the events that "drove
the Douglases to politics," wrote Ronald Brownstein, "—the rise of
fascism in Europe, the agony of the Depression at home—shook their
basic faith in American institutions." As her friend and fellow actress
Myrna Loy described their thinking at the time: "A liberal is one who
moves slightly left when the Fascists get too strong and slightly right
when the Communists get too pushy." But such nuances were lost
on Hoover and the right-wing element that was gaining ground in
America.

Helen's dedication to civil rights evolved gradually, but when the
first Ku Klux Klan cross burning ever to occur in Los Angles took
place in her congressional district—followed by the Klan-inspired
murders of two black couples in Georgia—she was outraged. She
sponsored anti-lynching legislation in the House, imploring her colleagues to attend to what she called the "unfinished business" of Reconstruction. Her bill passed the House but, not surprisingly, never
left the Senate Judiciary Committee.

In any case, she reserved her enormous zeal and focus for the issue
that would consume the rest of her political life: the control of atomic
energy. She saw it as the single most pressing matter of the twentieth
century. Overnight, the president and the Seventy-ninth Congress
"were faced with portentous decisions about what America should
do with its alarming new atomic power," as she put it. The military was
quickly maneuvering to seize control of its development, which
Helen thought extremely dangerous, for she firmly believed that who-
ever controlled the country's atomic energy would dictate the direction

of American foreign policy—and control the rest of the world—for decades to come.

Initially, Truman seemed to be on her wavelength, appearing before Congress on October 3, 1945, to urge the establishment of an Atomic Energy Commission under civilian rather than military control. The "release of atomic energy constitutes a new force too revolutionary to consider in the framework of old ideas," he told his audience. "We can't stand another global war. We can't ever have another war, unless it is total war, and that means the end of our civilization as we know it. We are not going to do that. We are going to accept that Golden Rule, and we are going forward to meet our destiny which I think Almighty God intended us to have."

Most members of Congress saw Truman as naïve and many of them later ridiculed his Pollyannaish reference to the Golden Rule. Helen thought Truman's remarks strangely out of touch with the reality and magnitude of the situation. The following day, in a blistering speech entitled "The Atomic Age," she criticized the president for failing to address the possibility of the U.S. sharing its scientific information with the Soviets. She shared the belief of the many scientists involved in the Manhattan Project that it was only a matter of time before all of the world's physicists were able to create an atomic bomb. Indeed, it had been Einstein's 1933 letter to President Roosevelt informing him of the recent scientific developments in nuclear chain reactions—and, especially, Einstein's warning that German scientists were on the verge of producing a massive bomb—that led Roosevelt to initiate the Manhattan Project. In a post-Hitlerian, post-Hiroshima world, Helen feared that maintaining atomic secrecy would usher in a dangerous arms race that could lead to the end of civilization.

Everyone in the world knew that the atom had been smashed, she argued, and to assume that we could keep such a secret was fallacious and misdirected. Like Einstein, who was widely espousing world federalism as a deterrent to world annihilation, Helen lobbied her colleagues for international control of nuclear energy. "As long as there will be man, there will be war," Einstein argued. "If the idea of world government is not realistic, then there is only one realistic view of our future: wholesale destruction of man by man!" But while Einstein envisioned a "supranational" entity comprising the United States, Great

Britain, and Russia, Helen was satisfied that the newly created United Nations would be the appropriate agency to monitor atomic developments and mediate disputes among nations. Though it had not yet held its first session, during the fall of 1945 she was enthusiastically optimistic about its potential to mediate international disputes and make war obsolete. A few years later Einstein would make his famous remark about the failure of the international community to control nuclear weapons. "I do not know how the Third World War will be fought," he told an interviewer, "but I can tell you what they will use in the Fourth—rocks."

For his part, Truman "was still in a quandary about the direction of the grand alliance of the United States, Great Britain, and the Soviet Union," as Churchill scholar R. Crosby Kemper III wrote, though some in the Truman administration were convinced that the Soviets had imperialist designs on Europe and Asia. "The State Department was a hive of conflicting voices. Though never as deeply charmed as was Roosevelt, Truman still felt he could handle 'Uncle Joe' Stalin on a one-to-one basis."

By the end of 1945, however, Truman's view of Stalin was beginning to harden as the Soviet leader's expansionist intentions became increasingly apparent. "Unless Russia is faced with an iron fist and strong language, another war is in the making," Truman wrote ominously to Secretary of State James F. Byrnes. "Only one language do they understand, 'How many divisions have you?'" Still, as the new year began, Truman remained publicly ambivalent on the subject of the Soviet Union's supposed designs on world domination.

On a sunny spring day in 1946, thousands flocked to the tiny Westminster College campus in Fulton, Missouri. They had come to greet their native son, Truman, and his celebrated cohort, Winston Churchill. The Presbyterian men's school had invited Churchill—the most famous orator in the world—to address the small academic community. Standing behind a podium in the school's gymnasium, Churchill gave what would go down in history as the most important speech of his long public career, one that would mark the inauguration of the cold war.

The recently deposed British prime minister drew on his longstanding observance of Soviet behavior, combined with a decade of unheeded warnings about Nazi Germany. While first gratuitously welcoming "Russia to her rightful place among the leading nations of the world," Churchill then issued a dramatic call for an Anglo-American bond in a speech that brought immediate worldwide attention: "From Stettin in the Baltic to Trieste in the Adriatic, an iron curtain has descended across the Continent."

Though Truman had approved in advance Churchill's "iron curtain speech," when the national reaction was overwhelmingly negative—with editorials roundly accusing Churchill of saber rattling and Stalin angrily denouncing it as a "call to war"—Truman began dissembling. He sought to mollify a livid Stalin by inviting him to present a rebuttal speech at the University of Missouri. Stalin, not surprisingly, declined the offer, and the stage was irrevocably set for a future of frigid relations between the U.S. and the Soviet Union.

With Russia now designated an opponent rather than an ally, Helen's support for sharing atomic secrets would come to be seen as anti-American. It was her fierce and passionate devotion to world peace—and her attempt to mobilize women against a nuclear arms race—that would soon define her public life and make her an enemy to the powerful military forces in America. The vicious attacks on her integrity and patriotism that would haunt her for years to come would now be set into motion.

The bill she sponsored with Connecticut Senator Brien McMahon, who had chaired the Special Committee on Atomic Energy, called for civilian rather than military control of atomic power, an exploration of peaceful uses of atomic energy, and an international exchange of scientific information. The McMahon-Douglas bill ran into heavy opposition in both houses of Congress. Helen was afraid the nation was about to set off "on a war program" the end of which "no one can see," and her fears about a third world war and warnings against genocidal weapons of mass destruction would later be seen as prophetic. But on the precipice of the cold war they seemed alarmist and far-fetched to many of her congressional colleagues. On July 18, 1946, she spoke to Congress in support of her bill. "One cannot legislate in a vacuum on atomic energy . . . One, the atomic bomb is a weapon of appalling destructiveness. Two, other countries of the world will be able to make atomic bombs. Three, no real military defense against the atomic bomb has been devised and none is in sight . . . Four, the secrets which we hold are matters of science and engineering that other nations can and will discover . . . Five, the peacetime benefits of atomic energy promise to be great indeed, particularly in medicine, biology, and many branches of research . . . Six, military control of atomic energy development, though necessary and useful during war, is a form of direction to which scientists in peacetime will not willingly submit."

James R. Newman—a brilliant mathematician, lawyer, and scientific historian who would eventually become Truman's White House counsel on atomic-energy legislation and helped draft the first Atomic Energy Act—advised both Douglas and McMahon. So impressed was Newman with the two legislators that he would dedicate his authoritative 1948 book, *The Control of Atomic Energy*, to them both—"two of the people's representatives who saw far and saw clearly." Newman's personal inscription in Helen's book was even more effusive: "For Helen, who is the best of us in heart, in spirit, in courage, in integrity, in sympathy, in forbearance, in vision, and in purpose. She evokes our love, commands our admiration and earns our fealty."

Throughout the summer of 1946 Douglas continued to align herself with the scientific community that was being squeezed out of the national dialogue about nuclear proliferation. She sent hundreds of telegrams to scientists around the world, including Einstein, Oppenheimer, and Nobel Prize–winning chemist Harold Urey and physicist James S. Franck, and forwarded hundreds more to the national press and the chairs of every college chemistry and physics department in the country. While more than a hundred scientists agreed to publicly support her efforts, Oppenheimer was notably reserved and reluctant, writing that he felt it "inappropriate" to endorse a "recommendation on political tactics and to which my technical knowledge and experience can make no valid contribution."

She became a national symbol for the role she felt women should play in international disarmament. Her venture into this male-dominated venue alarmed her political enemies. Her battle against nuclear proliferation, her appeal to women to lead the way toward world peace, marked her as a threat to the country's embryonic military-industrial complex. An avid believer in a strong and collaborative United Nations and unbending where it came to international control of atomic energy, she was a redoubtable force in the debate over civilian versus military control of the new technology—over whether there would be an arms race or arms control.

She saw the challenge as one of life and death, and with an evangelical urgency she sought to arouse the public, speaking at mass rallies throughout the country, urging women to rise to the challenge of saving the planet from nuclear annihilation. If women fail in this endeavor, she warned, the frantic pursuit of a thermonuclear bomb will send the planet "back to the molten mass of gas and flames it was before any life existed on it." Only women, she believed, as "the givers of life," could save the world. "Men," she once told a journalist, "haven't given up their age-old preoccupation with arms." Intelligent and lucid, Helen was capable of transcending "the unnavigable sea of nuclear physics, chemistry, and megatonnage, and foresaw almost intuitively the portents of a global nightmare," as a twentieth-century scholar put it. Perhaps most significant, she was able to make the unimaginable imaginable for laypeople.

For its part, the government ridiculed her doomsday predictions and diminished the possible dangers of nuclear war while subtly dismissing her as a hysterical woman. One government publication called *How to Survive an Atomic Bomb* claimed that there was no risk of cancer from exposure to radioactive fallout, and that fears of radiation were "mental." Nuclear attacks, while unsettling, were virtually safe, the government declared, as long as people remained calm. "Lots of people have little tricks to steady their nerves at times like that—like reciting jingles or rhymes or the multiplication table."

Predictably, the press focused its attention on her physical attributes, virtually ignoring the substance of the issues she raised. Writing about Helen meeting the heads of various national organizations who were lobbying against military control of the nuclear industry, the *Washington Post* reported that the "youthful looking" Douglas had her dark hair coiffed in a "long bob" and was "wearing what every woman instantly recognized as a well-cut suit, accented (dramatized, if you prefer) with a handsome lapel pin. She might have fitted into a movie role of a successful career woman. In fact, she was from Hollywood."

Her argument for arms control had overwhelming public support— four hundred thousand letters urging passage of her legislation poured into one congressional committee alone. But the military lobby was already entrenched in Washington politics. "Senators and representatives introduced a new rhetorical weapon to defend the military's desire for atomic control—hints of treason," was one scholar's analysis of the political moment. Minnesota Republican Senator Joseph Ball went so far as to accuse opponents of military control as Communist agents and Rankin, not to be outdone, began referring darkly to spies at the government's atomic bomb project in Oak Ridge, Tennessee.

Still, the issue was not partisan, and even the die-hard isolationist Republican Michigan Senator Arthur Vandenberg ultimately confessed that he did not believe the United States was capable of keeping the atomic bomb secret. "It is our task to develop through the United Nations organization a system of complete world-wide inspection which shall guarantee to civilization that no nation (including ourselves) shall use atomic energy for the construction of weapons of war," he wrote in his private papers.

When the debate was over, the House voted to permit the U.S. Army to continue manufacturing bombs, to reduce the AEC's regulatory powers, and to include the military on the commission. Though the defeat was a blow, Helen was widely praised by scientists throughout the world who opposed atomic secrecy. Inspired by her example, an untold number of American women joined the political process for the first time. Hundreds of women's groups—organized by Helen and other members of Congress—rallied in support of the peaceful control of atomic energy. She rose smoothly to the calling of role model. A "force of nature," a friend called her, "one of those rare human beings in whom life focuses itself, so that there is something irresistible about them, as about a great wind or a charge of electricity . . . Her effect on other people is something like that of a very potent cocktail."

She refused to let the setback dampen her commitment to her principles, and quickly found herself embroiled in yet another historically polarizing debate. Accusing Congress of allowing Rankin's Un-American Activities Committee (HUAC) to run roughshod over Americans' civil liberties in its search for Communists, she set off what the *San Francisco Chronicle* described as a "three-hour verbal brawl" on the congressional floor between Rankin and House Majority Leader John McCormack. Helen's outrage had been stimulated by a newspaper account of a HUAC investigator threatening a Columbia University professor: "You should tell your Jewish friends that the Jews in Germany stuck their necks out too far and Hitler took good care of them and that the same thing will happen here unless they watch their step." She thought it outlandish, she told her colleagues, that the threat had come from "a U.S. government employee, paid from tax funds, authorized by you—representatives of a free people." She railed against the interrogation abuses performed by the committee and expressed her alarm that it was bringing disrepute to the entire House of Representatives. "*We* are made a laughing stock. *We* become parties to the creation of a new Gestapo. *We* are completing the late Adolf Hitler's unfinished business."

Her remarks provoked Rankin to rise and accuse her of following the "communist line," which led McCormack—"every inch of his six feet two inch frame quivering with manly fury"—to gesture threateningly at Rankin. Rankin, "five feet six inches of Southern indignation, shouted back and the two then stood in the well shaking fingers under each other's noses." In a dramatic clash that would surely have led to a duel in an earlier time, the two congressmen ultimately had to be ordered to their seats by Speaker of the House Sam Rayburn. " 'I'll take the gentleman from Massachusetts anytime!' yelled Rankin and McCormack shouted back that he would 'answer the gentleman from Mississippi anytime, anywhere.' "

Rankin had set the tone for the anti-Jewish sentiments of HUAC, instigating his band of professional anti-Semites with his inflammatory rhetoric. "They whine about discrimination," he once publicly complained about the Jews. "Do you know who is being discriminated against? The white Christian people of America, the ones who created this nation . . . I am talking about the white Christian people of the North as well as the South . . . Communism is racial. A racial minority seized control in Russia and in all her satellite countries, such as Poland and Czechoslovakia, and many other countries I could name. They have been run out of practically every country in Europe in the years gone by, and if they keep stirring race trouble in this country and trying to force their communistic program on the Christian people of America, there is no telling what will happen to them here."

Rankin had fallen into the irritating routine of dismissing the liberal congressmen as "leftists" and calling the office hallway they shared Red Gulch. One day, while in the midst of one of his antiliberal tirades, Rankin had gestured toward a group of freshmen congressmen that included Helen and referred to them as "these Communists." She had finally reached the end of her patience and rose to address the Speaker. "Mr. Chairman, I demand to know if the gentleman from Mississippi is addressing me," Helen said, her voice rising toward Speaker Rayburn's empty chair. Rankin glared at her and continued talking. Two senior members rushed to her side and encouraged her to hold her ground. "He has to answer you," Congressman Wright Patman told her. "You don't have to ask again. Stand where you are."

Realizing there would be a stalemate until Rayburn arrived, for a point of order could not be made without the Speaker in his chair, one member went searching for Rayburn while another dashed to the coffee shop in search of Lyndon Johnson. "Douglas has taken on Rankin," the messenger told Johnson.

Johnson came running to the House, bounding up the stairs three at a time, and went to Rayburn's side. The Speaker had moved to his chair and was banging his gavel as Rankin was blatantly ignoring him. Determined to save his friend Rayburn from a humiliating standoff with an insubordinate colleague, Johnson whispered in Rayburn's ear. "Are you going to let the man from Mississippi run the House of Representatives?" Once more the gavel came down hard and Rayburn, glaring at Rankin, forcefully demanded that Rankin "answer the congresswoman from California."

Reluctantly, Rankin finally conceded. "I am not addressing the gentlewoman from California."

The incident led her to write a speech which she entitled "My Democratic Credo"—a long essay about her views of democracy and America, and which Johnson spent hours helping her edit. Lyrical and eloquent, the fervent speech became her rallying cry against the fear tactics gaining ground in American politics. "Mr. Speaker," she began her speech to Congress on March 26, 1946, "I think we all know that communism is no real threat to the democratic institutions of our country. But the irresponsible way the term 'communism' is used to falsely label the things the majority of us believe in can be very dangerous . . . The great mass of American people will never exchange democracy for communism as long as democracy fulfills its promise. The best way to keep communism out of our country is to keep democracy in it—to keep constantly before our eyes and minds the achievements and the goals which we, a free people, have accomplished and intend to accomplish in the future."

She ended the lengthy speech with a "flourishing paragraph" that Lyndon Johnson had composed in its entirety, and which she later regretted as hyperbolic. Still, he had been so helpful and supportive that she indulged him. "We, the members of this House, do not believe that Capitol Hill is a hill on which to kindle a fiery cross, but rather one on which to display the shining Cross which since Calvary has been to all the world the symbol of the Brotherhood of Man."

In addition to her efforts on behalf of atomic energy and against red-baiting, Helen was also deeply involved in other legislative issues of the Seventy-ninth Congress, especially the creation of a Jewish homeland in Palestine. She clashed regularly and fiercely with Undersecretary of State Dean Acheson and was proud of the fact that they were able to remain friends. Impassioned by her experience in prewar Germany and spurred by the injustices inflicted on Melvyn's ancestors, she was an avid and outspoken supporter of Israel. "Oil played a major role in our foreign policy even then, and there was a strong lobby in Washington that argued against recognizing Israel," she recalled. "Acheson . . . went along with the Arabs who were opposing Israel." Over lunch with Acheson one afternoon, she was "appalled" by what she thought a surprisingly unsophisticated attitude. "He said the Jews always were troublemakers in the world and shouldn't be encouraged."

Republicans swept the nation in the midterm elections of November 5, 1946—"scattering good Democrats everywhere," as Helen remembered it. It had been the first time in more than a decade that Democratic candidates could not rely on FDR's popular coattails. Helen managed to buck the national and state tide and win a resounding victory even though she had not campaigned in, or even visited,

California. Not only did she face several episodes of the total exhaustion that would plague her over the next decades—regularly requiring hospitalization—but she was too immersed in the pressing issues of the United Nations to find time to campaign in her congressional district. Sensing her political vulnerability, the Republicans "threw everything they had against me," as she recalled of the race, even importing "the heavyweight champion of the world, Joe Louis, easily the most admired black in the country, to campaign against me."

She had feared a massive black defection against her, following reports that Kyle Palmer, the influential political editor of the *Los Angeles Times*, was dissuading whites from challenging Douglas with the hopes that a black Republican would emerge. Indeed, a sixteen-year veteran of the State Assembly rose to the occasion. The appealing Frederick M. Roberts was a formidable opponent. If victorious, Roberts would have been the first black ever sent to Congress from California. With strong name recognition, experience, likeability, and the support of the powerful *Times*, Roberts posed a serious threat. "Ironically," as one political observer put it, "a factor that contributed to her illness [and inability to campaign] had been the workload she assumed on behalf of her constituents, in particular, the blacks."

It was the first campaign in which challenges to her patriotism arose. To her, the allegations were so preposterous she refused to credit them, and even when the *Los Angeles Tribune* mixed what one scholar described as "equal portions of red-baiting and reverse racism," Helen was more aghast than alarmed. "Maybe we're just old fashioned," ran a *Tribune* editorial, "but we can't see the rage for pink—pink toes or pink politics; and we'd kind of like to see a dark brown face in that sea of white up in Washington." But when a Los Angeles printing company printed seventy-five thousand copies of a Republican-sponsored anti-Douglas flyer claiming that she had made "a secret trip to Moscow" to meet with Stalin, she asked the U.S. attorney in Los Angeles to investigate the slander as a violation of federal election laws.

What her opponent hoped would be the coup de grâce came in a signed letter from candidate Roberts to the voters of the Fourteenth District. "This campaign is between a candidate endorsed and supported by the radical and left wing groups, and myself, a 100 per cent American,—a Negro,—and public servant," Roberts wrote. "This is not a fight between Democrats and Republicans. It is a severe test between advocates of State Socialism and Communism and our American system and way of life."

Still, while her staff and advisers worried, she always had faith that her black constituents would value the two years she had devoted to their needs. "I have long felt that the oppressed had a potential for loyalty far beyond anything you or I could understand," she wrote to the Lybecks in her certainty that the Fourteenth would not abandon her. In the end, she was proven right, and was one of the few Democratic incumbents reelected in 1946. Under such circumstances, her seat seemed safe for as long as she might want it. Grateful to her Fourteenth District constituents and more determined than ever to make a historic mark for herself, she hit the ground running in the fall of 1946. Her friend and colleague from the Twelfth District had not been so fortunate. Horace Jeremiah Voorhis, the handsome son of a Midwest business executive, had been a popular Democratic congressman for a decade. But in the 1946 general election, an up-and-coming California Republican had defeated him, using tactics never before seen in the state. Richard Milhous Nixon, a callow thirty-three-year-old lawyer with virtually no political experience, set out to portray his liberal opponent as a Communist—a technique that was so startlingly effective that he and his political cronies would perfect it for the future. During the Seventy-ninth Congress, "Jerry" Voorhis had been a conscientious member of HUAC, gaining attention for his forthright criticism of the procedures and abuses of some committee members. Nixon accused Voorhis of pandering to Communist spies, and in the nascent cold war tension of the moment, the charges stuck.

It was after this election that Helen began thinking seriously about expanding her political horizons, and observers began to note that she sounded and acted more like a seasoned statesman than a junior congressman. According to one analysis of the electoral results, "Not only did Douglas beat back the serious threat of a black opponent in her minority-populated district, and a Republican in a GOP year, but she actually doubled her margin of victory over 1944." Every week she received hundreds of invitations for speaking engagements, and her stump speeches took on an elevated tone. Her issues were the most vital of the day, and her ability to inform herself and then articulately reduce complicated subjects to a layman's understanding brought her large audiences.

Now forty-six years old, she had reached that stage in life in which all of one's faculties and talents, aspirations and resignations coalesce into the full measure of an individual. Though her sleep-deprived nights, frantic work schedule, and daily stress had led to high blood pressure, she seemed incapable of slowing down. Washington physicians diagnosed an enlarged heart, to which they attributed her sudden and debilitating periods of collapse. Still, she took her infirmities in stride, bringing stacks of books and files with her during her frequent hospital admissions. Meanwhile, her personal life was unsettled. Melvyn was living in the Hollywood Hills home and the two children—Peter and Mary—shuttled between two cities and two distracted parents. Most of the parenting was left to Evie, who alternated between resentment and sanguinity. When Helen decided to send the children to live with Melvyn, Evie was thankful. "You don't know what a relief it is not to have Mary Helen and Peter here," she wrote to the Lybecks, "as much as I love Mary Helen and can even tolerate Peter." For her part, Helen was torn between her professional commitments and spending time with the kids, but when she and Melvyn made the decision to enroll them in Chadwick boarding school in Los Angeles, she thought the stability would benefit them all.

Helen then turned her full attention to what would be the most rewarding personal and political experience of her lifetime: serving as an alternate delegate to the newly created United Nations. In April of the previous year, delegates from fifty nations had met in San Francisco to draw up the original charter for the organization. Then, in January 1946, the General Assembly met for the first time in London and adopted its first resolution for the peaceful use of atomic energy and the elimination of atomic and other weapons of mass destruction.

When President Truman appointed her as an alternate to the second session, to be held in New York City in October 1946, Helen was thrilled, for while it was a prestigious accolade it carried actual responsibility as well. There she would meet the world leaders who would inspire the next phase of her public life and introduce her to the international themes that would form postwar America. She, like delegate Eleanor Roosevelt, saw the United Nations as a natural home. "For her," she wrote about Eleanor's attachment to the UN, "it was a logical progression from the extension of her family to the 'family of man.'" Helen, too, held idealized, grandiose visions for what the organization could accomplish toward peace in the world. "The greatest engineering project ever undertaken by man," as she described it to the *Los Angeles Daily News*, ". . . building bridges to people the world over"—an entity that without the support of women's organizations would never have come to fruition.

So enthusiastic—or at least curious—were Americans about the UN coming to New York that an estimated 175,000 well-wishers lined the streets to welcome the motorcade of visiting delegates from fifty-one countries. The American delegation was one of only six countries that included women—of sixteen hundred delegates, seven were female—and was the only nation that sent two women, Helen Douglas and Eleanor Roosevelt. Predictably, Helen drew attention from the press. "A tall, well-tailored woman, she swings along through the U.N. corridors, her black topcoat tossed over her shoulders, the sleeves flying behind," the *Brooklyn Eagle* described her. "She greets those who know her with a breathless hello, an impulsive toss of her dark blond hair, and a large grin, distinguished by the brightness of uncommonly white teeth."

Other members of the American delegation were among the most distinguished statesmen in Washington, and Helen felt honored to be in their company. Staying at the Pennsylvania Hotel—the building surrounded by staggering numbers of Secret Service agents—the American delegation ate, drank, and breathed foreign policy. Helen voraciously read the documents they were given, determined to fully grasp every issue before them. "They send the stuff up here by the bushel, most of it marked 'secret' or 'very secret' or 'top secret,'" she wrote to Melvyn, who warned her to be circumspect and discreet where secret documents were concerned. "It wouldn't help . . . if you were suddenly accused of discussing State Department Secrets," he wrote with a prescience of the looming witch hunt of Communists in government.

Assigned a place behind Eleanor and between New York Congressman Sol Bloom and presidential adviser John Foster Dulles, Helen had a ringside seat to a historic experiment in international peace-keeping. Secretary of State James F. Byrnes was the delegation's leader. The other delegates were Senators Warren R. Austin, Arthur Vandenberg, and Tom Connally. Joining Helen as alternates were New Jersey Representative Charles A. Eaton and foreign policy adviser Adlai Stevenson.

Lorena Hickok, Eleanor Roosevelt's friend who had lived for an extended period of time in the second-floor residential quarters of the Roosevelt White House, now moved in with Helen to serve as her secretary. A journalist for many years, Hick, as she was nicknamed, had frequently helped Helen with her congressional and campaign speeches. She had accompanied Eleanor to New York to act as her helpmate and had generously offered her assistance to Helen as well. "Mrs. R says she is doing a magnificent job," Hick wrote of Helen's work at the UN.

Helen was assigned to a committee that dealt with the shortage of cereal in the world—the United Nations Relief and Rehabilitation Association (UNRRA)—where she came to the uncomfortable realization that American delegates were expected to vote in lockstep with each other. "Someday we may have a Parliament of Man where each delegate will be independent to vote his or her conscience," she would later write of the experience. "Today the United Nations isn't remotely like that. The delegates are bound hand and foot."

Still, if the experience left her with less optimism than when she began, she would meet the man who ignited the passion for disarmament that would shape the rest of her life. "Throughout those long weeks of the Assembly, I really never thought of anything except of being with Helen," was how Philip Noel-Baker would wistfully recall the period.

Author of the much-acclaimed 1926 book *Disarmament* and a leading authority on the subject, the erudite Philip Noel-Baker was a British pacifist who spoke seven languages and who had been Lord Robert Cecil's assistant at the 1919 Paris Peace Conference. A distinguished Member of Parliament and a foundation member of the League of Nations, the future Nobel laureate was instantly smitten with Helen. Although he was a decade older than she—and entangled in both a long-standing and unsatisfying marriage and another complicated extramarital affair—the attraction was swift and mutual. An avid rock climber, swimmer, and one-time Olympic silver medalist for the fifteen-hundred-meter race, at fifty-eight Noel-Baker had a physique as fine and impressive as his mind.

Born in 1889 into a Canadian Quaker family, Philip John Baker was raised in London, where his father had moved and established a manufacturing firm. The elder Baker was a well-known humanitarian who served several terms in the House of Commons. He had devoted his political life to trying to prevent World War I and espousing a strong British-American alliance. Philip—who was raised in an affluent milieu of political activism and intelligentsia—was educated at Bootham School in York and Haverford College in Pennsylvania. He then studied history and economics at King's College in Cambridge, where he was president of the debating society and the University Athletic Club, and at the Sorbonne in Paris. Energetic, charming, and creative, he envisioned the idea and then orchestrated the reality of Oxford and Cambridge men running against Harvard and Yale men. The Cambridge University magazine, *Granta*, outlined Noel-Baker's busy summer of 1912 schedule, which included Olympic track events at Stockholm, various Alpine climbs, fishing in Scotland, and cricket "at Lords and at the Oval." A legendary long-distance runner, he performed with the British Olympic team at Stockholm in 1912 and captained the British teams at Antwerp in 1920 and Paris in 1924. The exploits of the 1924 games were depicted nearly sixty years later in the Academy Award–winning *Chariots of Fire*, though Noel-Baker's role was not dramatized.

In August 1914, one day after the war began with Germany, Baker announced his organization of a Quaker ambulance unit for conscientious objectors to go to the front in France. There, after having witnessed firsthand the reality of trench warfare, he determined to "carry on what my father had tried to do . . . to get rid of war and armaments and the militarism from which war and armaments begin." He married a hospital field nurse ten years his senior named Irene Noel, and, with a commitment to gender equality unusual for the time, officially hyphenated his name to Noel-Baker.

After World War I, and with his father's help, he landed a position with the powerful Cecil in the Foreign Office of the League of Nations. There he rose quickly in British foreign policy circles, attracting attention and making a name for himself as an eloquent orator with an incisive intellect. Before pursuing politics, he had a stellar academic career as a professor of International Law at the University of London and a guest lecturer at Yale University. His academic research led him to write and publish several renowned books and to pursue a four-decade-long political career with Great Britain's Labor Party. "I have only one real concern in public affairs—*peace*," he once wrote to his longtime mistress, Megan Lloyd George, who was the first female Member of Parliament.

The quintessential diplomat, the lean, virile, and handsome Noel-Baker had everything that Melvyn Douglas and Lyndon Johnson were missing. Where Melvyn was emotionally inaccessible, Philip was effusive and capable of unabashed adoration. Where LBJ could be moody and crass, Philip was cordial and refined. Finally Helen had met someone who was truly her peer, who could match her on all levels, and the spark between them that ignited during that moment of history would last until each of their deaths.

On the opening day of the General Assembly, as the Belgian foreign minister began his introductory remarks, Philip glanced down the front row, past Dulles, who was seated next to him, and toward the American delegation. "I did not know her. I did not know who she was, so ignorant and ill-informed a Britisher was I. I looked along the bench, past the men, and I saw this lovely young woman." He could barely contain himself, so eager was he to meet her, and when the morning session ended he rushed over to introduce himself. As they shook hands, he recalled that they had a mutual friend in the French film producer Louis Dolivet, who was living in New York City.

"I went straight from the assembly hall to a telephone and I rang up Louis Dolivet, and I said, 'Louis, you have to ask me to dinner with Mrs. Helen Gahagan Douglas.'"

"Sure," Dolivet replied. "What night would suit? Thursday? Friday? Saturday?"

"Not Thursday, Friday, Saturday. Tonight!" the Englishman answered.

That night they met at Dolivet's, and when dinner was over Philip offered to take her home in a taxi. As they passed the Plaza Hotel, he

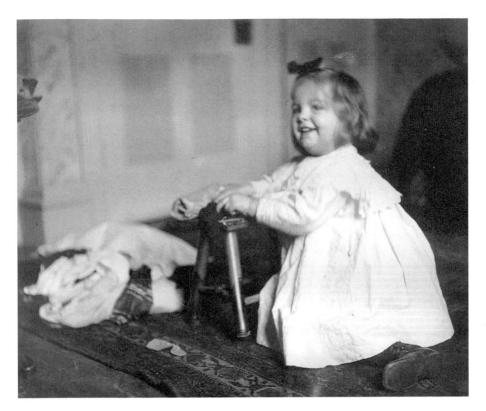

The cherubic Helen was a precocious and curious child. At three years old, she was already the center of attention in the lively Gahagan brood. (Unless otherwise noted, all photographs are courtesy of the Carl Albert Center Congressional Archives, University of Oklahoma.)

A natural-born actor, Helen argued passionately with her father, who forbade her theatrical pursuits and insisted that she attend college. Determined to make her way to the Broadway stage, she set her sights on Barnard—an elite women's college—because of its location in New York City. As a twenty-one-year-old student, Helen found her niche in the drama society of Wigs and Cues.

As the Ethiopian slave girl in Verdi's *Aida*, Helen debuted at a Viennese opera house. A lyric dramatic soprano, the twenty-nine-year-old Helen abandoned her lucrative and critically acclaimed stage career in order to pursue singing.

In 1933, Melvyn Douglas had an epiphany in the middle of the night: "It came to me that we should get on a ship and sail away." The young married couple embarked on a nine-month around-the-world tour. Helen later thought the journey life changing—a primer for her career in world affairs. Their trip was cut short when Melvyn contracted malaria and Helen became pregnant with the couple's first child.

By the end of the 1930s, Helen had made her transition from actress and singer to politician, heading the John Steinbeck Committee and bringing national attention to the plight of migrant workers. First Lady Eleanor Roosevelt threw her full support behind every issue Helen deemed important, and in 1940 accompanied Melvyn and Helen on a tour of ditch bank settlements in California's San Joaquin Valley.

This photograph of an eighteen-year-old mother from Oklahoma was taken by Dorothea Lange in 1937. Commissioned by the Federal Farm Security Administration, Lange and her economist husband, Paul Schuster Taylor, conducted a thousand-mile fact-finding tour of migrant communities for the Roosevelt administration. Lange and Taylor would become ardent friends and supporters of Helen.

Helen adored being a mother to the couple's firstborn, Peter. She acted as if she had been the first to discover the pleasure of babies. "I'd have twenty of them—they're so nice—if I only had the time."

Lyndon Baines Johnson, a lanky Texas congressman, stopped in to welcome Congresswoman Helen Gahagan Douglas on one of her first days on Capitol Hill. He draped "his long frame in one of my easy chairs," Helen remembered. For several years to come, the two were inseparable. Their relationship over the next two decades, however, would come to emblemize the shift in American politics from the New Deal to the quagmire of Vietnam.

Daughter Mary Helen, born in 1938, was a free-spirited young girl who idolized her mother. Seen here in their lavish Hollywood Hills home, the two cherished the time they spent together, which was difficult to find given Helen's demanding bicoastal existence.

Congressman Richard Nixon is seen here campaigning in the 1950 Senate race from the back gate of a station wagon in Azusa, California. (Courtesy of Richard Nixon Presidential Materials, National Archives and Records Administration, College Park, Maryland.)

DOUGLAS-MARCANTONIO VOTING RECORD

Many persons have requested a comparison of the voting records of Congresswoman Helen Douglas and the notorious Communist party-liner, Congressman Vito Marcantonio of New York.

Mrs. Douglas and Marcantonio have been members of Congress together since January 1, 1945. During that period, Mrs. Douglas voted the same as Marcantonio **354** times. While it should not be expected that a member of the House of Representatives should always vote in opposition to Marcantonio, it is significant to note, not only the great number of times which Mrs. Douglas voted in agreement with him, but also the issues on which almost without exception they always saw eye to eye, to-wit: Un-American Activities and Internal Security.

Here is the Record!

VOTES AGAINST COMMITTEE ON UN-AMERICAN ACTIVITIES

Both Douglas and Marcantonio voted against establishing the Committee on Un-American Activities. 1/3/45. Bill passed.

Both voted on three separate occasions against contempt proceedings against persons and organizations which refused to reveal records or answer whether they were Communists. 4/16/46, 6/26/46, 11/24/47. Bills passed.

Both voted on four separate occasions against allowing funds for investigation by the Un-American Activities Committee. 5/17/46, 3/9/48, 2/9/49, 3/23/50. (The last vote was 348 to 12.) All bills passed.

COMMUNIST-LINE FOREIGN POLICY VOTES

Both voted against Greek-Turkish Aid Bill. 5/9/47. (It has been established that without this aid Greece and Turkey would long since have gone behind the Iron Curtain.) Bill passed.

Both voted on two occasions against free press amendment to UNRRA appropriation bill, providing that no funds should be furnished any country which refused to allow free access to the news of activities of the UNRRA by press and radio representatives of the United States. 11/1/45, 6/28/46. Bills passed. (This would in effect have denied American relief funds to Communist dominated countries.)

Both voted against refusing Foreign Relief to Soviet-dominated countries UNLESS supervised by Americans. 4/30/47. Bill passed 324 to 75.

VOTE AGAINST NATIONAL DEFENSE

Both voted against the Selective Service Act of 1948. 6/18/48. Bill passed.

VOTES AGAINST LOYALTY AND SECURITY LEGISLATION

Both voted on two separate occasions against bills requiring loyalty checks for Federal employees. 7/15/47, 6/29/49. Bills passed.

Both voted against the Subversive Activities Control Act of 1948, requiring registration with the Attorney General of Communist party members and communist controlled organizations. Bill passed, 319 to 58. 5/19/48. AND AFTER KOREA both again voted against it. Bill passed 8/29/50, 354 to 20.

AFTER KOREA, on July 12, 1950, Marcantonio and Douglas and 12 others voted against the Security Bill, to permit the heads of key National Defense departments, such as the Atomic Energy Commission, to discharge government workers found to be poor security risks! Bill passed, 327 to 14.

VOTE AGAINST CALIFORNIA

Both recorded against confirming title to Tidelands in California and the other states affected. 4/30/48. Bill passed 257-29.

VOTES AGAINST CONGRESSIONAL INVESTIGATION OF COMMUNIST AND OTHER ILLEGAL ACTIVITIES

Both voted against investigating the "whitewash" of the AMERASIA case. 4/18/46. Bill passed.

Both voted against investigating why the Soviet Union was buying as many as 60,000 United States patents at one time. 3/4/47. Bill passed.

Both voted against continuing investigation of numerous instances of illegal actions by OPA and the War Labor Board. 1/18/45. Bill passed.

Both voted on two occasions against allowing Congress to have access to government records necessary to the conduct of investigations by Senate and House Committees. 4/22/48, 5/13/48. Bills passed.

ON ALL OF THE ABOVE VOTES which have occurred since Congressman Nixon took office on January 1, 1947, HE has voted exactly opposite to the Douglas-Marcantonio Axis!

After studying the voting comparison between Mrs. Douglas and Marcantonio, is it any wonder that the Communist line newspaper, the Daily People's World, in its lead editorial on January 31, 1950, labeled Congressman Nixon as "The Man To Beat" in this Senate race and that the Communist newspaper, the New York Daily Worker, in the issue of July 28, 1947, selected Mrs. Douglas along with Marcantonio as "One of the Heroes of the 80th Congress."

REMEMBER! The United States Senate votes on ratifying international treaties and confirming presidential appointments. Would California send Marcantonio to the United States Senate?

The Pink Sheet became notorious in the annals of political dirty tricks, earning the sobriquet "Tricky Dick" for its behind-the-scenes creator, Richard Nixon. Used to imply that Helen was a Communist, the document would result in her branding in history as "the pink lady."

Near the end of their long and productive lives, Melvyn and Helen finally created the kind of family life that had eluded them for four decades. Standing together here on the long staircase leading down to Lake Morey at the family's Cliff Mull estate in Vermont, the couple remained lifelong devoted friends and dedicated parents.

boldly asked: "What about stopping here and dancing for a little while?" At first she declined, citing her nine o'clock meeting the following morning—"So after a little argument, I beat down her feminine resistance." They danced for several hours and then settled at a table and talked for several more. "As soon as we sat down," recalled Noel-Baker, "I said, 'Look, I ought to understand. Supposing you tell me the story of your life?'"

Helen complied, beginning with her childhood, then the stories of her stage and opera careers, her marriage, and her entry into politics. "From that day," he recalled three decades later with a distinctive dose of understatement, "we worked rather closely." As leader of the British delegation, Noel-Baker had an overwhelming schedule of obligations, from public speaking to meeting with the Australians, Canadians, South Africans, Americans, and New Zealanders. "But all the time, I was only waiting for the moment when I got the opportunity to begin talking to Helen and being with her again. That went on through the evening almost every day. Whenever I could, I got her not only for lunch, but for dinner as well. You may draw your own conclusion," he told an interviewer near the end of his life, smiling warmly for emphasis.

They had lunch and dinner together nearly every day. "Gradually we found that on every aspect of foreign policy on armaments, on militarism, on economic cooperation, on help to the poorer nations, on international disputes, on the international court, on the proper use of the Security Council and the Assembly, we were in complete agreement. Our minds always clicked together. If Helen said something, it was as though I'd said it myself."

When the UN session was over, and Noel-Baker had been called back to England by Prime Minister Clement Attlee, he was "immensely reluctant" to leave Helen and had to practically be kidnapped. "I was bundled into an aeroplane," he said, and flown to London.

Just as Philip returned to his full and demanding life in Great Britain, Helen returned to Washington to take her seat in the historic Republican-dominated Eightieth Congress. In the 1946 midterm elections, Republicans had swept into both chambers of Congress for the first time since the Great Depression—"an era so distant to most people," as Truman biographer McCullough wrote, "that it seemed another world." What had appeared to be the Democrats' inevitable hold on Washington had been suddenly and shockingly broken, and the president and his party were now in the minority. With the sweep of one election, the New Deal that had defined the past decade and a half seemed destined for oblivion.

Scholars and political observers attributed the Democrats' defeat to everything from the divisions in the party between Northern liberals and Southern conservatives to maritime and railroad strikes to housing, automobile, and food shortages. Unemployment was high and the cost of living had jumped more than 6 percent despite a thriving economy. But political squabbles and domestic discontent aside, the stark fact remained that Harry Truman could not escape the shadow of Franklin D. Roosevelt, who had died the year before. FDR's "impact on American politics was so profound that even the most powerful Republican leaders believed privately that their party might be permanently in the minority," the eminent author David Halberstam wrote of FDR. But such fears were unfounded, for Truman—with his connections to Kansas City's corrupt Pendergast machine and his country-bumpkin manner—was a boon to the opposition party.

Watching his standing in the polls plummet and his influence weaken, he was resentful of his critics. "There have been only two or three Presidents . . . as roundly abused and misrepresented . . . as I," he wrote to a confidant. But he could not escape the pulse of the nation. The mood was unmistakable. Americans were turning outward, focusing on a belligerent Soviet Union that had its sights set on Europe, threatening world peace. Truman had been dolefully unprepared in foreign policy, rarely briefed, and often ignored altogether by Roosevelt's advisers if not by the president himself. As it was, he was in lockstep with his countrymen, harboring personal anxiety over Communist expansionism. "It was a mean time," Halberstam wrote in *The Fifties*. "The nation was ready for witch-hunts. We had come out of World War Two stronger and more powerful and more affluent than ever before, but the rest of the world, alien and unsettling, seemed to press closer now than many Americans wanted it to." The Eightieth Congress would be the stage from which the next half century of foreign policy would unfold.

Despite congressional support by the Seventy-ninth Congress for civilian control of atomic power, Truman, in a special message to the new Congress, pushed for the unification of the army, navy, and air force under one Department of Defense that would also control atomic energy. Such a concentration of power under a single cabinet secretary was resisted by many, including, especially, the navy, which feared a dilution of its influence. In the event, the Soviets saw the move as an alarming signal. "For whatever reason, and some of us thought that bellicose moves by the United States were a factor," Helen wrote of the militaristic climate, "the Soviet [sic] was becoming increasingly difficult."

Helen and Philip had frequently and thoroughly discussed foreign policy and were in agreement that the Russian Communists were "tiresome," that Stalin's Middle East expansionism was belligerent, and that the U.S. and Great Britain should treat the Soviets in a friendly but firm and uncompromising way—"not letting them think they could carry out sponsored revolutions," as Philip put it. Both also firmly believed in the possibility of peaceful coexistence between the U.S. and the Soviet Union. But by early 1947, Stalin's lack of interest in peaceful diplomacy with the West was no longer debatable. He had obvious designs on Turkey, opposed Allied plans for the unification of Germany, and had rejected both the efforts toward international control of atomic power and the establishment of a United Nations peace force. It had become clear to the American foreign policy establishment that a hard-line diplomatic stance was necessary.

As a member of the Foreign Affairs Committee, Helen was deeply involved in the debate surrounding the containment of Communism abroad. She was confidently outspoken on the subject, emboldened by her experience with the UN and by her extensive dialogue—and continuing correspondence—with the foreign policy expert Noel-Baker. The tensions between the U.S. and the Soviet Union escalated when Great Britain, in late February, informed the Truman administration that it could no longer afford to provide military and financial aid to Greece. In a top secret message from the Atlee government to the White House, the bankrupt British asked the U.S. to take over the responsibility. Since 1945, the British had supplied forty thousand troops and untold millions in economic aid to Greece in support of an oppressive royalist regime engaged in a civil war with insurgents. In response to Britain's formal announcement of withdrawal, the Soviets mobilized on the Turkish border, which, as Helen recalled the moment, "sent shock waves through the West" and prompted the Turkish government to seek military aid from the U.S. "just as fighting broke out in Greece between the government and Greek communists supplied from Yugoslavia."

Though the president was uncomfortable with the rapid pace with which events were unfolding, he was convinced that Soviet domination of Europe and the Middle East was at stake and that the U.S. needed to act immediately. According to his biographer, David McCullough, "Truman felt he faced a decision as difficult as any ever to confront a president . . ." The money for Greece was only the beginning." Truman began writing the speech his staff sensed would be the most important of his career, and on March 12, 1947, he addressed a joint session of Congress. As Republican Senator Arthur Vandenberg had said, Truman would have to "scare hell out of the American people" in order to get them to support a peacetime proposal for military intervention in a faraway civil war. The eighteen-minute speech never mentioned the Soviet Union, but the Truman Doctrine, as it would become known throughout history, was the firing shot in the cold war and set a precedent for a U.S. military commitment during peacetime.

Calling for four hundred million dollars in aid to Greece and Turkey, the president was greeted with overwhelming enthusiasm for his courage, if not total support for his program. For her part, Helen was supportive of aid to Greece—though skeptical that the money would get into the right hands with the reactionary monarchy at the helm—but she thoroughly opposed shoring up the military government in Turkey. In any case, she believed the two should not be linked together and, especially, that the proper venue for addressing Turkey's complaint against the Soviet Union was the United Nations Security Council. She agreed with the influential journalist Walter Lippmann, who elevated the term "cold war" into the international idiom it would become, and who advocated aid to Greece but objected to Truman's imperialistic doctrine. Not totally convinced that the Soviets intended to conquer the world—viewing them not as revolutionary fanatics but rather as fearful and paranoid—Lippmann supported a show of force but rejected Truman's "vague global policy which sounds like the tocsin of an ideological crusade."

Helen clashed yet again with Undersecretary of State Acheson, who strongly opposed her recommendation that the proposed bill be delayed until the UN could address the situation. "Sending arms to Turkey was old-style, pre-atomic-bomb diplomacy," she argued with Acheson. "The nuclear age demanded a saner approach, that of airing grievances in the United Nations." Irritated, Acheson pointed to the Soviet veto power on the Security Council, and, in any case, thought the apparatus too slow-moving for such an urgent international crisis—a crisis she felt he and Truman exaggerated for political expediency. Even George Kennan, the Soviet expert within the administration who had penned the famous "Long Telegram" warning that Stalin would never deal reasonably with the U.S., opposed provoking the Soviet Union.

"If we tried to frighten the Soviet," Helen argued before Congress, "it would only make the Soviet more frightened of us." Pushing Stalin into a corner, she reasoned, would provide him with justification for severe retaliatory measures that might lead to the use of atomic weapons. She feared that the U.S. was on a path that "should have been avoided at all costs: America and Russia locked head to head."

Her opposition to the Greek-Turkish aid bill would further incite her numerous enemies, and she would be officially branded as soft on Communism, if not a "commie" herself. As a Democrat opposing a Democratic president's initiative, the attacks on her would be bipartisan, and even though this was the only Truman bill she had not supported, the administration took it as further evidence that she was not, and never would be, a team player. When Truman, to appease conservatives in both parties, instituted a loyalty program for two million government employees—"to the horror of many of us"—she broke from the Democratic congressional pack to oppose it, further alienating herself from the president.

Indeed, Helen presciently sensed that America was taking the first step down a slippery foreign policy slope of supporting *any* government—regardless of its corruption or tyranny—as long as it was anti-Communist. Helen "saw too clearly the Faustian bargain of Cold War foreign policy," according to the historian Roger Morris. "It began with weapons and money for oppressive but anti-Soviet regimes in Athens and Ankara and led off decades later into the mists of Vietnam and Central America. Helen Douglas instinctively bridled at the start."

Into this maelstrom of fear and agitation, ignorance and xenophobia, fanaticism and opportunism, rose the newly revitalized House Un-American Activities Committee and its star witness, J. Edgar Hoover.

The FBI director told members of the committee that Communism was being spread by "the diabolic machinations of sinister figures engaged in un-American activities" who had "hoodwinked and duped" American liberals into joining them. In his unprecedented testimony before Congress in March 1947, Hoover claimed that the U.S. had been massively infiltrated by traitors and Communist spies. There were more Communists per capita in the U.S. than in Russia at the time of the Bolshevik Revolution, he told them, and he recommended an aggressive national policy of rooting out subversives.

"Is there any one area in which the communists are more dangerous and more deeply entrenched than any other?" Richard Nixon, a junior congressman from California, asked Hoover.

One of the hotbeds of this penetration, Hoover answered, was the country's motion picture industry. The Hollywood film community had been a favorite target of both Communists and Communist hunters since the founding of the writing and acting guilds in the 1930s, which had divided the industry between Left and Right. In 1934, leaders of the International Alliance of Theatrical Stage Employees (IATSE) reported that Soviet Communists had financed the takeover of the studios—and infiltrated AFL unions, according to IATSE representative Roy Brewer—in order to use the movies as pro-Russian propaganda. "To kick off its postwar campaign, HUAC needed a headline grabber," author Griffin Fariello wrote, "and what better than Filmland?" Producing more than six hundred films a year, Hollywood "was the focus of the nation's fantasies . . . and the purge of its Communists captured the public's attention."

Compliantly, HUAC turned its attention to Hollywood. "The result was to be a spectacle of pounding gavel and theatrics on all sides as the panel confronted a group of militant and defiant screenwriters, the famous Hollywood Ten," as one Nixon biographer portrayed the frenzied moment that Dalton Trumbo would famously refer to as "the time of the toad."

Hoover's sensational and inflammatory testimony was the clarion cry for the reactionary forces in Congress. "If the communists take over this country there will be no Baptists in Missouri," Congressman Rankin predictably railed, appealing to Truman as a Missouri Baptist; "there will be no Methodists in Mississippi, or Presbyterians in Iowa, there will be no Catholics in Louisiana or New York, there will be no Episcopalians in Virginia."

A "handful of us," as Helen referred to "the vanishing moderates" that included herself, Harry Byrd, Jacob Javits, Vandenberg, and a few others, fought unsuccessfully against the rising red-baiting tide. Helen voted against funding for HUAC, introduced legislation guaranteeing the right of defense to citizens dragged before the committee, called the hearings a "tragic farce," and was one of only seventeen representatives to oppose the contempt citations against the Hollywood Ten. Her opposition stimulated Hoover to expand the already existing FBI investigation of her and her political activities—a dossier that he had personally begun in 1939 and that would eventually swell to several hundred classified pages.

She redeemed herself somewhat with the Truman administration as a fervent supporter of the Marshall Plan, ironically drawing vitriolic criticism from the Communist Party. Beginning in July 1947, the massive reconstruction plan for America's World War II allies—the European Recovery Program, as it was officially titled—was primarily the brainchild of George Kennan following a multinational conference in Paris. Based on what was called the Kennan Report, which had been directed to Secretary of State George C. Marshall, the plan would offer millions of dollars in economic aid to war-torn Europe while providing an economic stimulus to American industry, which would manufacture the exports and grow the food to feed a starving continent.

Marshall announced the plan—with little fanfare and no attending press—in a graduation address to Harvard University on June 5, 1947.

"It is logical that the United States should do whatever it is able to do to assist in the return of normal economic health to the world, without which there can be no political stability and no assured peace. Our policy is not directed against any country, but against hunger, poverty, desperation and chaos. Any government that is willing to assist in recovery will find full cooperation on the part of the U.S.A."

Helen thought the plan masterful and representative of the UN's most noble and moral aspirations, "a model of economic and social assistance welcomed by liberals because it was humane and by industrialists because it would restore world trade." The national press had not been invited to hear Marshall's unveiling of the plan because the administration feared the American public—in dire need of housing programs and health insurance—would not support pouring millions of dollars into rebuilding Europe. "The answer was to tout the Marshall Plan as a bulwark against communism," as Helen explained the administration's strategy, with which she reluctantly agreed. "The line was that France and Italy would become communist unless prosperity was restored." Even Eleanor Roosevelt halfheartedly supported the tactic.

The Soviet Union "cooperated splendidly" by invading Czechoslovakia, as Helen put it, ushering in a quick bipartisan approval of Truman's five-billion-dollar aid plan in early 1948. "Ironically, despite the hope many of us had that the Marshall Plan would be supported because of its decency, it succeeded in the Eightieth Congress mainly because of the Cold War."

Meanwhile, Helen found herself in the middle of the drama of the 1948 presidential election that was playing out on the floor of the Eightieth Congress. Overworked, exhausted, disillusioned, and emotionally drained by the constant discord, she was far more interested in presidential politics than in her own upcoming reelection campaign. In fact, she almost decided not to run, so disenchanted with the process had she become.

In the run-up to the Democratic National Convention, Helen met regularly with a group of liberal Democrats for Sunday dinners at the Cosmos—the exclusive intellectually based social club founded in the nineteenth century by John Wesley Powell. The group unanimously viewed the Truman presidency with ambivalence. Disappointed by the resistance his domestic policies met in Congress and alarmed by his "bellicose foreign policies," they discussed possible challengers. When Henry Wallace, a member of the group, announced his intention to run against Truman as a third-party candidate, they were mortified. "There was an embarrassed silence," Helen remembered. "Wallace's statement lay on the table like a hot potato. None of us wanted to touch it." Suddenly, people rose and began to make excuses about leaving early. "They said good night pleasantly to Henry and piled out of the door as if fleeing a bad odor."

The mass exodus made Helen feel uncomfortable. She thought they were being hypocritical and evasive, and that they owed Wallace an honest response. She waited until nearly everyone else had left and then cleared her throat. "Mr. Secretary," she began, "I won't support you if you head a third party. I don't think anyone here tonight will support you."

She was deeply touched by Wallace's pained expression. She had great regard for him but thought his third-party candidacy naïve, if not pathetic. She knew that he hadn't felt the same about the Democrats since Truman's decision to send military aid to Greece and Turkey. She knew as well that he held fast to the belief that "conciliation and peaceful coexistence with the Soviet Union was possible." After the Soviet aggression in Czechoslovakia, she thought Wallace's policy of appeasement to be "dangerous nonsense." But she knew as well that he had little experience with realpolitik and suspected that he was unwittingly allowing "manipulators"—Communists and fringe radicals—to use his "good name" to advance their agenda. When, at the first meeting of the Progressive Party, many liberals "walked out in protest of communist domination of the organization," Wallace seemed oblivious to the seriousness of their concern. Helen thought it all a tragedy, and agreed with labor leader Walter Reuther when he pronounced Wallace "a lost soul."

Still, though she hated to abandon her old friend Henry Wallace, she was eager to find a different Democratic challenger to Truman. To that end, she and her California colleague, Congressman Chet Holifield, made a reconnaissance mission to New York City to meet with General Dwight David Eisenhower of the U.S. Army. As the Allied commander in chief, Eisenhower had returned to the U.S. with a hero's welcome at the end of the war and was serving as president of Columbia University. Several members of Helen's Cosmos group had decided they should approach Eisenhower to feel him out about running for president. First they needed to determine whether or not he was a Democrat.

Helen thought the meeting very revealing, and though she found Eisenhower charismatic, attractive, and extremely masculine, she was stunned by his lack of erudition. "We had a pleasant chat with the general, who appeared to be neither a Democrat nor a Republican. He gave the impression that he was a man with so little interest in politics that he had made no distinction between the two parties." Convinced that he would not suffice as a Democratic candidate, Helen reported back to her Cosmos cohorts that Eisenhower's "ignorance of government was embarrassingly apparent."

In the spring of 1948, it was clear that Truman faced an uphill battle for the nomination. Southern Democrats—thinking Truman's Fair Deal domestic policies too similar to Roosevelt's New Deal— were backing the racist South Carolina Governor Strom J. Thurmond. Truman was certain to face opposition from the liberal wing of the party as well—alienated New Dealers who had joined the new Americans for Democratic Action as a "non-Communist liberal response to the Wallace movement," as McCullough depicted the ADA— and were searching for an alternate candidate while the country at large had embraced a new conservatism.

She knew that Truman had two major problems that could not be addressed head-on but that were the elephants in the living room— Jews and blacks—and unless he assuaged the reservations of both of those constituencies, his candidacy would be doomed. In the most generalized and simplistic terms, she thought that Jews found him weak and irresolute about recognizing the state of Israel and blacks saw little evidence of his dedication to racial equality. "The Negroes don't cotton to Truman worth a God damn," Helen's campaign manager, Ed Lybeck, wrote to her. "They seem to realize fully that it doesn't matter what a guy says if what he does is just the opposite. And he comes from too far South to suit most of 'em anyway. As for the Jews—they're so sick and disgusted over the Palestine sell-out that I doubt many of them will actually vote Democratic."

Ultimately, she had no choice but to stand firm for Truman, whom she admired deeply despite their differences. "I had disagreed with his Greek-Turkish aid bill and other aspects of his foreign policy but the Marshall Plan was superb and his domestic policies, though thwarted by the Republican Congress, had been humane." She had been asked to present a major speech at the convention—the first Democratic convention in sixteen years without FDR leading the party. For weeks she worked on the speech, perfecting and strengthening it, and along the way had determined to focus her attention on the legacy of Roosevelt and the New Deal rather than the polarizing candidacies of Truman and Wallace.

In early summer she learned that there was a campaign under way, led by a group of young activists along with what she described as "influential Democrats who were highly placed in the Washington establishment," to nominate her for the vice presidency. She dismissed the idea as preposterous. Not only did she feel the country was not ready to elect a woman to such a high national office, but she could not fathom the possibility that Truman would ever go along with a Truman-Douglas ticket. Apparently, the Helen Gahagan Douglas for Vice President Movement was far more advanced than was commonly known. "I was generally astonished. The idea of a woman running on a presidential ticket had never crossed my mind." The *Washington Post* called it the "first genuine boom in history for a woman for vice-president [and] heralded what may happen sooner than we think, even possibly in 1952." Disaffected New Dealers, progressives who could not abide a Wallace candidacy, and the few women who had risen to relatively lofty positions in the Roosevelt and Truman ad-ministrations thought her an inspired choice.

In the end, she felt like a woman in a no-man's-land: The leftists thought her too conservative, the moderates thought her too liberal, and the conservatives considered her a radical. When rumors swirled on Capitol Hill that Kentucky Congressman Alben W. Barkley was seek-ing the vice-presidential nomination, Helen greeted the news enthusi-astically and asked her supporters to abandon their draft-Helen efforts.

Back home in her California district, as the primary election battle was raging on largely without her, gender had become a full-fledged issue. Her constituency of blacks and labor was solidly behind her, and she was widely favored to win reelection. Though her seat was deemed safe by all the pundits and operatives, the press hammered away at what were known as her market basket events—a series of cost-of-living antics that involved bringing a market basket full of food to the floor of Congress to demonstrate the rising cost of groceries. Food prices had gone up by 50 percent, which she blamed on Republicans' refusal to institute price controls. National news reports were overwhelmingly favorable, and she received mailbags full of letters from women throughout the nation. "Can't the women of the country elect you as their representative at-large?" wrote one. "You seem to be the only one concerned with our problems of food, clothing, and housing."

The Los Angeles press was characteristically snide. "Congressmen were drooling, but not at Mrs. Douglas's basket," the *Los Angeles Daily News* wrote regarding the reaction of Helen's male colleagues. Among the most sexist was an item appearing in the *San Francisco News*. "Douglas is an experienced shopper. Like your lady and mine, she wants her money's worth. She gives the bananas a squeeze with thumb and forefinger. Same for the tomatoes . . . Mrs. Douglas, looking trim in her modest sharkskin suit, with the skirt slit just right to show the old look in legs through the new, moved away from the liver department."

Her National Convention speech in Philadelphia in July "unfurled with the grace of a wind-swept flag," as one political scholar put it. Some members of the press used the historic 1948 Democratic National Convention—and the role of Helen Gahagan Douglas—to mark the one hundredth anniversary of the first women's rights convention in America, held at Seneca Falls, New York, in July 1848. But much of the fanfare was lost on Helen, who chose to "resurrect even just the shadow of the former President" as one observer put it, to make Franklin Delano Roosevelt the dominant figure of the convention. Launching a full-force rhetorical attack on the Republican Party, she lambasted the Eightieth Congress for its retrograde unraveling of all that Roosevelt and the Democratic Party had accomplished. She attacked what she saw as widespread posturing and obfuscation at the Republican National Convention, held three weeks earlier in the same city, to nominate the Thomas Dewey–Earl Warren ticket.

"All of the oratory, all the carefully-planned, synthetic demonstrations, all the well-rehearsed sound and fury, was merely a smoke-screen to obscure the shameful record of the Republican hatchet-men in Congress who spent an entire Session, feverishly chipping away at the pillars of New Deal liberal legislation—and who were afraid that the people would find them out. And well they might be afraid!"

Unfortunately, party leaders had assigned her a midnight speaking slot—a pointed signal to her and the delegates that her political clout had died with FDR. While some in the press noted her artic-ulate delivery, most reports centered on her attire. When it was over, she literally disappeared. Neither Chavoor nor Lybeck could find her. Finally they learned that she had collapsed from fatigue and had been hospitalized in New York City. Her doctor was adamant about her total isolation, and for more than a week she received no visi-tors, phone calls, or mail. When she emerged from her forced respite, she threw herself into what had become a vicious presidential pri-mary campaign in which Democrats accused Wallace of being a tool of Communism and Wallace blamed Truman for launching the cold war. "To some degree both sides were correct," Helen thought, ". . . which made it difficult for voters to sort fact from fiction. The President did contribute substantially to escalating the Cold War with Russia, and Wallace certainly did have fanatical communists close to him."

Whatever the bitterness of the 1948 Democratic primary, the real drama would play out in the general election between Truman and Republican Thomas Dewey, who, given Truman's 36 percent public approval rating, was the front-runner. The national press unwaver-ingly predicted Dewey's imminent victory, with the *Chicago Tribune's* banner headline DEWEY DEFEATS TRUMAN going down in political in-famy, as Truman would win with 303 electoral votes.

Despite a bitter reelection campaign in the Fourteenth District—prompting Lybeck to remark that Helen's enemies' "hatred of you is psychopathic"—Helen won by a phenomenal fifty-thousand-vote majority. Conventional wisdom now held that the seat was hers for as long as she wanted it. The voters of California had given her an overwhelming mandate; Democrats in the state outnumbered Republicans by one million voters, and Hollywood celebrities including Ronald Reagan and Rita Hayworth had supported her with money and campaign appearances. With Truman winning the White House and a Democratic majority in the Eighty-first Congress, her political future seemed assured. But history's trajectory would send her on a different path.

Helen and Melvyn rarely saw each other during her years as a congresswoman, though they spoke often on the telephone—more about politics and parenting logistics than personal emotions. Their estrangement—or arrangement—seemed to concern Melvyn more deeply than it did Helen. "I miss your intelligence, your quiet understanding," he wrote her, "and I miss, too, the meaningful noise and restless activity with which you sometimes disturb the atmosphere. It all adds up to a chunk of my existence which is irreplaceable."

The children remained in boarding school in California, though during the summers they traveled between Vermont, California, and Washington, attending camps and pursuing various enthusiasms. Helen's social life in Washington revolved around intimate dinners and small gatherings with a few New Deal friends to play bridge or charades. She became a fanatical solitaire player and took up painting as well, using that artistic venue as a means for relaxation. The times she most enjoyed were when her mother or sister visited her.

Her relationship with Lyndon Johnson, while still warm, had grown distant. Ever pragmatic, Johnson was careful not to be painted by the "red" brush that now seemed to follow Helen. Noel-Baker had replaced Johnson as her intellectual mentor and object of affection, and she increasingly felt that she could not rely upon LBJ in matters of foreign policy. "He had no yardstick in foreign affairs as he did in domestic matters," she recalled, worried about his increasingly close bond with the military while looking hopefully to him to keep FDR's New Deal coalition together. "I was never sure whether some of Lyndon Johnson's votes were cast out of conviction or out of judging what Texas politics required."

The Eighty-First Congress proved as problematic for Helen as the previous one, beginning with the intensification of HUAC and the rise of the man who would become her nemesis—Richard Nixon. When Truman was inaugurated in January 1949, his popularity was at an all-time high and he was ecstatic at having been elected president in his own right. "He had made the greatest political comeback in American history," wrote Michael J. Ybarra. "His party was in control of both houses, and his approval rating climbed to 57 percent." Finally outside the shadow of FDR, Truman confidently put his Fair Deal domestic program before Congress, a no-holds-barred liberal agenda. Helen supported it wholeheartedly and optimistically submitted more than two dozen of her own bills. Her proposals included the establishment of a Civilian Conservation Corps–type study of the employment problems of middle-aged citizens; relief for grain growers; an increase in the minimum wage; a low-income, low-interest housing bill; funding for kindergarten; tax deductions for domestic help; equal pay for equal work; and the establishment of a presidential commission to study the status of women in America.

The later events in her life would overshadow her many legislative accomplishments. Called a "superanimated whirlwind" by *Fortnight* magazine, she was known for her fastidious attention to detail, her diligence in studying the issues, and her unswerving courage in facing off her opponents. "As a Congresswoman, she led the liberal vanguard," wrote one scholar. But by the late 1940s her golden moment of the New Deal was passé, and her strident idealism was overly quixotic for the new era of pragmatism. Blithely unresponsive to the changing mood of America, she increasingly seemed a caricature of an earlier time, a celebrity ideologue who had lost her tether with the passing of her mentor and protector, FDR. Accustomed to entrée into the highest levels of government, she was now relegated to the fringes of political influence. Though she seemed oblivious to the reality, despite her striving for independence, much of her power had indeed been derived through the men in her life—her father, Melvyn, FDR, and LBJ. With all of them now gone, she had lost her grounding. Yet she charged forward, eschewing the Washington game of party politics and failing to establish the kind of supportive network she would need for the future.

Her attention to foreign policy issues continued unabated, but fortunately no international crises were on the immediate horizon. With the death of Sol Bloom—the chairman of the Foreign Affairs Committee and a dear friend—Helen became the de facto leader of the committee and seemed to rise in stature overnight. She also had hardened, according to Evie Chavoor, who described Helen in this period as short-tempered and inflexible; those closest to her worried about her physical and emotional frailty. Now forty-nine years old, her five-foot-seven frame still trim and fit, she drove herself at a pace others could not maintain. "I am getting one hell of a reputation around Capitol Hill about what a bitch I am," she confessed to Chavoor.

By March 1949 she had become consumed with the possibility of challenging Senator Sheridan Downey in the 1950 California primary. In fact, she had had her sights on the U.S. Senate from the beginning of her political career—prompting Lybeck to advise her as early as 1945 to be patient and "in general, act like the Senator-to-be." The time would come, and only when the timing was right should she make her move, he counseled her, often signing his letters "G'night Senator." Though she had always followed Lybeck's flawless political advice, she could no longer contain her ambition and desire and began to chafe at his caution. The 1948 victory of Margaret Chase Smith of Maine as the first elected woman senator, combined with the heady discussion of Helen as a vice-presidential contender, bolstered her ego. Highly competitive and determined, she "must have looked on Smith with a mix of envy and anticipation," as Douglas scholar Colleen M. O'Connor conjectured.

The impetus for settling on the 1950 senatorial race was her mounting disdain for the rightward-shifting Downey. Once a populist New Dealer who had run unsuccessfully for lieutenant governor with Upton Sinclair in the 1934 California gubernatorial race, Downey was swept into the U.S. Senate in 1938 on a left-wing platform. His progressive credentials were impeccable, thanks to his support of a pension for the elderly, his commitment to the United Nations, and his advocacy of the international control of atomic energy. But Helen had watched with surprise and contempt as Downey became increasingly beholden to the oil and agribusiness interests in the state.

At the core of her disagreement with him was an issue known as the 160-acre limit—long-standing California legislation that severely curtailed irrigation to farms larger than 160 acres in size. Passed during a progressive era in state politics as part of the 1902 Reclamation Act, the law was intended to protect small farmers from the monopolistic absentee ownership of large tracts of farmland. But by 1949 the two-billion-dollar state reclamation project was channeling water into the Central Valley, where corporate growers owned the majority of the irrigable acres and were fighting to repeal the limit. The sixty-six-year-old Downey had once come down firmly in support of the limit but was reneging on his promise and siding with the oilmen who sought to have the law changed. As it turned out, the onetime End Poverty in California (EPIC) activist had undisclosed holdings of his own in the Central Valley.

In the heightened atmosphere of red-scare America, even a water issue in the West was elevated to a battle between Marxism and capitalism. One congressman went so far as to accuse the proponents of the 160-acre limit of forcing "communism upon the people of the San Joaquin" and warning that it encouraged "undesirables" such as the Japanese to squat on the land. Downey himself had become consumed with the idea that Communists had infiltrated the Bureau of Reclamation and were plotting a sinister takeover of the Central Valley. The slight, silver-haired senator had been "elected by the little people of California, but promptly went over to the side of the corporate landowners and the Pacific Gas and Electric Co.," the Los Angeles–based *Frontier* magazine later wrote of his political metamorphosis.

Helen had studied the issue in depth, guided by such experts as former Interior Department officials Harold Ickes and Arthur Goldschmidt and celebrated Berkeley economist and agriculture authority Paul Taylor. She was not only passionate about the subject but saw it as a perfect centerpiece for a possible senatorial campaign.

While state and national pundits predicted an easy third term for Downey, rumors were circulating in both California and Washington that he was in ill health. Indeed, he was suffering from a painful ulcer but had every intention of seeking reelection. Helen had heard the rumors, and regardless of their validity, she had set her sights on knocking him out—either herself or by encouraging another candidate. At the same moment, and "with precisely opposite estimates of the political present and future," as Roger Morris wrote, Richard Milhous Nixon was setting his sights on the same seat.

Born January 9, 1913, in Yorba Linda, California, Richard Nixon was the firstborn son of Francis A. and Hannah Milhous Nixon. A devout Quaker—as members of the Society of Friends were known—Hannah gave birth to the eleven-pound baby on a freezing winter day in a one-story bungalow built by her husband. Raised in the spartan Quaker traditions that prohibited drinking and dancing, and by a mother who still used phrases such as "thee" and "thou," Nixon lived a childhood of poverty and financial despair. Known for his violent temper, Francis Nixon "would not hesitate to use the strap or rod" on his children, as Hannah recalled.

When the family farm—a lemon grove carved out of a ditch—failed to produce a reliable income, they moved to Whittier, where Francis opened a grocery store. Graduating second in his class from Whittier High School, Richard Nixon was one of a handful of the 1930 graduates to attend college, and even though he was invited to apply for scholarships to both Harvard and Yale, he didn't have the financial wherewithal to head East. He enrolled instead at Whittier College, a small Quaker school where he "stood out from the beginning," as one of his biographers put it. There he was elected freshman–class president and became a star tackle on the school's eleven-man team. Five feet eleven and 150 pounds, the lean, dark-haired young man was a strong debater and drama enthusiast, and after he again graduated second in his class he received a full scholarship to the Duke University School of Law.

He had returned to California in 1937 and was practicing law when he met a Whittier schoolteacher named Patricia Ryan. A "rugged individualist" who had "come up the hard way," as one of her cousins described her, Pat finally accepted Nixon's numerous proposals and the couple was married in 1940. "He had wed a woman of matching resolve, of comparable if not larger ambition, of perhaps greater strength, and he had won her in a supplicant's courtship," Morris wrote. After Nixon's stint in the U.S. Navy during World War II, a group of prominent Whittier bankers approached him about challenging liberal Democratic incumbent Jerry Voorhis. A five-term congressman from

California's Twelfth District, Voorhis was an inveterate New Dealer who cut his political teeth in the EPIC movement. In one of the dirtiest campaigns in California history, Nixon's 1946 challenge traced its roots to the 1934 gubernatorial campaign against EPIC's founder, Upton Sinclair—a campaign masterminded by Murray Chotiner. Called a "young, brilliantly combative Los Angeles attorney" by journalist Greg Mitchell, Chotiner devised the Nixon camp's strategy for not only winning, but demolishing the opposition.

Across the floor of the House of Representatives, Helen often caught Nixon staring at her. While she was disappointed that he had defeated her friend Voorhis and she thought him overzealous in rooting out Communists as a member of HUAC, he seemed relatively harmless. She saw him as shy and insecure but affable enough, and when the references were inevitably made to the two of them as potential rivals for Sheridan Downey's seat, she took it in stride. When a magazine endorsed both of them with a tongue-in-cheek assessment—calling Helen a liberal with "some conservative ideas" and Nixon a conservative with "some liberal tendencies"—she good-naturedly sent a copy of the article to Nixon with a personal note. "Dear Richard. Have you seen this? I thought it would amuse you. Sincerely, Helen." In any case, she did not consider him a formidable opponent if indeed he was to become the Republican nominee.

Throughout the spring and into the summer she wrestled with her decision about running against Downey. Many of her advisers in the district opposed the idea, thinking California was not ready to support a woman for the U.S. Senate. Some party loyalists tried to dissuade her from taking on Downey, with at least one powerful boss, Bill Malone, essentially guaranteeing the full support of the party in 1952 against Republican Senator Bill Knowland if she held off running in 1950. Malone, who had appointed her vice-chairman of the party, was distressed that she would split it. The press and establishment Democrats thought it disloyal to go after a fellow Democrat who had supported the Truman administration on what the *San Diego Union* calculated to be "95%" of the issues.

Snubbing the power brokers of her own party was at once naïve and grandiose, if characteristic. She was accustomed to bucking the system and landing on top and no doubt felt she could do it again. She had taken an unconventional path to stardom, had successfully digressed into a singing career, and stealthily maneuvered her way into Congress. She had skillfully resisted the dictates of many powerful men in her life, beginning with her father, and was stubbornly determined to do so again. She seemed carelessly unaware that the stakes were now higher, that the U.S. Senate—arguably the most powerful and elite governing body in the world—was not only a bastion of male dominance but the centerpiece of party politics. "This was the big leagues, and she refused to play ball with the big boys," a contemporary observer remarked. Her critics saw her as self-aggrandizing, while supporters thought her courageous. Intimates worried that her impatience and sense of entitlement would lead to her downfall. In any case, her refusal to play by the implicit, unbending rules of party politics would have severe consequences.

Lybeck was pessimistic and tried to dissuade her. When he realized he could not stand in her way, he became resigned: "I'd rather lose you in a hell-bending race for the United States Senate than lose you just because you got bored." Mostly, Lybeck worried about money, calculating that it would take $150,000 to win—a staggering amount. Despite his fears that she was a long shot against the incumbent Downey, he put forth a confident public face, telling doubters: "If she makes up her mind to run, she'll run the hell out of the whole damned state and anybody who happens to be on the ticket will just get swept in with her." Both Helen and Lybeck were focused entirely on the primary, never taking Nixon seriously as a strong general-election rival. Lybeck was also concerned about finding a strong candidate to replace Helen in the House, and the two discussed approaching Ronald Reagan, whom Lybeck thought a "stellar attraction on his own" and a strong orator.

Some were concerned that while Helen had legendary support in Southern California, she was virtually unknown in the northern part of the state. Still others thought her chances of winning were slim and that she should hold on to her congressional seat and continue to build seniority in the House. National labor leaders from the CIO who valued her position in the House did not want to risk losing her, while the California AFL chieftains whose unions were often used for racketeering purposes had never been supportive of her and were committed to Downey.

Many Democratic insiders thought it political suicide to challenge a fellow incumbent Democrat, regardless of his politics. Even her assistant Chavoor thought it a half-baked idea and dreaded the prospect. "If Helen decides to run for the Senate I will be nuts," Chavoor wrote to Lybeck, telling him it was "hell living through the uncertainty." Meanwhile, Roosevelt's son, Jimmy, had decided to run for governor against Earl Warren—"a scheme that seemed foolhardy to many observers," as Helen remembered it—and Roosevelt supporters had conducted a secret poll that indicated his own chances would be elevated if Helen were in the Senate race. While Lybeck advised her to distance herself from the Roosevelt campaign, her loyalty to Eleanor and the memory of FDR overrode such expediency.

Others, such as her dear old friend Harold Ickes, tried to discourage her from running, certain that she would not be able to defeat Richard Nixon in the general election. "After all, Nixon will be running on a ticket with [Governor Earl] Warren and it is to be expected that Republicans will make every effort to put across a big vote for both," Ickes wrote her on April 13.

When Easter recess passed and she had still not made up her mind, she set a deadline of July 15 for making a decision. She and Melvyn were named "Mr. and Mrs. American Citizens of 1949" by the Beverly Hills chapter of B'nai B'rith just as they were busy quelling rumors and innuendo of an impending divorce. She apparently had not yet sought Melvyn's counsel on the decision to run for the Senate, but during the summer congressional recess she returned to California. She used the opportunity to test her popularity in the outer reaches of the state, touring reclamation projects in the north with photographer Dorothea Lange and scholar Paul Taylor. Filling the car with reference books and notebooks, the three made the outing an "intensive study expedition" in order for Helen to immerse herself in the issues with which she intended to challenge Downey. In a whirlwind excursion they met with everyone they could—newspaper editors, small farmers, legislators, ranchers, agribusinessmen, civic leaders, reclamation officials. When the tour ended, she had finally decided.

She felt an obligation to "remove one of the most dedicated enemies of the Reclamation Act from Congress." Helen Gahagan Douglas would become the first woman in California history to run for the U.S. Senate.

"Her entry brightened my prospects considerably," Nixon later wrote.

4

PINK LADY 1950

*The blacklist was a time of evil. No one on either side who
survived it came through untouched by evil . . . Some suffered less
than others, some grew or were diminished, but in the final tally we
were all victims because almost without exception each of us felt
compelled to say things he did not want to say, to do things he did
not want to do, to deliver and receive wounds he truly did not want
to exchange. That is why none of us—right, left, or center—
emerged from that long nightmare without sin.*

—Dalton Trumbo

I T WAS SEPTEMBER 11, 1950. Eleanor Roosevelt addressed
the record crowd on a balmy Southern California afternoon. Journalists noted that she wore a gray suit over a black blouse, and the *Los
Angeles Daily News* reported on her "right nice hair-do." Fashion and
triviality aside, the former First Lady and widow of FDR was eloquent and animated in her speech to the thousands that had gathered.
She had traveled here from New York to support her dear friend,
Helen, who was locked in one of, if not *the*, most bitter senate campaigns in U.S. history.

It was here, at Bixby Park in Long Beach, while Mrs. Roosevelt
appealed to the crowd, that Helen's supporters first noticed Republicans
passing out pink slips of paper. "The Pink Sheet"—implying that she
was a Communist, "hinting darkly at secret ties," as one historian put
it—would become notorious in the annals of political dirty tricks. It
would earn for its creator the sobriquet of Tricky Dick. The nickname,

which Helen attached to her adversary, would haunt Nixon for decades to come. Forever branded as the Pink Lady, Helen was the first Hollywood figure to rise meteorically in national politics, the first female to gain entrée into the male-dominated, smoke-filled rooms of a Democratic National Convention, the first American woman seriously considered as a vice-presidential contender.

This day in the park, Helen laughed at the ludicrousness of the Pink Sheet, dismissing it as an unsophisticated, sophomoric attempt to deflect attention from the many real issues and challenges facing the nation. Eleanor Roosevelt was less sanguine, urging her friend to "set the record straight." Helen was neither a Communist nor a Communist sympathizer. She was a New Deal progressive, an unabashed liberal. "I failed to take his attacks seriously enough," she later remarked upon realizing that her enemies had distributed more than half a million copies of the slander sheet throughout California. "I just thought it was ridiculous, absolutely absurd." Only later did she grasp the full impact.

Helen and Nixon had served two simultaneous terms in Congress from 1946 to 1950. He was the thirty-seven-year-old upcoming star in the increasingly reactionary national Republican Party. She was the Democratic Party's bright and shining hope—rich, smart, and charismatic—who, as one of the first women in the U.S. Senate, would be a powerful voice for an enlightened social policy. At the beginning, she was widely favored to win. But the " '50 campaign" would go down in American history as the dirtiest ever—the contest that historians and scholars have concluded was pivotal in gender politics.

"Did you know that she's married to a Jew?" So began the telephone slander campaign against her, Nixon himself calling her Helen Hesselberg and inciting the terror of the "movie Jews" conspiring to take over the country. "You can't elect this woman that sleeps with a Jew" was one of the soon-to-be-familiar slogans.

The race between Tricky Dick and the Pink Lady, as it came to be known, would become the focal point for the Right and the Left in America as both sides struggled to define the postwar national ethic and the business of electing officials. Symbol and metaphor of the direction the country would take, the Douglas-Nixon match was the breeding ground for unseemly tactics that would dominate politics for decades to come—teaching a generation of campaigners how using fear-based smear and sexist stereotypes could transform the electoral process and assure huge victories at the polls. The first mass-media campaign of its type—the first marriage of television and politics—it would be marked by slush funds, slander, voter intimidation, and ad hominem attacks and signal the beginning of the unparalleled influx of money into the political process.

The campaign had begun a year earlier, on October 5, 1949, when Helen announced her candidacy to ambivalent California Democrats who feared she would divide the party. It was a precarious moment in America, a time of cold war national anxiety over what Nixon and his cronies described as an "axis" of evil conspiracies. In a period of four months in 1949—beginning with the detonation of a Russian atomic bomb on August 29—the country had moved into a period of grave international insecurity. The Soviet Union had secretly exploded the bomb in Kazakhstan, and the U.S. only learned of it nine days later when a U.S. Air Force weather plane picked up radioactive readings over the Pacific Ocean. The news came as a great shock even to Oppenheimer and other scientists, who thought the Soviets were three to five years away from building an atomic weapon.

Helen, like others in the disarmament movement, had hoped the evidence of the bomb would finally convince Truman to seek an atomic partnership with the Soviet Union. Instead, the news galvanized the president's cold war stance and ultimately persuaded him to pursue an accelerated program for the construction of a thermonuclear, or hydrogen, superbomb. Ten times more powerful than the bombs dropped on Hiroshima and Nagasaki, the H-bomb, as it became known, was considered a "genocide machine" by many Manhattan Project physicists.

The Soviet detonation was only the opening salvo in a series of shocking events. Just as the debate over the hydrogen bomb was reaching its zenith—and at the same moment that Republicans in both houses of Congress were accusing the Truman administration of being riddled with Communists—the FBI announced that a Soviet spy had infiltrated the Manhattan Project. Klaus Fuchs, a German-born

British physicist, had been in Oppenheimer's inner circle and had given nuclear secrets to the Soviets voluntarily and without reward as a deterrent against a U.S. monopoly. Fuchs would soon confess to providing secret atomic data to Russian intelligence officials between 1945 and 1947. The Fuchs revelation spawned a chain of events that elevated Republican Senator Joseph McCarthy of Wisconsin into the national headlines, where his accusations of Truman's being "soft on Communism" were a steady drumbeat. The previously unknown junior senator claimed to have a list of more than two hundred members of the Communist Party working in the State Department, setting off a congressional inquisition that would later be defined by its own term. "As McCarthyism entered the language, christening an era as well as a political method, HUAC flourished," wrote one historian.

Meanwhile, a Communist army of a million men drove Chiang Kai-shek from mainland China, despite the two billion dollars in aid the U.S. had invested to defeat the Maoists. And Alger Hiss—president of the Carnegie Foundation and formerly a high-level State Department official in both the Roosevelt and Truman administrations— was facing trial on perjury charges stemming from allegations that he passed government secrets to a Communist spy. HUAC "was creating the hottest news in the country with its daily accusations of espionage in high places," Helen later wrote. Nixon, the rookie congressman on the committee, "was to play a prominent role in HUAC's biggest catch, Alger Hiss, the brilliant adviser to the State Department who was accused by magazine editor Whittaker Chambers of carrying American secrets to the Soviet."

"The air was so charged with fear that it took only a small spark to ignite it," remembered the political cartoonist Herb Block, who is credited with adding the term *McCarthyism* to the national lexicon. That Helen Gahagan Douglas failed to accurately gauge the depth and breadth of the fear and paranoia that gripped the nation during 1950—a crucial year in American history—would have fatal consequences for her.

"I know that it is rumored around the Capitol that I am the most irritating thorn in the side of the corporate Republican body and that every effort will be made to destroy me," she wrote a friend. But she managed to maintain a resolute optimism and faith in the intelligence of the electorate and seemed strangely unaware of the forces arrayed against her. Or perhaps she merely misjudged the lengths to which her opponent would go to defeat her, never fully grasping the new brand of politics that would be embodied by the "'50 campaign."

For his part, Nixon looked forward to a divisive clash among the Democrats that would serve him well regardless of the winner. If Sheridan Downey defeated Helen Douglas, Downey would straggle into the general election weakened by her. And if by some chance Douglas managed to win in the primary, she and her liberal New Deal agenda would be easier to beat than a conservative Democrat.

"The Democratic Party has been captured and is completely controlled by a group of ruthless, cynical seekers after power who have committed that party to politics and principles which are completely foreign to those of its founders," Nixon said in his formal announcement on November 3, 1949. "They can call it planned economy, the Fair Deal, or social welfare. It's still the same old socialist baloney any way you slice it."

Seeking a solution that would unite the party, the "back-room strategists," as Helen described the Democratic leaders, tried to lure Downey into stepping aside by offering him a plum federal judgeship. But Downey, personally insulted by Helen's preemptive challenge, wanted none of it and announced his intention to stay in the race.

Most of the state's newspapers had opposed Helen in the past; she fully expected them to do so this time around, and that she would be depending primarily on the support of the liberal *Los Angeles Daily News*. From the start, Nixon cultivated the press, and by the time he had decided to run he had already polled sixty-two papers from San Diego north to the Central Valley. Of those, thirty-five had promised to support him, while the majority of the rest were leaning toward him. It had been Kyle Palmer, the political editor of the powerful *Los Angeles Times*, whose phone call to Nixon in late 1949 convinced him to run for the Senate. When Nixon replied that he was willing to run if he could raise the money, Palmer made one telephone call to the chief fund-raiser for the state GOP, insurance magnate Asa Call. "That's all it took," wrote David Halberstam in *The Powers That Be*. "Two men."

Front man for the powerful Chandler family, which had owned the *Times* for half a century, the diminutive Palmer was known as "Little Governor" for the absolute control he wielded over the California legislature. "Political power at the *Times* during the 1950s remained vested in a graying, curly-haired gnome named Kyle Palmer and his small army of string-pulling assistants," observed Otis Chandler biographer Dennis McDougal. A rabid proponent of the anti-Communist mania of the moment, Palmer relished the opportunity to knock Helen Douglas out of California—and national—politics once and for all.

Indeed, it would be a crude and brutish Palmer who advised her opponent to "slap her around a bit."

A "so-called Democrat," as nationally syndicated columnist Drew Pearson described him, Downey, citing ill health, finally withdrew from the campaign in favor of Elias Manchester Boddy—the editor and publisher of the *Daily News*. Helen's onetime supporter, Boddy was now the favorite of the disaffected Democrats who had been offended by Helen's brazen flouting of the party leaders who had implored her not to run. With a Horatio Alger background as an encyclopedia salesman who had come to Southern California with a mere fifty-five dollars and a striving for the American dream, the handsome, silver-haired publisher accepted his call to public service with characteristic pretense. "If my entrance into the race can relieve your anxiety and help you concentrate on getting well you may be sure I will make as strong a campaign as possible," he wrote to Downey.

His campaign literature depicted a Lincolnesque boy born in a log cabin who had managed to graduate from high school before serving his country in World War II. "In short," as one scholar put it, "Boddy represented the working man's patriotic Democrat, a studied opposite to the liberal, patrician Douglas." His motto—"Manchester Boddy, the Democrat Every Body Wants"—was aimed at moderate Democrats and crossover Republicans. Calling her a maverick who failed to support President Truman in the Greek-Turkish aid bill—which, on a subliminal level, naturally called her patriotism into question—Boddy became the instrument of the mainstream Democrats' "revenge."

Boddy came out swinging against Helen, determined to make her liberalism—wildly popular during the New Deal but a liability in postwar America—the centerpiece of his agenda. He even went to lengths to depict her as a radical on the fringe of "sound liberals," implying a level of kookiness in her personality and candidacy. The liberals "on his team," as he described them, ". . . are genuinely alarmed because a relatively small minority of redhots strive to win this election in order to use the sound gains achieved by the Democratic party as a beachhead from which to launch an un-American attack against the United States on behalf of Communist Russia." Even Sheridan Downey arose from his sickbed to make a statewide radio broadcast accusing her of giving "comfort to the Soviet tyranny by voting against aid to Greece and Turkey."

There were vague allusions to Helen as Stalin's favorite pinup girl and innuendo about an alleged secret trip to Moscow—spurious allegations that gave voters pause while stirring J. Edgar Hoover's FBI agents into a full-court press of surveillance and intelligence gathering. References to the FBI "investigation" routinely found their way into the press and to HUAC, which was conveniently probing Hollywood leftists.

According to one of Nixon's biographers, "Richard Nixon greeted Downey's exit and the Democratic bloodletting with private glee." He and his campaign manager, Murray Chotiner, sat back and let Boddy and other Democratic Party leaders bloody Helen in the primary so they could knock her out in the general. By then, they felt assured, she would be firmly identified as a "commie" in the minds of voters, and they would seem clear of the smear.

Helen saw Boddy's candidacy as "a crippling blow"—not only for the loss of the only newspaper she could count on but because she considered Boddy a friend. In fact, he had recently called her "one of California's great women." His defection baffled her until many years later, when she learned that Boddy's newspaper was more than two million dollars in debt to California oil interests: He had no choice when they handpicked him to run. The virulently reactionary Hearst newspaper organization pressured Boddy to enter the race as well. What was not known then was that the Hearst company had been keeping the *Daily News* "afloat with $250,000 options to purchase, which it paid annually," Helen later wrote after learning of the relationship. It had been William Randolph Hearst who first described

Helen's political ideology as "softly suffused with pink, like the sky at morning, when tenderly touched by the rosy fingers of the dawn."

Helen had established a campaign headquarters on South Broadway in Los Angeles. She hired Harold "Tip" Tipton, a former student of Paul Taylor's at Berkeley, as campaign manager; he replaced Ed Lybeck, who felt his strength lay in local rather than statewide politics. Ruth Lybeck took over as strategist for the southern part of the state. From the beginning the campaign had a jerry-rigged feel to it. While Helen had enough self-confidence to single-handedly wage the battle, most of her friends harbored serious doubts, not least Ed Lybeck, who privately voiced concerns about her electability. "We are going to win this fight and it will be the first fight of its kind since Hiram Johnson ran against the Southern Pacific Railroads," she wrote to a longtime supporter, referring to the candidate who had designed California's open primary system in order to thwart political bosses and machines. "It will be in the great Western tradition."

Many thought Tipton a strange choice. He had relatively little political experience but possessed an air of sophistication and polish Helen thought would be useful in the northern part of the state. "I'm scared to death but ain't showing it," Tipton privately admitted to a friend.

Most of California's moneyed interests lined up behind Boddy, including oil magnates, power company executives, and agricultural industrialists. Helen had the support of many Democratic women whom she had recruited into the process during her stint as national committeewoman, but many more opposed her. The California Democratic Women's League urged its members to vote against her because she had fought funding for HUAC. As Ed Lybeck remarked, "the hardest thing about Helen was selling her to women." Women—more than men—worried about whether she had the toughness to fight Communists. While conservatives disliked her liberalism, liberal women rejected her because of her opposition to the equal rights amendment. She had opposed the ERA in the Seventy-ninth Congress with the belief that it would undermine protective labor laws. Instead she had cosponsored an equal pay and equal status bill—neither of which passed the House—but those efforts did not satisfy the feminists in her district.

When the Boddy campaign first raised the specter of Vito

Marcantonio—the sole American Labor Party congressman, from New York—Helen was shocked. The Nixon-Chotiner camp had defeated Congressman Jerry Voorhis four years earlier with a document titled "How Jerry and Vito Voted" that compared how many times Voorhis had voted with the avowed leftist Marcantonio. She had expected such tactics from Nixon. "The whole GOP campaign this year will consist of crying 'communism,'" she had warned fellow Democrats during the primary, because Nixon was a predictable "demagogue who will try to win by fear and hysteria." But she was blindsided by the assault from within her own party and was never able to reconcile herself with that reality and regain her equilibrium.

Newspapers had called her "pink" and "red," but when Boddy's *Daily News* dubbed her "the pink lady" on April 28, 1950, the label stuck. At the same moment, Richard and Pat Nixon began touring the state in a woody—a flashy 1949 wood-paneled Mercury station wagon. Equipped with a loudspeaker and record player, they drew crowds in communities throughout California, downplaying his Republican affiliation and seeking the support of Democrats. "As One Democrat to Another," read one of his numerous campaign flyers that purposely blurred the distinction and implied that he was a Democrat. In a state that allowed crossover voting, if Nixon won the Democratic and Republican primaries, there would be no general election. "Is Helen Douglas a Democrat?" another circular asked. "The Record Says No!" Groups calling themselves Democrats for Nixon sprung up throughout the state, urging voters to support "the man who puts country above party."

In the first two weeks, Nixon gave more than thirty-nine speeches and two radio interviews per day, according to his campaign spokesmen. Chotiner described the Nixon tour that would become part of American campaign lore: "The car will stop at some suitable place in a particular community. The driver of the car will play a couple of records to attract a crowd, and Dick will then make a five or ten minute informal talk to those who gather." While Nixon spoke, his wife handed out thimbles to the women in the crowd embossed with the slogan "Safeguard the American Home." His road show made its way from Los Angeles to the San Francisco Bay Area, where he spoke to a large crowd in front of Sather Gate at the University of California at Berkeley. Alarmed at his eloquence and anti-Communist vitriol, a university student—a debate captain—wrote to Helen: "He gave a magnificent speech. He is one of the cleverest speakers I have ever heard . . . Indeed, he was so skillful—and, I might add, cagey—that those who came indifferent were sold . . . If he is only a fraction as effective as he was here you have a formidable opponent on your hands."

Raising the issue of a Russian attack on the West Coast by the "godless would-be 'supermen' of the Kremlin," he called for a trade embargo against the Soviet Union, and at virtually every appearance he spoke of the Communist threat and the recent conviction of Alger Hiss. Eager to take the credit for Hiss's guilty verdict, Nixon used every opportunity to insert Hiss into the political dialogue in California. Dignitaries such as former president Herbert Hoover had applauded his efforts as a congressman to root out the evil "stream of treason that existed in our government." Smug and serious, "wearing the satisfied mien of the successful spyhunter," as one historian described his demeanor, Nixon feigned an aloofness from the subject while tacitly linking Helen to Hiss. "There's no use trying to talk about anything else," he disingenuously claimed, "because it's all the people want to hear about."

Nixon himself rarely mentioned Helen Douglas, relying instead on his supporters in the press—and the Democrats themselves—to attack her. A Santa Monica newspaper called her an "ally of Communist Partyliner Vito Marcantonio," and the Santa Ana Register opined that she had "traveled the 'pink fringe' sufficiently long that whether she actually believes in the communist form of government is unimportant."

For her part, Helen was too preoccupied with her congressional responsibilities in Washington to campaign effectively in California, and it was only gradually that she began sensing a dangerous "mood of pure hatred" that would come to dominate the entire campaign season. She also grew increasingly alarmed at the cold shoulder she was receiving from the press. At first she thought the newspapers were not covering her because of the topics she raised, and she began an earnest attempt to address issues she hoped would gain their attention. But it was soon

obvious that she was the victim of an orchestrated news blackout—
that her "heretofore copious press coverage had evaporated on cue."

Ed Lybeck was livid when he realized she was being intentionally
censored. "Last year she was all over the paper; this year, they wouldn't
even know how to spell her name if it wasn't for the Fashion Academy!" he railed. In a humiliating gesture, she was forced to buy advertising space in her opponent's newspaper in order to receive any
coverage at all. That spring saw a vicious whispering campaign as
well, with references to Helen's supposed Communist ties being
promulgated at social and business functions throughout the state. She
was never able to figure out a strategy for challenging the ubiquitous
rumors, for they were amorphous and elusive. Still, while she personally thought Nixon a "pipsqueak . . . a peewee who is trying to scare
people into voting for him," she initially discounted his involvement
in the smear against her. In fact, she would later say that she was
"scarcely aware" of Nixon during her embattled primary with Manchester Boddy. "I was too busy defending myself from Democrats."

The Democratic National Committee, while officially remaining
nonpartisan in California's Democratic primary contest, was watching it closely, along with other national campaigns such as that of
Claude Pepper in Florida. The New Deal senator was in the battle of
his career against right-wing Democrat George Smathers. As with
Helen's contest in California, the opposing strategy was based solely
on labeling Pepper a Communist. Smathers would call him "Red
Pepper," a label that would stick and lead to Pepper's defeat. "Anti-
Communist fervor had a grip on America," Pepper recalled the
spring of 1950. "The words *left* and *liberal* began to take on ominous
connotations. The so-called upper classes that Franklin Roosevelt so
effectively 'betrayed' saw their chance to brake the New Deal social
revolution, and even to reverse it." Other progressive Democratic senators who were in ferocious contests in which the Communist issue
was pivotal included Majority Leader Scott Lucas in Illinois, Frank
Graham in North Carolina, Millard Tydings in Maryland, and Elbert
Thomas in Utah.

Rumors circulated in both Florida and California that President
Truman considered Helen a traitor to his foreign policy agenda. He
thought Helen especially a political liability and did not intend to

campaign for her in the fall. She began to wonder if she could count on the support of the national party at all.

Just as her press coverage dried up, so did the money. While Boddy campaign managers boasted that they intended to spend more than two hundred thousand dollars in the final two weeks of the primary, Helen had difficulty raising a few thousand. Her campaign was even more straitened by her frequent rejection of contributions that had strings attached—"conditioned on a slight reversal of my thinking on certain subjects," as she described the distasteful quid pro quo. Eleanor Roosevelt held a fund-raising party for her in New York. Actors and screenwriters, sometimes reluctantly and sporadically, came through for her, though the industry was increasingly worried about what was being described as a "Hollywood witch hunt" in the HUAC hearings. Lillian Gish, Myrna Loy, Ronald Reagan (who was now president of the Screen Actors Guild), Eddie Cantor, Lena Horne, and Philip Dunne began holding small fund-raising parties, but throughout most of the primary she was dependent upon money raised outside the state. Heirs and overseers to the Bloomingdale, Carnegie, Marshall Field, and Bingham fortunes, among others, raised money in their circles, while Washington luminaries such as Daisy Harriman and Mary Norton rounded up contributions in the capital.

An eternal optimist, Helen never doubted that she would win. She wrote her old friend Harold Ickes that she was confident of victory and expressed her hopefulness to a supporter, calling the Boddy campaign one of desperation. "I am convinced that no amount of smearing and no amount of propaganda, no matter how libelous, can change the final vote."

On the night of June 6, a triumphant Helen won 735,000 Democratic votes to Boddy's 379,000—an overwhelming margin that no one had predicted. She had also received 154,000 Republican votes. Her mood was dashed only by the disturbing news that Nixon had won 319,000 *Democratic* votes. Those, combined with the 740,000 Republican votes he collected, put him a hundred thousand votes ahead of her. Clearly he was carving into her Democratic Party base while she was making relatively minor inroads with the Republicans.

"It gives me the greatest of pleasure to congratulate you on your nomination," Truman wrote to her on June 8. "You can count on the National Democratic Committee to do everything possible to see that you become a member of the United States Senate." Helen fervently hoped she could depend on the president in what was shaping up to be a titanic contest.

"What my campaign now needed was some luck," she remembered Ed Lybeck telling her.

"We got it—all bad," she wrote many years later, reflecting on the events that followed.

Less than three weeks after the primary election, the North Korean Communist government invaded South Korea, sweeping its anti-Communist regime off the peninsula. "For a shocking while it appeared possible that the Soviet and China would support North Korea and the United States would help defend South Korea," Helen recalled the moment. "We would have a Third World War, this time with atomic weapons on both sides."

Suddenly it "appeared that communists were advancing upon us from all sides," she would write, and she had an immediate and visceral feeling that despite her own strident anti-Communism, she was facing the political fight of her life.

Paul Ziffren always insisted he was born in Davenport, Iowa, on July 18, 1913, to a Lithuanian mother and German father. In 1931, with ten dollars in his pocket and a small scholarship to Northwestern University—or so his legend goes—he finished high school, moved to Chicago, and rose meteorically in that city's Democratic political machine. While his familial origins have long been a matter of speculation, his connections to Chicago's Jacob M. Arvey have never been disputed. Boss of one of the nation's most powerful big-city political operations, Arvey was so close to Ziffren that many associates assumed Ziffren was Arvey's illegitimate son. "The natural parentage of Paul Ziffren, if ever learned, could explain his exceptional and early acceptance in Chicago political and organized crime circles," the FBI reported of Ziffren's background, "upon which associations, coupled with his acknowledged intelligence, are based his phenomenal economic and political career."

Indeed, the unprepossessing, scholarly looking young man excelled in college, got his law degree with the generous support of Chicago's Pritzker Foundation, and by 1938 was an assistant U.S. attorney. A brilliant tax lawyer, Ziffren soon went to work for the law firm that had represented Prohibition-era gangster Al Capone. There he shared a suite with Sidney Korshak, a fellow lawyer who would become his lifelong closest friend and associate. At the time of his death in 1996, the FBI would consider Korshak the most powerful lawyer in the world. But forty-five years earlier, in postwar America, Korshak was the point man between Chicago organized crime and its California investments—what legendary FBI agent Bill Roemer described as "the most important contact that the Mob had to legitimate business, labor, Hollywood, and Las Vegas." Known as "the Fixer" for his middleman role between the organized-crime-controlled Teamsters union and the Hollywood film companies, Korshak emblemized the symbiotic relationship between union and management, wielding enormous influence in California politics. As Nick Tosches wrote with characteristic flair, "In the land of dreams, Sidney Korshak was a shadow among shadows, a wisp of smoke curling around the brighter lights . . . His was the hidden mystery at the heart of the furnace of illusion and delusion. To some, he was evil incarnate; to others the nicest guy in the world."

How his lieutenant, Paul Ziffren, became the primary fund-raiser for Helen Gahagan Douglas's 1950 campaign for the U.S. Senate raised eyebrows in her inner circle. "The Democrats' Man of Mystery," as award-winning 1950s crime writer Lester Velie called him, Ziffren had arrived in Los Angeles in 1943, a virtual unknown at thirty years old. "Within seven years he was sporting all the trappings of a well-fixed man: a twelve-room home with swimming pool on five acres of gardens rivaling those of his movie-star neighbors in the wealthy Coldwater Canyon section of Beverly Hills."

Helen's own memoirs are vague regarding Ziffren and his role in her campaign. "Paul Ziffren raised money in the south," was the sole oblique reference to him in her lengthy and otherwise revealing autobiography, *A Full Life*. What she apparently did not know at the time— or if she did, never mentioned publicly—was that while raising money for her campaign, Ziffren was under investigation by the Los Angeles

Police Department's intelligence unit for his connection to organized crime figures. In fact, Ziffren had moved to Los Angeles in order to set up shell companies to buy, at bargain-basement prices, Southern California real estate that had been seized by the U.S. government from Japanese Americans after Pearl Harbor. According to Velie, "Chicago underworld cash was flowing into California and was putting solid, legitimate enterprises secretly into some of the uncleanest hands in America."

While she had been preoccupied in Congress with issues of grave national and international urgency, the Chicago-based organized crime syndicate was muscling in on her California district. In a scenario rivaling the most insidious scandals of the twentieth century, a group of Chicago political operatives acquired hundreds of millions of dollars' worth of Los Angeles real estate, gaining control of a sizable block of California's economy while building a formidable political machine along the way. Under the auspices of the benign-sounding Office of Alien Property, the U.S. government had frozen all the bank accounts and seized the property belonging to the 120,000 Nisei in California—the second-generation Japanese Americans who were interned in concentration camps at the outbreak of World War II. The Federal Reserve estimated the property—mostly hotels, warehouses, and lush farms that Anglo Californians had coveted for decades—at approximately $2.7 billion by today's standards. By 1950, as Helen was battling to expand her own political power base, nearly all of the Nisei property in her congressional district had moved into the hands of the old Capone mob and its allies through the machinations of what one federal investigator described as "an insider gravy train."

Ironically, even while Ziffren—the man acquiring the Nisei real estate—was embedded in her campaign, she was pleading with the U.S. Justice Department to unfreeze the bank accounts of her Japanese American constituents. Obviously unaware of Ziffren's role in the acquisition and control of this property—and oblivious to the fact that Chicago organized crime elements now owned the valuable real estate in question—she was naïvely drafting legislation for the return of $367 million worth of assets to persons "of Japanese ancestry." Such an obvious conflict between the interests of her constituency and the interests of her "money man" would inevitably doom the campaign even as the full implications remained beneath the surface.

One thing was clear: Helen Gahagan Douglas posed a major threat to this new California consortium of underworld and upper-world titans. They could not allow her to ascend to the U.S. Senate and beyond, could not afford to have her form an investigating committee to probe the massive land grab, and Ziffren became their point man to sabotage her campaign. But it would be decades after the deaths of both Helen Douglas and Paul Ziffren that the full extent of the forces at play were exposed. At the time of his death in 1991, Ziffren would be widely considered the most influential person in the California Democratic Party, eulogized by the *Los Angeles Times* as the "soft-spoken civic leader" and "hardworking patriot for Los Angeles." By then the brutal Douglas-Nixon match of 1950—the race that broke the spirit and betrayed the soul of the California Democratic Party and kept California from sending a woman to the U.S. Senate for the next forty years—seemed like ancient history.

"Isn't it interesting how all these 'civil libertarians' ended up with the confiscated Japanese land?" an investigator with the California attorney general's office later reflected.

While the Nixon camp was flush with money, the Douglas campaign, housed at the Alexandria Hotel in Los Angeles, was operating on a shoestring. Gifford Phillips, the putative chairman of Helen's finance committee, couldn't get a straight answer from Paul Ziffren about how much money was being raised and from what sources. All he knew for certain was that there was not enough to mount a serious effort. A young Colorado businessman, Phillips had recently moved to Southern California where he was starting a progressive magazine called *Frontier*. The Washington, D.C., native and Yale graduate had been a member of the Democratic State Central Committee, and though he was well connected in national New Dealer circles, he was new and naïve in California politics.

"I got a call from Paul Ziffren one day," Phillips remembered nearly seventy years later. "He asked me to be Southern California finance chairman for Helen." Ziffren told the young publisher that he would be "the front man"—that Ziffren himself would really be running the operation. Ziffren claimed to be controversial because of his recent divorce and said he needed to remain behind the scenes. "It didn't ring true, but I liked Helen Gahagan Douglas, so I agreed."

It was only later that Phillips learned of what he called Ziffren's "mob clients in Chicago." In 1950, Phillips knew nothing about Ziffren except that he had unique access to Hollywood's wealthy Jewish community and "the movie people."

"When I tried to determine the sources Paul was tapping, I got nowhere," Phillips told *Reader's Digest* in 1960. Phillips mostly sat around waiting for Ziffren to disconnect from his long-distance telephone calls to Chicago. "He wasn't going to let me know those sources." An enduring mystery, for Phillips and others, was how the campaign could be so broke if Ziffren was so connected to the big Hollywood and Chicago donors. Only years later did it become clear that Paul Ziffren never had Helen's best interests at heart. His association with Sidney Korshak and Korshak's "men"—Richard Nixon and Nixon's chief strategist, Murray Chotiner—superseded his ideological loyalty to Helen Gahagan Douglas.

A few campaign insiders wondered about Ziffren's apparently close relationship with Chotiner, whose gambling and bookmaking clients were linked to the Chicago outfit as well. "Chotiner and Ziffren both answered to the same people: Korshak and Arvey," says Chicago investigator Jack Clarke. "They sold her down the river."

"Helen . . . is still a beauty," mused a Hollywood writer, "but hard campaigning has deepened the lines of character in her face and she no longer has the appearance of a movie star."

Indeed, the stress and exhaustion were beginning to show, and while Helen and her supporters were elated with the primary results, their hiatus from the rigors of the campaign would be brief. The outbreak of war in Korea and the rise of the Maoists in China created high anxiety in the U.S. When American troops landed on July 1 in South Korea under the blue flag of the United Nations, they were defeated in every one of their engagements. "The panic was most acute in California," Helen reflected, "which saw itself closest to the outbreak of hostilities on the far side of the Pacific." She steeled herself as international tensions and domestic hysteria escalated.

Republicans blamed Truman's foreign policy for the "loss" of China and Korea and Helen braced herself for a fresh onslaught of attacks on her liberalism. Washington columnist Drew Pearson issued the first salvo in the California general election, reporting that a California politico was seeking wire service photos "linking Congresswoman Helen Douglas with Paul Robeson, Henry Wallace, Claude Pepper, or Moscow." Nixon had initially planned to challenge her on domestic issues, on her unwavering devotion to Roosevelt's New Deal policies. But all of that changed with the new developments in Korea, and the Nixon camp was clearly not wasting a moment.

Nixon met with his advisers the weekend after the primary to strategize. They were in agreement that the theme of the campaign was to be national defense and "a strong America." Holed up in a secret location near Santa Barbara, the group of men disagreed about the extent to which the red-baiting should continue, some thinking it had reached its maximum effectiveness. But Chotiner—alternately described as the "Machiavelli of California politics, master smear artist, and Svengali to Nixon's Trilby"—had found a formula that worked and was not about to temper his instincts. A man who genuinely equated Democrats with Communists, Chotiner had perfected the technique of fear and smear, of scaring the voters with an outside enemy and then tainting one's opponent with "ties" to that enemy. Some thought his approach diabolical. Others, such as Nixon himself— "a man with kindred tastes and kindred political morality," as his biographer Fawn Brodie put it—thought it shrewd and pragmatic.

Short and chunky, a sartorial mess with greasy, thinning hair, a foul mouth, and a wicked sense of humor, the forty-one-year-old son of a Pittsburgh cigar maker had been a notorious figure in California politics for nearly two decades. The youngest graduate of Southwestern College of Law in Los Angeles, he was a sole practitioner in Los Angeles whose clients were a seedy collection of bookmakers, gamblers, and bail bondsmen. Sneaky, extremely partisan, and unabashedly amoral, Chotiner maintained the motto "Hit 'em, hit 'em again, and hit 'em again." Such a philosophy was in keeping with that of Nixon, who often quoted his mentor and college football coach's adage "Show me a good loser and I'll show you a loser." Chotiner also well understood the necessity of keeping Nixon above the fray so that the candidate could be "shocked, shocked!" to see dirty tricks going on.

Most of the debate within the Nixon camp centered on how to handle a female opponent. Nixon was keenly aware of the danger of appearing "ungallant," as he put it in his memoirs—that it was a fine line between bullying and firmly needling. He had little regard for the aptitude of women, or what Nixon's press secretary described as "a total scorn for female mentality." Believing that women universally and biologically functioned on an emotional rather than cerebral plane, he held special enmity for a beautiful and intelligent woman like Helen, "who could hold her own with any man in spitting out the sharp and cutting epithet." Such gifts threw him off balance and he reacted with a vengeance, making it clear from the beginning he had no intention of treating her as an equal.

"No club in America has been, and has remained, harder for women to penetrate," historian Brodie wrote of the U.S. Senate, and Nixon was personally affronted by the sheer brazenness of Helen's ambition. "Not only was Nixon contemptuous of women's intellect generally, but he was also oblivious to women as individuals." He expected women to be pleasant adornments who shored up their husbands, and was notorious for his contemptuous dismissal of Pat if she dared to inject herself into "the man's world of politics," as Henry Kissinger, Nixon's later alter ego, put it. In that male sphere, according to Kissinger, Pat Nixon "was a silent patriot . . . a loyal and uninterfering female . . . speaking only when spoken to and not sullying the cigar smoke with her personal opinions."

Fully expecting the red-baiting, Helen was taken aback by the ferocious and insidious antifemale bigotry that gained purchase in the campaign. She crisscrossed the state in a two-seated helicopter—a flashy and daring campaign tactic recommended by her friend Lyndon Johnson—that by its counterintuitiveness drew even more attention to her gender. Dubbed the "Helencopter" by one of her supporters, it had no roof, which meant her hair was usually windblown and casual in an era of tightly-coiffed updos. Helen seemed to love the freewheeling, adventurous aspect of the craft, but her detractors thought it "unladylike." Blessed with natural beauty, she rarely wore makeup—a lack of pretension that some less favored women resented. A Nixon supporter watched with a combination of astonishment and derision when she disembarked in San Fernando dressed for a formal dinner. Wearing a long black evening gown, elbow-length gloves, and a stylish hat accessorized with a rose, she amazed the crowd that had gathered. Her "hair was an absolute mess," as one account described the jarring scene, while she seemed utterly indifferent.

Republican Party propaganda referred to Helen's "blushing complexion" and warned voters they needed to "bear down" if they intended to "shove the 'Pink Lady' out of the picture." One GOP official wrote that the candidate "expects to devote her campaign to convincing the citizenry that, being a woman, she has the right to change her mind, and her record." A woman speaker at a Los Angeles luncheon sympathetically told her audience that women "would naturally like to support a woman for public office, but when a woman does not measure up we must turn to a man."

For his part, Nixon went to lengths to inject gender into the political dialogue, always referring to Helen as his *female* or *woman* opponent, making crass sexual remarks if he was in an all-male gathering—even smirking and hinting that she was sexually involved with Truman—and using every opportunity to dismiss her intellectual attributes with a reference to her sex. In this period decades before the women's movement, the innuendo fostered little if any outrage. Even when he made the most bizarre remark of all—that Helen Douglas was "pink right down to her underwear"—Nixon received no condemnation for his crude condescension. A newspaper cartoon depicted Helen on a stool, her underwear showing beneath her skirt as she reached for jars of red apples, red peppers, and red herrings.

Chotiner devised a scheme that pitted Pat Nixon against Helen in the battle for female propriety—suburban housewife versus clawing professional. While Pat was the quintessential homemaker, keeping the hearth fires burning for the family, Helen was the ruthless elitist who had abandoned her children and husband in her unwomanly ambition and grasp for power.

"Of all the contrasts between Nixon and Douglas, none was more striking and more exploitable in 1950 than their family lives," wrote Greg Mitchell in his masterful analysis of the Nixon-Douglas Senate race, *Tricky Dick and the Pink Lady*. "Douglas's rich, famous Jewish husband was rarely around, at least one of her kids always seemed to be away at camp or across the country, and her posh home in the hills hardly reflected middle-class living. Richard Nixon, on the other hand, had it all, at least in terms of voter identification: a starter home in an all-American community; a pretty, Irish Protestant wife usually at his side when she wasn't cooking and sewing and looking after the house, and two cute little daughters close by."

Events moved quickly during the summer of 1950. Three of the Hollywood Ten who had been cited for contempt of HUAC—Dalton Trumbo, John Howard Lawson, and Ring Lardner Jr.—had exhausted their legal appeals and were heading to jail. As one of only seventeen in Congress who had opposed contempt citations against the black-listed screenwriters, Helen would be labeled a Communist appeaser. The regents of the University of California voted unanimously to fire 157 faculty and staff members who refused to sign a loyalty oath. U.S. Attorney General J. Howard McGrath claimed there were half a million Communists trying to undermine America, and the FBI announced there were 6,977 dangerous Communists in California alone.

The undeclared Korean War presented an apocalyptic prospect and monopolized the nation's headlines, as Americans heard stories of Russian and Chinese troops massed on the Korean border. In the first week of July, General Douglas MacArthur requested thirty thousand American ground troops, and just days later requested twice as many more. The *Los Angeles Times* published a daily list of American casualties, and Truman aides were secretly recommending a military appropriation of fifty million dollars—three times the current military budget.

"The Korean War came as a kind of fearsome vindication of Richard Nixon's Senate candidacy," wrote Nixon biographer Morris, "and his campaign thrived in the political climate." Money poured in to the Nixon campaign—an estimated $1–1.5 million—which gave him the ability to saturate the state with radio and television ads and erect nearly fifteen hundred billboards. The early seed money came from Mickey Cohen, king of the Los Angeles gambling underground, who had been solicited early on by Chotiner. "I was asked by Murray Chotiner to raise funds for Nixon's campaign," Cohen told syndicated columnist Drew Pearson during an interview from Cohen's cell in the federal prison at Alcatraz. "During that time I was running most of the gambling and bookmaking in Los Angeles. I reserved the banquet room in the Hollywood Knickerbocker Hotel on Ivar Street in Hollywood for a dinner meeting to which I invited approximately 250 persons who were working with me in the gambling fraternity." Chotiner told Cohen the "guests" would not be allowed to leave the banquet until the quota of $25,000 in contributions was met. Cohen later claimed that his orders to raise money for Nixon came from the organized crime boss Meyer Lansky.

Though Ziffren was apparently successful at fund-raising, the campaign remained strangely bankrupt, calling into question Ziffren's loyalty to Helen. "She always had all the money she needed until she posed a potential threat to the mob," veteran Chicago private investigator Jack Clarke said recently. "Ziffren kept her focused on the migrant workers and the Tideland Oil controversy and away from the Southern California real estate scam in which Ziffren, Korshak, Arvey, and the Chicago outfit was invested."

Whether or not Ziffren infiltrated her campaign and then betrayed her was probably irrelevant, for she could not have withstood the conservative tide that was sweeping the nation. The FBI was investigating the reading habits and political proclivities of American citizens. Communities were banning from public libraries books deemed un-American, and Hollywood was self-censoring movies that were even slightly "controversial." Such films as *Mission to Moscow*, *None but the Lonely Heart*, *North Star*, and *Song of Russia*, created when Russia was an American ally, were suddenly considered New Deal propaganda. Griffin Fariello characterized the moment: "Neighbors informed on neighbors, students on their teachers . . . Seven war-era concentration camps were dusted off, and lists prepared of the radicals to fill them."

Reporting to Washington in August to attend to congressional business, Helen approached Sam Rayburn on the Speaker's platform. Rayburn congratulated her on her primary victory and then nodded toward Nixon, who was seated near the dais. "His is the most devious face of all those who have served in Congress in all the years I've been here," Rayburn said.

Before Congress that day was the McCarran-Wood bill—legislation

that would outlaw Communism, and which Helen thought was a violation of the U.S. Constitution. President Truman had declared his
opposition to it as well, vowing to veto it if it passed the House and
Senate. After a stormy debate, she called Lybeck back in California
and told him of the impending vote.

"You know what I'm going to do," she told him.

"Yes, Helen, we know," he answered resignedly.

There was a tense silence in the chambers as the roll-call vote began.
"One by one, California congressmen squirmed through the narrow
space behind our seats and pleaded with me. 'Don't vote "no" on this
bill, Helen,' each said. 'It'll cost you. Why jeopardize your campaign?
This bill is going to pass overwhelmingly. Your vote won't matter. Anyway, Truman will veto it.'"

"He'll beat our brains in," a colleague whispered to her, referring
to Nixon.

She knew they were right, but could not bring herself to vote
against principle.

When they got to the Ds and called her name, she stood up and said,
"No."

The vote passed overwhelmingly, and she had been one of only
twenty to vote against it.

"How does it feel to be a dead statesman, Helen, instead of a live
politician?" one of her colleagues asked her when she retired to the
House cafeteria.

That afternoon, Nixon was feted on the floor of the House for his
"untiring service" in the fight against Communism. Helen somehow
managed to smile at him, unusual enough under the circumstances
for it to be remarked upon by journalists.

The pundits and the pollsters, seasoned analysts and grassroots activists, were predicting her demise. But Helen was overtaken by a
strange sense of calm. "I believed the worst was over."

In fact, the worst had just begun.

"If Vito Marcantonio had not existed in the late 1940s and early 1950s,"
wrote Frank Mankiewicz in *Perfectly Clear: Nixon from Whittier to Watergate*, "Richard Nixon (or, more properly, Murray Chotiner) would have
had to invent him."

On August 30, Bernard Brennan, Nixon's campaign manager in Southern California, escalated the attack on Helen. "During five years in Congress, Helen Douglas has voted 353 times exactly as has Vito Marcantonio, the notorious Communist Party-line congressman from New York." Printed on legal-sized, pink-colored paper stock—and described that same day by the *Los Angeles Times* as "a red-hot broadside fired into the Douglas camp"—the Pink Sheet was crammed with "facts" about Helen's voting record. Linking her with the radical New York congressman, the Pink Sheet would become part of American political infamy.

Chotiner had picked the colored paper because "it just seemed to appeal to us for the moment," he later claimed when the choice was widely attacked as a calculated smear. He had ordered a first printing of fifty thousand copies, and within days California had been blanketed with the pink flyers. Soon there would be half a million more copies circulating the state. Nixon would later claim that though his campaign committee issued the Pink Sheet, it had been inspired by Democrat Manchester Boddy's attacks against Helen in the primary: "All we added was the mordant comment of the color of the paper." Uncharacteristically, Chotiner downplayed his role, telling a colleague shortly before his death that "we didn't get Helen Douglas, other Democrats got her." But many political observers held Nixon and Chotiner personally accountable for decades to follow. "Helen Gahagan Douglas was one of the really great women who should have been in politics in this country. I mean, you don't get a good woman like that very often," noted professor Shaw Livermore said of the race twenty-five years later. "Nixon cut her to pieces with that dirty lying rot he put out about her in that campaign." Some in the Nixon campaign were ashamed of the tactic. Herb Klein, who as an erstwhile journalist wrote press releases for the campaign, later admitted he was glad not to have participated in its origin, calling it a "smearing distortion."

In retrospect, Helen thought she should have bought radio airtime and straightened out the charges immediately. Every time she considered challenging the lie, she got mired in the confusion of the congressional voting patterns that allowed Marcantonio—who belonged to neither the Democratic nor the Republican parties—to vote with either party. In fact, on foreign policy issues she had voted the bipartisan containment-of-Russia line every time except for the Greek-Turkish aid bill, and had voted against Marcantonio in several critical roll-call votes. "I don't know to this day whether Marcantonio *was* a communist," she wrote in her 1980 autobiography. "He certainly was very, very left." In any case, she knew that their similar voting patterns were not relevant, and she also knew that Nixon shared a significant number of votes with Marcantonio as well. Still, the Pink Sheet damage was done and she was never able to gain back the offensive position.

Chotiner instructed Nixon campaign workers to refer to Helen as "a supporter of the socialist program running on the Democratic ticket"—a deliberate lie that was repeated endlessly throughout the state. While the Pink Sheet was first being distributed, Eleanor Roosevelt arrived to campaign for Helen in Bixby Park in Long Beach. The former First Lady urged Helen repeatedly to set the record straight, to address the false charges head-on.

"I don't know why I didn't," Helen reflected near the end of her life. "My only excuse is that I was always off-balance, working so hard and fast to cover the state." Indeed, by early September her campaign had virtually no money to spend on newspaper advertisements, airtime, or flyers—this despite Paul Ziffren's supposedly tremendous fund-raising talents.

While Nixon was tarnishing her with Communist ties, Kyle Palmer and the *Los Angeles Times* made a full-frontal gender attack. Calling her "an emotional artist . . . a veritable political butterfly, flitting from flower to flower," he contrasted her metaphoric flakiness with the manly Nixon, who had "pulled up the weeds, sprayed the plant lice, squashed the snails, killed the worms, and tilled the soil." Some Nixon insiders thought that Pat Nixon was appalled by the tactics her husband and Chotiner were using against Helen, and that the 1950 campaign left her with a lifelong hatred of politics. Historian Fawn Brodie wrote of the future First Lady: "The effect of the 1950 campaign on Pat Nixon, as she watched her husband destroy the actress-politician—a role not altogether unrelated to her own—can only be guessed at."

On the heels of the Pink Sheet came the whispering campaign, begun earlier with random remarks and now evolved into the carefully crafted dissemination of innuendo. Rumors of Helen's Communism, her marriage to a Jew, her anti-Americanism, were repeated in restaurants, bars, golf clubs, churches, grocery stores, in newspapers, and on the air. Then there were the paid hecklers at all of her public appearances and the anonymous half million phone calls to registered voters in which a Nixon supporter would say, "Did you know that Helen Douglas is a Communist?" and then hang up. "Richard Nixon never said openly that I was a communist," Helen later wrote. "He didn't have to—his people took care of that."

Calling Senator Joseph McCarthy "a political madman who insulted America's intelligence," she became one of the first public figures in the country to stand up to the man she depicted as "the national hero of the Red hunt," which only drew more ire from her opponent. At the height of his power, McCarthy had managed to intimidate his critics into silence. To challenge McCarthy at the apex of the Red Scare was to ensure that one's own loyalty to America would be scrutinized; predictably, she would be marked as a traitor.

By the end of September, the death knell to her campaign came with the defection of sixty-four prominent Democrats led by George Creel, a onetime friend and avid supporter who could not forgive her for challenging Sheridan Downey. The influential seventy-four-year-old Democrat, who had been paid sixteen thousand dollars by the Nixon campaign to come out publicly against Helen, had once been a progressive administrator under Woodrow Wilson in the Red Scare of the 1920s. Now the increasingly conservative and cantankerous Creel was heading the "Democrats for Nixon," a group that author Carey McWilliams described as "political has-beens."

She felt she could have handled the Pink Sheet, "which was being waved at me wherever I spoke," alone, but she felt ambushed by the massive desertion of leading Democrats. She sent a telegram to friends throughout the country: I HAVE RUN INTO A FRIGHTENING CRISIS. I NEED YOUR HELP, YOUR ADVICE, YOUR SUPPORT. She became increasingly desperate and began asking Washington friends and colleagues to record radio and television ads for her. Some, such as Lyndon Johnson, Alben Barkley, and Sam Rayburn, responded loyally if not always eagerly. Even Ickes, who had opposed her decision to run, made his first and only television spot, urging California voters to support her. "She has convictions and the courage to fight for them," Ickes said in his one-minute ad. "She has not spent your time or my time hunting for a Red under the bed. She has fought Communism in the only way in which it can be effectively fought—by improving the economic and social conditions of the underprivileged." He also sent her a cash contribution and made an appeal for donations through his column in the *New Republic.*

President Truman—"mostly trying to maintain a nonpartisan commander-in-chief image," according to a biographer—answered a telegram entreaty with a benignly polite letter. "I hope everything is going well with you," the president wrote. But when she asked him to campaign for her in California, he declined. Soon she was literally begging him to come, prompting one of Truman's aides to refer to her as "one of the worst nuisances."

"They have lost all proportion," President Truman said of the Nixon campaign and the misrepresentations of Helen by the Los Angeles press, "all sense of restraint, all sense of patriotic decency." For all his posturing, however, Truman refused to come to California to campaign for her—a gesture most political analysts doubted would have turned the tide, but would surely have offered moral support to the much-beleaguered candidate at a very trying moment. Truman, "like many Democratic politicos, had at best mixed feelings about her," concluded Alonzo L. Hamby. "Partly, he did not think politics should be a woman's game, however much he respected Eleanor Roosevelt." As Hamby noted, Truman "was a cultural traditionalist who considered his wife the epitome of American womanhood" and who was further "cynical about starry-eyed reformers with little grounding in practical organization politics," such as Helen and her milieu. Like many political men in Helen's orbit, he no doubt half believed the allegations against her.

At first she had tried to rise above what she saw as gutter tactics, and then, too late, she realized she had taken a terribly wrong turn. "Perhaps I shouldn't have been so above-it-all, sticking to my record all the time with Gahagan stubbornness," she wrote thirty years later. "I don't mean I should have played his game—winning isn't everything— but that I should have defended myself better."

It would only be later that she learned the shocking full extent of her abandonment by Democratic power brokers. In one of the great ironies of American politics, former ambassador Joseph P. Kennedy—father of John F. Kennedy, who would run against Nixon for the presidency a decade later—gave a staggering $150,000 to the Nixon campaign. Calling it an investment that "came back to haunt him," the reactionary patriarch later told U.S. Speaker of the House Tip O'Neill that he was "against Helen Gahagan Douglas because he believed she was a Communist."

The campaign was brutal and took a physical toll on Helen. On the campaign trail, she found little time for what a reporter called the "feminine necessities" of getting her hair and nails done, and her ten-pound weight gain from skipping meals and eating candy bars became a topic for the press. "A man goes straight to bed at night after a final speech," wrote one campaign observer, "but a woman has to get a shampoo at midnight. She has to go to bed with her head in a towel to dry while she sleeps." She had been pelted with stones, spit upon, doused with seltzer, showered with hay, barraged by raw eggs, and still she tried to hold her head up high and maintain a buoyant front. She felt that "Nixon and Chotiner had woven a spider's web of sticky lies" from which she could not extricate herself, "a deadly whispering campaign that was impossible to fight."

Those closest to her thought she had lost her effectiveness as a campaigner. She spoke too long and her voice was too shrill, but no one in her inner circle had the courage to tell her. Addressing the crowds she could *feel* the defections—"Democrats, Catholics, union people from the building trades"—even though they were mostly polite and promised to vote for her. Many Democrats felt she had betrayed the party by challenging the incumbent Downey. The Catholics had not forgiven her for denouncing the fascist Spanish dictator Franco. While she maintained her support from both the AFL and the CIO, the building trades—which were controlled by Ziffren partner Sidney Korshak—were solidly against her.

The movie industry became increasingly ambivalent about her; while many had supported her in the primary, the HUAC investigation of the film colony was at a fever pitch and had "torn the community apart," as she recalled. Ronald Reagan remained one of her staunchest allies. But near the end of the campaign his future wife, Nancy Davis, took him to a Nixon rally where he heard the actress Zasu Pitts rail against the Pink Lady. He was converted on the spot. Though Reagan's defection was apparently never known to Helen, he hosted a clandestine impromptu fund-raising dinner for Nixon shortly after the Pitts speech. While a relatively few small donations came in to the Douglas campaign, only a handful of Hollywood celebrities wanted to be publicly associated with her, and, in stark contrast to all of her previous congressional campaigns, she was unable to coordinate a single movie-star gala. Only the die-hard loyalists—Myrna Loy and Eddie Cantor—came forward enthusiastically. Instead, it was Nixon who garnered the most Hollywood support with such bigwigs as Cecil B. DeMille, Howard Hughes, Anne Baxter, John Wayne, Rosalind Russell, and dozens more.

On October 27, her longtime close friend and supporter, the Jewish actor Edward G. Robinson, finally agreed to answer HUAC investigators' questions about the political activities of his Hollywood colleagues. Robinson had done so reluctantly, out of fear of being professionally blacklisted, but it was widely seen in their circle as a betrayal of his liberal friends in the film community. While she could empathize with Robinson's predicament, she saw it as a devastating personal and political setback. Rather than face contempt, Robinson set a precedent of answering the very kinds of questions Helen had been calling unconstitutional. Robinson's testimony set off the period in Hollywood referred to as "naming names" and sent fear throughout the film community. "The question of naming names was at some level a struggle between the right and the left within the Jewish community," author Victor S. Navasky wrote of the Hollywood Red Scare. "As the cold war heated up, so did the Jewish community's fear of McCarthyite anti-Semitism. First, it was a fact that many Jews were or had been in the socialist movement, and the professional patrioteers were unable or unwilling to distinguish between socialist and Communist." Nixon had managed to gain the support of Rabbi Max John Merritt—a strong Jewish leader in Los Angeles—and with his endorsement came money from Hollywood tycoons and executives including Louis B. Mayer (MGM), Harry Cohn (Columbia Pictures), and Darryl Zanuck (Twentieth Century-Fox).

Even Vito Marcantonio, apparently lacking any sense of irony, sidled up to Nixon when the two found themselves waiting to cross a street near the Capitol. "I hope you beat that bitch out there in California," Marcantonio said—a remark Nixon would retell with relish for the rest of his life.

The Nixon-Chotiner camp never relented. In the final days of the campaign, thousands of postcards were mailed to voters in the white suburbs and Northern California communities. Signed by a fictitious organization called the Communist League of Negro Women, the postcards carried the message VOTE FOR HELEN FOR SENATOR. WE ARE WITH HER 100%. Then cities were showered with leaflets offering prizes of silver tableware to people who answered their telephones saying "Vote for Nixon" rather than "Hello."

Smears had happened before in political history, but not with such blatant lies and sophisticated orchestration. Columnist Drew Pearson called it "one of the most skilled and cutthroat campaigns . . . I have ever witnessed" and branded the Pink Sheet "one of the most skillful pieces of propaganda I have seen."

As for the men in Helen's life, Lyndon Johnson was verbally supportive but, like most high-level Democratic men in Washington, went to lengths to distance himself. No political figure, regardless of power, could afford to be painted with the red brush of "Communist," and what was happening to Helen in California only validated the danger. For his part, Noel-Baker was extremely worried about her. He thought the race "a great disaster" and blamed her fellow Democrats for urging her to run against Nixon and then betraying her.

Melvyn was virtually missing from the campaign, though he made some financial contributions and offered advice by telephone from time to time. "After all, it's your job and you do it very well," he had written to her early in the campaign. But in the final days he could no longer stand silently by, so outraged was he by the lies and attacks. On election eve, speaking from a radio station in Cincinnati where he was on tour with a play, Melvyn delivered a poignant and eloquent speech, introduced by Humphrey Bogart. Melvyn's seething fury and irrepressible pride were palpable.

I had not intended to make a campaign speech for my wife. But I am angry. In California a congressman named Nixon is pursuing the same course being used by the Republicans throughout the country. And what is this course? Let us be frank about it . . . It is a course based on the refuge of all reactionaries—do nothing and attack your opponent as radical or subversive. Men and women in government who have sound policies, based upon their respect for and responsibility to their constituents, are always attacked. They strive for the best interests of human beings. It is easier—as a matter of fact it is the easiest thing in the world—to call people of goodwill dirty names, to call them Communists.

Well, I resent this with all my heart and all my soul . . . In my book, doing something to alleviate the shameful lacks in our society is the best possible way of fighting the Communists. That is what I believe, and that is what my wife believes. For years we have worked side by side, honestly, frankly, and openly, on the side of human decency—honestly, frankly, and openly, against dictatorship, against Fascism, against Communism . . .

I also understand that my wife is being criticized because of her career in the theater. It is true. My wife was an actress. I am an actor. I will not speak of myself, but I will tell you my wife was an extremely good actress, and made a very fine living at it. I will tell you that while she was an actress and raised two children, she read the newspapers and listened to the radio, and her heart bled—and she decided to do something about it. She knew and I knew the kind of criticism we'd have from the Nixons, the Tafts, and the McCarthys. She knew and I knew that she'd be attacked as just-an-actress. It's pretty funny, ladies and gentlemen. Anybody who's ever been in show business will tell you what courage and fortitude, what disappointment and perseverance, go into the life of an actor. But she knew and I knew that the voters of this country would judge her on her merits, on her accomplishments, on her reputation as a human being. They judged her three times and three times they sent her to Congress. They judged her and they nominated her for the United States Senate. I'm very proud of that.

Nobody discounts the real menace of Communism, both in the world and in the nation—but the McCarthys and the Nixons are taking advantage of this menace in their frantic, grasping thirst for political power. I don't think the people of the State of California, or the people of America, like this kind of thing. And the only way to show it is on November seventh when, in the voting booth, you can vote against what is the most un-American of all un-American activities: false witness against thy neighbor, libel and slander against good and honest public servants.

And so, with no modesty whatever, I ask you to vote for my wife, Helen Gahagan Douglas, for the United States Senate. I have known her a long time. I have loved her a long time. What is strongest and best in Helen is what is strongest and best in America. All her life she's lived by one thing alone—her love for her fellow man. I know of no better quality in a wife. I know of no better quality in a senator.

Helen's reaction to her husband's tender and immodest outpouring was not recorded; perhaps she saw it, like Truman's lukewarm and backhanded endorsement of her, as too little, too late.

On Monday morning, November 6, 1950, Californians—along with the rest of the nation—awakened to banner headlines. M'ARTHUR IN THREAT TO STRIKE AT REDS IN CHINA, blared the *Los Angeles Times*. It was election eve, the day before the 1950 midterm elections, in which Communism had played a pivotal role in campaigns throughout America— perhaps nowhere as much as in California. FRESH COMMUNIST TROOPS POURING INTO KOREA BATTLE, continued the *Times* headline.

The day marked an escalation of the unofficial Korean War as the Chinese marched deep into North Korea virtually undetected by U.S. forces. Caught by surprise, the U.S. troops crossed the thirty-eighth parallel and continued on to the Yalu River, where, according to one account, "they were about to be hurled back to the old postwar Korean boundary in one of the bloodiest retreats in modern history." But although that fate was still weeks in the future, the effect on the American public was already sealed—the only clarity being that "uncertainty, danger, and more war lay ahead," as Roger Morris put it.

Chinese soldiers were killing young American men as Americans went to the voting booths. Helen would have needed a miracle to survive this latest development, and down deep she knew it. She thought she might have had a chance even after the Korean War started in July. But with the Chinese intervention, she knew her candidacy was doomed. "There was the United States fighting communism and I was the person who said we should limit the power of the military and try to disarm the world and get along with Russia."

She had been making ten to fifteen speeches a day, often too tired to drag herself out of the car and up to the podium, yet determined to go on even if she knew it was all over. "The worst moment, a sight I couldn't shake, was when children picked up rocks and threw them at my car, at me. I knew that in order to survive I would have to accept the rocks and the Nixon campaign, shrug them off and move on. I wondered if I would be able to do it."

When the vote was tallied on November 7, she was not surprised. Nixon had defeated her by nearly 700,000 votes, the largest margin— 59 to 40 percent—of any senatorial race in the country. While a jubilant Nixon made the round of victory celebrations, playing "Happy Days Are Here Again" whenever he found a piano, Helen's headquarters was "a desolate scene."

Composed and stoic, Helen consoled her distraught staff. Finally, a newspaper photographer decided to cover the story. Her employees and volunteers had all dissolved into tears while Helen stood in the center of them wearing a strangely calm smile. She had worried about becoming embittered, about the possibility that she would lose hope for America's future. "I was so pleased that I had escaped the terrible burden of hating Richard Nixon that I was almost elated." She was eager to tour the state, to thank all of those who had worked for her, and the next day she hurried off to San Francisco. At the airport in Los Angeles, a black skycap approached her to help with her baggage. "Oh, Mrs. Douglas," he said, tears streaming down his face. "Oh, Mrs. Douglas, what have we done to you?"

Against insurmountable odds, Douglas had waged a valiant battle, though she was never able to combat the erroneous perception that she was a Communist, or that, as a woman, she was unqualified to enter the male bastion of the U.S. Senate. Even in a clean campaign, she would have been in trouble. "The Cold War was at its height," wrote David Halberstam in *The Powers That Be*. "Stalinism seemed a dark and immediate threatening specter. The country, disillusioned, was turning inward from the liberalism of the thirties and forties. Mrs. Douglas seemed the embodiment of a period that people were now turning away from, liberalism on domestic issues, trust of the Soviet Union."

The pundits' postmortem examination of the campaign began immediately and continued for several decades, as the Nixon-Douglas race became a part of national political legend. She had been up against the most powerful interests in California at a moment when the state was turning sharply right. Even if Richard Nixon had not been the candidate and Murray Chotiner had not engaged in trench warfare, the odds were markedly against her. In the end, though Douglas suffered an overwhelming defeat—and it would be forty more years before California elected a woman to the U.S. Senate— she refused to let the experience define her, refused to see herself as a victim. Future political scientists concluded that she never had a chance in the Senate race, that the electorate was not yet ready to entrust a woman with such power. The Nixon camp kept her constantly on the defensive, and no candidate could ever have overcome the total press blackout she faced. The *Los Angeles Times* never published a single photo of her during the campaign, and the owner of one of the largest radio stations in Los Angeles told his newscasters that Helen Gahagan Douglas "should receive nothing but critical notices."

Renowned American historian William Manchester would lay the blame squarely on the Democrats. "Mrs. Douglas had been crucified alright," Manchester wrote in his magisterial *The Glory and the Dream*, "but the worst spikes had been driven into her by fellow Democrats. It was a conservative Democrat who had first called her the Communist candidate, making her primary triumph a pyrrhic victory and assuring her defeat before the Republicans had chosen their nominee." But even granted the Brutus-like betrayal, nothing could have saved her from the massively financed, impeccably organized, and extraordinarily vicious campaign waged against her. She had stood against an immense tide of opposition and was arguably fortunate to have survived it intact.

What remained hidden to the public, though, was the length to which organized crime figures went to ensure her defeat. *Los Angeles Mirror* reporter Art White would later write that Ziffren and his asso-

ciates "had gained control of an enormous block of California's economy. They could finance political campaigns with the best of the native barons." So why would Helen's campaign be perpetually strapped
for cash? She had no way of knowing the strength of the organized
crime elements that had infiltrated her district, her party, and even her
campaign. She had no way of knowing that Paul Ziffren, her finance
director, was the Chicago syndicate's representative in California and
that he never had her best interest at heart. According to one account,
"The trio of Korshak, [MCA head Lew] Wasserman, and Ziffren . . .
were the triumvirate of absolute power in Hollywood. When they
moved in concert, there was not a candidate that could not be elected
or ruined, not a problem that could not be caused or solved, not a
deal that could not be made or killed." So how and why did they fail
Helen Gahagan Douglas?

"They were never going to let someone they couldn't control join
that exclusive club," organized crime investigator Jack Clarke concluded.

In the carefully orchestrated whispering campaign of smear, fear,
and innuendo that would go down in American history as the dirtiest
ever—while also becoming the model for the next half century and
beyond—her rival exploited America's xenophobia and reflexive chau-
vinism with devastating consequences.

Murray Chotiner introduced his own brand of dirty tricks to the
new medium of television in 1950. Five years later, he spoke to a Republican National Committee school for campaign workers about the
Douglas-Nixon race and political strategy for the future. Even though
the session was closed to the press, the *New York Times* obtained a copy
of Chotiner's fourteen-thousand-word syllabus, which was essentially
a GOP dirty-tricks manifesto. It would be one of many secret lectures
Chotiner would give to "GOP schools" over the next two decades;
these sessions would also be where he would meet the protégés who
would succeed him, Lee Atwater and Karl Rove.

The Chotiner formula, as laid out in his manual, was simple—a
theory based upon the belief that voters vote *against* someone rather
than *for* someone, so one must reveal as many negative things as possible about one's opponent. "Discredit your opponent before your
own candidate gets started—organize a separate group of Democrats

or independents to support your candidate—associate your opponent with an unpopular idea or organization, with just a suggestion of treason—if your opponent objects to defamation, complain that he is using unfair political tactics by calling you a liar—above all, attack, attack, attack, never defend."

In any case, it was the making of Richard Nixon and thus of an era, and the race seemed to haunt Nixon even more than her. "His enemies, like Abou ben Adhem's tribe, increased tenfold, and with them grew the myths of Nixon's 'reprehensible conduct' during that campaign of 1950," wrote one of his biographers. Nearly a decade later, as Nixon was preparing to run for the presidency, a British journalist asked him how he reconciled the dirty tactics of the 1950 campaign with his revised posture of a moderate candidate—a new man for a new decade. In the off-the-record exchange, Nixon reportedly paused before answering in quiet tones, "I'm sorry about that episode. I was a very young man."

Soon after publisher David Astor reported this remark, the ever-dissembling Nixon issued a denial of the exchange and reiterated his justifications of the campaign against Helen Douglas, stating: "The impression that she was pro-communist is both due to and justified by her own record."

For her part, once she fully gauged the depth, strength, and corruption of her adversaries, Helen turned away from public life for good. "There's not much to say about the 1950 campaign," Helen wrote near the end of her life, "except that a man ran for Senate who wanted to get there, and didn't care how."

5

HUMANITARIAN 1951–1980

I felt a funeral in my brain,
And Mourners, to and fro,
Kept treading, treading, till it seemed
That Sense was breaking through.

—Emily Dickinson

THOUGH SHE COULD easily have recaptured a congressional seat, and probably could have become the first female Speaker of the House, she refused to run for office again. Supporters tried to persuade her to run for the Senate from either New York or Nevada; friends encouraged her to become involved in Americans for Democratic Action in New York; colleagues lobbied Truman to have her appointed to a government position. But it was as if she had seen into the heart of a dark beast and wanted only to escape unscathed. Her retreat from public life, at least initially, was complete.

For the most part, she had been a loyal supporter of Truman's foreign and domestic agendas, but she had watched with disgust as he purged the intellectuals from government, replacing them with party hacks and cronies. The transition from Roosevelt to Truman had underscored the divisions of class in America, as the Ivy League–educated policy makers were replaced with Horatio Alger characters. Still, repulsed as she was, she remained a stalwart Democrat, if a lonely remnant of her idealized and idolized New Deal.

After the 1950 campaign, she and Melvyn sold their California home and moved back to New York, where Melvyn returned to the stage. She became an international spokesperson for peace and multi-lateral nuclear disarmament—a cause that put her at odds with those who favored unilateral disarmament. She was at the forefront of the antiwar, ecology, nuclear-freeze, and feminist movements, long before any of them were christened as actual movements.

"I have always thought the Douglases' gain was our country's loss," Melvyn later wrote of Helen's return to the family. "Not once during the remainder of her life did she display the slightest personal rancor over this shabby episode in American politics . . . she was happy to return, full-time, to a family which needed her." But the marriage remained one more of convenience and logistics than traditional husband and wife. "They were de facto separated," Gifford Phillips recalled of their unique relationship. "They were amiable and affectionate, but separated; they went their separate ways."

She kept her hand in both the theater and politics, but from a decidedly less center-stage role. She played the lead in *First Lady*, a shallow remake of a 1930s play, and began singing lessons again with her old coach, Madame Cehanovska, who had never forgiven Eleanor Roosevelt for wooing Helen into politics to begin with. But after several performances, and even though "the critics were kind," she was forced to admit that the prime years of her voice were behind her. It was after a recital at Carnegie Hall in September 1956 that she decided to end her singing career for good. She came to the unmistakable realization that "it was not possible for me, at fifty-six, to have a first-rate voice." She turned her attention then to learning about the world, making three study tours of the Middle East and two of South America. She spoke in support of Israel and performed at numerous fund-raising concerts and poetry readings. As for politics, she campaigned ardently and passionately for Adlai Stevenson in 1952 and 1956 for the Democratic nomination for president. She thought him a man of enormous intelligence and dignity, a statesman who would have directed the country in an honorable and upstanding way. "There are things more precious than political victory," Stevenson had said after defeat, in a remark that held special meaning for Helen; "there is the right to political contest. In much of the world partisan controversy is forbidden and dissent suppressed. God bless partisanship, for this is democracy's lifeblood!"

By 1960, neither Melvyn nor Helen continued the façade of a marriage, and Melvyn, apparently suffering a bout of depression, left the cast of *The Best Man* and moved to Spain. Writing her from Malaga, Melvyn offered her an ambivalent apology of sorts and described his trouble-free existence of swimming and sunbathing and sleeping. "This is the fate of man," he wrote, "the struggle between fireside and adventure—as old as Odysseus." She worried about his melancholia— a lifelong condition that seemed to be deepening—while also expressing frustration at his inability, or unwillingness, to address and resolve it. "This business of you not being happy unless you are pursuing your own desires . . . but torn with guilt in the process should be faced and cured if possible," she wrote, somewhat testily.

They returned to the issue of divorce, which had been tabled more than twenty years earlier. "You say when questioned by me on our marriage that you want it to continue. I wonder do you really. The reason I raise the question again and at this time is so that you may be freer to examine your own inner needs and desires." A close reading of their correspondence during this period suggests they had reached the culmination of two decades of ambivalence, disappointment, and inertia, and were finally addressing what had been too painful to confront while the children were still at home. "It is too ridiculous to continue a life that makes you ill," she wrote. "I keep asking myself if I have been unkind to you in not getting a divorce."

While many of Melvyn's letters are missing from the public record, judging from Helen's extant responses to him he fervently wished to stay married. All she wanted, Helen wrote him repeatedly, was for him to become healthy—"emotionally as well as physically." In the end, they stayed married and he remained in Europe for several months, sparking a round of press reports that they were formally separated. When he returned to the U.S. to play in the Chicago stage production of *The Best Man*, Helen joined him there. Their relationship deepened when he faced a life-threatening perforated stomach ulcer. She never left his side during a lengthy hospitalization, and they began a new phase in their marriage. They moved back to New York City together, and while they both continued to live their separate lives, they joined their grown children in fashioning a close-knit extended family.

Peter had attended Columbia University, where he received a graduate degree in sociology. Married with three children, he was a practicing therapist in New York. Mary Helen grew into a free-spirited young woman who lived on a kibbutz in Israel before joining the Peace Corps. An artist and weaver, she traveled the world teaching her craft. For the first time they created the kind of intact family that had eluded them during the 1940s and '50s.

Helen campaigned for Adlai Stevenson in 1960 and wrote a narrative to accompany photographs of Eleanor Roosevelt following Eleanor's death in 1962. The book was well received and brought her back into the public eye—at least among those nostalgic for the New Deal. She traveled the world advocating peace and disarmament, and was a much sought-after speaker on the issues that always motivated her—arms control, atomic energy, and civil rights.

It was November 22, 1963. Flanked by a blood-spattered Jacqueline Kennedy and his wife Lady Bird, Lyndon Baines Johnson took the oath of office aboard Air Force One just hours after John F. Kennedy had been assassinated in Dallas. Watching the historic and tragic event unfold on television along with the rest of America was Helen Gahagan Douglas—Johnson's former congressional colleague, fellow New Dealer, and onetime paramour. "We look forward to your leadership with confidence and loving admiration," she telegraphed him a few days later. Within weeks she would act as the president's emissary to Africa, and shortly after that she would carry a secret and hopeful dispatch to him from the Kremlin.

In the spring of 1964—during a frosty period of the cold war—Helen boarded a chartered airplane in Moscow bound for London. She bore a stirring message from the wife of Soviet Prime Minister Nikita Khrushchev to LBJ, which she transcribed on the flight and then delivered to the U.S. embassy for conveyance to the president by diplomatic pouch.

"Dear Lyndon, dear, dear Lyndon," she wrote. "Nikita Khrushchev is an old man and he wants to help the cause of peace in his final active years. He needs reassurance that you are sincere in saying that peace is your prime concern. He is fearful of putting his head in a noose. Such assurance could be a letter from you delivered by someone he trusts.

There are those who oppose efforts to reach disarmament agreements, but if Khrushchev is convinced, many things are possible."

Helen believed that Khrushchev was reaching out to President Johnson in earnest—that he needed to produce successful disarmament negotiations with the West if he was to hold his political power amid the gathering opposition in the Soviet military. But LBJ's nascent presidency—in which Helen bestowed such "confidence" and "admiration"—was already in thrall to the U.S. military, perpetuating an arms race and heading toward war in Southeast Asia.

For nearly two decades, she had been a friend and lover to LBJ, who was now suddenly, by tragedy and fate, the president of the United States. With the new circumstances, their relationship was at once changed. Her defeat a decade earlier for the U.S. Senate by Richard Nixon, who accused her of being a Communist—combined with the FBI's identifying her as a radical, and now her conspicuous international peace activism—had saddled her with a scarlet letter of red-baiting and misogyny. So when she appeared from behind the Iron Curtain with stunning information from the front lines, as it were, LBJ ignored her and her message. It would not always have been so.

There was a time when Helen Douglas's political trajectory seemed as dynamic as that of Johnson's. Once rated the second most outstanding representative of Congress, she had also been ranked as one of the twelve smartest and most influential women in the world. But her path to power had been thwarted by forces seen and unseen.

After Lyndon Johnson became president in 1963, Helen was the first woman he appointed to anything. "Happy New Year, sweetheart!" Johnson bellowed into the telephone on January 1, 1964. He began with some ingratiating small talk aimed at Helen's disarmament and humanitarian sensibilities. "I'm cutting down the military bases—some of these archaic, old, out-fashioned things, and Khrushchev's cutting his down too . . . and I'm taking that money and putting it into poverty," he told her. Helen had been urging him to distance himself from the military and focus on his domestic program—what would be his Great Society agenda—and at first it seemed he might have been taking her advice seriously.

"That's wonderful! That's terrific," she responded enthusiastically.

"I want you to do something for me. I want you to go as my representative . . . to Liberia for their hundredth anniversary of the relations between the United States and Liberia. I'd like to go myself . . .
But I can't do it. And it's this Saturday."

"This *Saturday*?"

"Yeah," the president answered, "it's this Saturday. What you shout-
ing about? That's four days longer than you usually have."

Helen laughed and said she would have to ask Melvyn. "I thought
you ran your own house. Don't tell me that you got to clear things
with Sidney!" the president joked, referring to the accusations by the
Republicans in 1944 that Franklin Roosevelt "cleared" every decision with labor leader Sidney Hillman.

Two months later, according to Johnson biographer Randall B.
Woods, Helen was staying with LBJ at the White House. "He had
supplied her apparently with my nightgown and robe and there she
was on the third floor," the First Lady recorded in her diary. Woods
and other biographers of both Lyndon and Lady Bird Johnson have
suggested that the First Lady accommodated Lyndon's extramarital
affairs. But "her husband's flaunting of Douglas hurt," according to
Woods. "So at breakfast I called her to come down in her robe (my
robe) and have breakfast with me in my room while we watched Lyndon depart by helicopter from the South Lawn . . . She is indeed the
same vivid person I knew back in 1949–50, somewhere along there . . .
She's an extraordinarily handsome woman, with an enormous appetite
for life, and encyclopedic accumulation of information and a regular
machine gun way of imparting it—rat-a-tat-tat."

Throughout 1964 Helen communicated with President Johnson
through back channels—emissaries who could hand-deliver letters to
Johnson. "Dear Jack Valenti, Please be so kind as to give this note to the
President," one cover letter asked of Johnson's close confidant. "Dear
Bill Moyer[s]," read one sent to the president's press secretary: "En-
closed is Philip Noel-Baker's 'The Way to World Disarmament—
Now' . . . He is a very close friend of mine, and I wanted the President
to meet him." Early in the year, she wrote the president that she was
planning to go to Russia. "Do you have any objections?" she asked.

In 1965, Helen spent several weeks with Noel-Baker in London.

Their close relationship had continued throughout the years, and after he won the Nobel Peace Prize in 1959 following publication of *The Arms Race*, they began meeting frequently in Europe and New York. By now, both his wife and his mistress had died, and Helen was married in name only. "I left New York feeling that I wanted to take you out to dinner every night for a year, instead of two nights in ten years," he wrote her in 1959, referring to their original parting after the United Nations session more than a decade earlier. Philip remained as smitten as he had been upon first meeting her in 1946, and though Helen was circumspect about their relationship in her personal writings, anecdotal evidence suggests the admiration and devotion was mutual. He was never able to relinquish a deep sadness about what had happened to her in 1950—and, especially, how she had been neutralized as a national political force. "While she was with me, Lyndon Johnson made his marvelous speech to a joint session of Congress about civil rights," Philip told an interviewer in 1976.

It had been March 15, 1965, and Johnson's speech was in response to recent racial violence in Selma, Alabama, that had resulted in the death of a civil rights activist. Thousands of citizens were planning a march from Selma to Montgomery, led by Reverend Martin Luther King Jr., to protest voting discrimination. President Johnson used the phrase "we shall overcome," the motto of the civil rights movement, bringing national and international attention to the festering racial divides in America. In what would go down in history as one of his most eloquent speeches, Johnson famously called for every American to join him in the struggle for civil rights. "At times, history and fate meet at a single time in a single place to shape a turning point in man's unending search for freedom. So it was at Lexington and Concord. So it was a century ago at Appomattox. So it was last week in Selma, Alabama."

Helen and Philip were ecstatic. They truly believed that Johnson was elevating the national dialogue and taking a historic step toward civil rights. Philip pronounced it "one of the epic orations of all history on the equality of the races, on the vital necessity of cooperation and non-discrimination, non-segregation, and the building of a single multiracial nation." Johnson's speech was greeted in Great Britain with wild enthusiasm, and the English press treated it as one of history's great events.

Then, three weeks later, Helen and Philip were further elated by what would become Johnson's "peace without conquest" speech. He had been elected in 1964 as the peace candidate, and Helen had tremendous hopes for him in those first years of his presidency. "Vietnam is far away from this quiet campus," Johnson addressed the crowd at Johns Hopkins University. "We have no territory there, nor do we seek any. The war is dirty and brutal and difficult." Helen listened raptly to the speech, thrilled to hear Johnson's reference to a proposed billion-dollar American investment in humanitarian programs for the Vietnamese, and especially of his mention of the ability of the Mekong River to "provide food and water and power on a scale to dwarf even our own TVA."

Helen saw the speech as a great turning point in the president's attitude toward the Southeast Asian conflict. "Lyndon has made the speech about foreign affairs that we wanted him to make!" she enthusiastically shouted down the hallway in Noel-Baker's London home. But very soon it was clear that Johnson had no intention of retreating from Vietnam. "Helen and I were both wrong," Philip remembered of their disappointment. "Lyndon Johnson did not stop the bombing of Vietnam, and it became obvious very soon . . . that the North Vietnamese and the Viet Cong would not negotiate while they were being bombed, just as the British people would not dream of talking to Hitler while he was bombing London and Liverpool and Manchester and other cities."

Helen and Philip both saw Johnson's entanglement in the Vietnamese civil war as a blatant violation of the UN charter—unlike the Korean War, which they were convinced had been instigated by Stalin and which therefore justified American intervention. "The Russians will never have allies who are not satellites," Yugoslavia's leader Josip Broz Tito had once confided in Noel-Baker, who took the warning to heart.

Still, for a time Helen remained fond and protective of Johnson, attributing his misguided foreign policy to a perennial and deep-seated inferiority complex and unquestioning faith in the military. She thought Johnson's intervention in Vietnam "was against everything he did and believed in at home." She thought the president parochial and naïve, uninformed and unworldly, neither well-read nor conversant with the lives of other people. She knew that he did not trust the

UN and that he viewed Vietnam, somewhat simplistically, as a mess that needed cleaning up—"a stump in the way of the plow." Patriarchal and paternalistic, LBJ "was not indifferent to the suffering of the Vietnamese people but he could not relate to them as he did to his own people," as Helen described his "Great White Father" attitude. By condescending to the Vietnamese, he was able to "rationalize the suffering," as she saw it. He genuinely believed that once it was all over, "he would make things right with the people of Vietnam." He would turn the Mekong Delta into another Tennessee Valley and they would all love him and forgive him. She thought his philosophy tragically flawed and unsophisticated.

As the war dragged on, claiming more and more American lives, she grew increasingly exasperated with Johnson's stubbornness and disenchanted with his motives. She lobbied him endlessly on disarmament, believing as she did that it was the most important matter in the world. And yet she was unable to convince Johnson of the evils of nuclear weapons. Truman's containment policy had led to the arms race, she argued, which in turn led to the cold war with Russia, which then spawned the hot war in Southeast Asia. Johnson tried to appease her with what she saw as "token gestures." When he bragged to her about closing a run-down New York army base, she countered, "Oh, Lyndon, when will you really begin to cut the meat out of the military? . . . Eliminating the Brooklyn base is not cutting back on the arms race."

Meanwhile, during his five years in office, LBJ escalated American involvement in the Vietnam War from 16,000 to 550,000 American soldiers. Once he authorized ground troops, Helen broke with him and became an outspoken opponent of the war, speaking at massive protests throughout the country: "I didn't try to contact Lyndon." She felt after his silence following her trip to Moscow as a member of the Jane Addams Peace Association Delegation, which resulted in her letter to him about Khrushchev—the letter in which she wrote "Khrushchev is an old man and he wants to help the cause of peace in his final active years"—that her efforts were futile. "It was no use," she finally concluded. "He couldn't listen."

In December 1968—at the end of his term—his popularity was at its lowest. Young American soldiers were dying at a rate of one thousand a month, and Richard Nixon was elected to succeed him as president. That month, Helen was among a large number of longtime Johnson supporters invited to one of the president's last White House receptions. She entered the receiving line and made her way toward the man who was once her friend, colleague, and lover. She held out her hand to shake his. He stood mute, his arms at his side, and gave her a glassy stare. Publicly snubbed, she faltered for a moment, unable to move. Shaking her head in despair, she backed away. It "struck me as sad," she later reflected. "Not only for me, but for his misery and that of the country. What we all had suffered."

EPILOGUE

If the national security is involved, anything goes. There are no rules.
There are people so lacking in roots about what is proper and
what is improper that they don't know there's anything wrong
in breaking into the headquarters of the opposition party.

—Helen Gahagan Douglas after Watergate, 1973

H ER ISSUES WERE a prototype for foundering progressives over the next half century. "She was a light in the window for liberals at a time when things were very dark," said one of her earliest supporters. First as an unwavering FDR New Dealer, and then as a supporter of Harry Truman's Twenty-one Points, she sponsored legislation on full employment, affordable housing, collective bargaining, cancer research, public education, an increase in the minimum wage, federal health insurance, the extension of Social Security, aid to farmers, the plight of migrant workers, and water and mineral rights in the American West.

What happened to Helen Gahagan Douglas at the hands of Nixon and his henchman, Murray Chotiner—the mentor of contemporary hardball political operative Karl Rove—has been often told by journalists and historians. "He is way beyond anything Nixon had at his disposal," former White House counsel John Dean said about the twenty-first-century Republican strategist Rove, comparing him to Chotiner, who could "cut off an opponent at the knees so quickly the person did not immediately realize he had been crippled."

The 1950 Nixon-Douglas campaign was not only a grave and

disturbing omen of what would become politics as usual in the twenty-first century: Its further tragedy was how it froze Helen Douglas in a time and place, overshadowing not only the accomplishments and complexities of her long and fascinating life but allowing the press, her male political colleagues and rivals, and her later biographers to define her and then dismiss her from the national stage.

It was not until efforts to impeach Nixon were under way and criminal charges were filed against the plumbers—as Nixon's campaign operatives would be known throughout history—that Helen finally began to speak publicly about her nemesis. It had been Dean who first blew the whistle on the plumbers; beginning with the June 17, 1972, break-in at the Democratic national headquarters at the Watergate hotel in Washington, D.C., and ending with Nixon's ignominious and historic resignation in August 1974, the Watergate scandals included illegal burglaries, secret slush funds of laundered money, hush money paid to silence witnesses, and a cover-up of massive proportion. At the center of it all stood Chotiner and his band of dirty tricksters.

When details of the Watergate break-in first began to come to light, Helen held an uncharacteristic press conference. "I raised the matter of the strange incident in the Watergate apartments where five men with close ties to the Republican Committee to Reelect the President [known as CREEP] were arrested in the Democratic party's national headquarters. It was clear that they were spying on behalf of Richard Nixon and it seemed essential for the country to know whether the President had condoned or authorized the crime." Once the conspiracy behind the Watergate burglary had unraveled, exposing Nixon as culpable and deeply involved, Helen no longer sat on the sidelines. "I threw myself into the movement to impeach the President," she later wrote, though she found no pleasure in the process. "I don't feel the need for vindication," she told a reporter at the time, "—and satisfaction is *totally* out of place."

After President Nixon resigned in 1974 while facing certain impeachment, bumper stickers appeared throughout California: DON'T BLAME ME, I VOTED FOR HELEN GAHAGAN DOUGLAS.

"People rather expected that she would be gloating over Richard Nixon finally being found out," her secretary, Nan Stevens, wrote of her at that moment, "but she was only sad. She thought it was terrible for the country and for America's reputation abroad. I know that makes her sound almost too good to be true, but she *was* good. I'm not saying Helen didn't have feet of clay, because she did. But you had to look awfully hard to find her tiny clay feet."

In the end, the combination of gender and cold war politics shaped the historic Douglas-Nixon match into a paradigm for political women over the next decades. In another of the many ironies and complexities that distinguished Helen Douglas, she never considered herself a feminist and often lashed out at women. In 1972, she appeared on the cover of *Ms.* magazine, but though she became a feminist icon during that decade's women's movement, she never embraced the role, believing that many women activists of the time were embroiled in petty jockeying and infighting. She was particularly disappointed in women's apparent lack of commitment to disarmament, convinced as she was that the main issue women should be fighting for was peace.

In fact, she saw women as the greatest obstacle to other women. "There are more women in this country than there are men," she once said. "Women themselves fail women. Women don't support women. They keep talking about 'getting the power.' They *have* the power." She often compared housekeeping to world politics, and tried to use the analogy to inspire women to run for office, to expand their horizons from domestic duties to political obligations. "Since government is only housekeeping on a large scale, it seems to me that women can play an important and constructive part in building world peace and healthy, sound communities at home. Who knows more about running the home than the mother? . . . From the time she is born, a woman is a politician. At home she must be housekeeper, mother, teacher, judge, and sometimes even jury."

She never saw herself as a token female but as a voice for the working class, for world peace, and against imperialism. Still, she often spoke out in favor of women's rights. "I was not one of those 200,000 women a year who gave birth to their children without medical attention," she once remarked, referring to her position as a white woman of privilege. "I do not belong to a minority—at least, I do not think the Irish are considered a minority in America anymore."

As brilliant and competent as any male colleague—"as smart as she is beautiful," mused columnist Drew Pearson—Douglas had been blindsided by the sexist assault against her. Her beauty and wealth only added to her plight. As relevant today as decades earlier—and symbolic of where the nation was headed—she was at the center of some of the most dramatic and historic events of the twentieth century.

As Hillary Clinton battled through the 2008 presidential race, Congresswoman Nancy Pelosi ascended to the highest office ever held by a woman, and Sarah Palin became the first female Republican candidate for vice president, the 1950s-style trivialization of women in politics was alive and well. In the national political contest of 2008, gender played a central role, bringing a timeliness and freshness to the life and times of Helen Gahagan Douglas. In rhetoric that seemed a throwback to a previous, unenlightened era—with only slightly more subtlety—female political figures were marginalized by the media. MUTED TONES OF QUIET AUTHORITY was the *Washington Post* headline to a November 2006 article about Pelosi's wardrobe, sense of style, and selection of jewelry, describing her Armani suit as a "tool for playing with the boys without pretending to be one."

In Hillary Clinton's historic and vicious race, she was called a "hellish housewife" and an "anti-male" "she-devil" whose laugh sounded like a "cackle." She faced hecklers with blatantly sexist messages of "Iron my shirt." Conservative radio commentator Rush Limbaugh went so far as to say, "Will this country want to actually watch a woman get older before their eyes on a daily basis?" And in a backhanded sexist compliment meant to enhance her stature, Limbaugh called Palin a "babe" who "doesn't have to wear pantsuits." Palin's image was "plastered on suggestive action figures, risqué T-shirts, and pornography on the Internet." Indeed, the Internet was brimming with sexist and gender-related chatter throughout the presidential campaign. "Everyone is treating Sarah Palin like a vapid celebrity and it is just so patronizing!" wrote one blogger. "Here she is, four thousand four hundred miles away from her tanning bed, meeting all these important people with accents in her very most distinguished Nancy Pelosi outfits and the president of Pakistan tells her she is 'more gorgeous' than he expected her to be!"

What Helen Douglas might have thought of both the sexual politics and the dirty tricks of the 2008 presidential campaign—more than a half century after her race against Nixon—can only be guessed. "I feel sure that at some time along the line between 1950 and today," Philip Noel-Baker told an interviewer in 1976, "if Helen had stayed in the House of Representatives, she would have been the presidential candidate, and the first woman president of the United States. I think she would have had an enormous influence on American public life, on the position of women in every country in the world, and on the success of the United Nations. That's another of the ifs of history." Indeed, when she accompanied presidential candidate Jimmy Carter to a campaign event in 1976 she received a standing ovation, prompting Carter to remark: "It's you who should be running."

Someday there will be a woman president, she had come to believe near the end of her life—after serving three terms in Congress, advising two presidents, and enduring a mudslinging U.S. senatorial campaign that set back the cause of women in California politics for fifty years. But only when they entered politics "as individuals, not as a woman."

As complicated as their marriage was, the relationship between Helen and Melvyn was by all accounts marked by mutual admiration, almost adoration. Even so, the 1950s, '60s, and '70s found them most often apart, Melvyn sometimes living in Europe, and each linked with other romantic partners. Emerging from Hollywood's "gray list," if not blacklist, Melvyn would win two Academy Awards, for his roles in *Hud* and *Being There*. Although he was never called to testify before HUAC—or officially accused of being a Communist—Melvyn's career had been negatively affected by the 1950s Red Scare. It had been Melvyn who first introduced Helen to progressive politics. Melvyn had been cofounder of the Hollywood anti-Nazi league, California state chairman of the Americans for Democratic Action, avid and public supporter of the Hollywood Ten, member of antifascist and civil rights committees suspected by the FBI as Communist fronts, and union activist, and his liberal credentials had thwarted both of their careers.

The 1970s saw Melvyn performing some of the best parts of his life and winning awards, ironically, for his roles as political figures. In *The Candidate*—a 1972 film about a liberal politician loosely based on California Governor Jerry Brown—Melvyn played the father of the

Senate candidate. In 1979 he costarred in *The Seduction of Joe Tynan*—
another political roman à clef, inspired by U.S. Senator Edward
Kennedy, about the rise of a liberal senator and the inescapable corruption that surrounded him. Considered one of the finest actors
ever produced by the United States, Melvyn would win all three of the
entertainment industry's highest awards—two Oscars, a Tony for *The
Best Man*, and an Emmy for *Do Not Go Gentle into That Good Night*.

"I cried when I was moved," Melvyn wrote near the end of his life.
"It was Helen who always kept a stiff upper lip in times of trouble.
This mechanism had served her well in the face of public difficulty of
the sort she had encountered during the late 1940s."

During the last years of her life, she spent winters with Melvyn in
Mexico and summers at the Gahagan family retreat in Vermont—the
place Helen loved above all others. "I get great delight from so many
things," she told a journalist near the end of her life, while gazing out
toward her favorite mountain. "Looking at the sunset or the sunrise,
just seeing the color of things, how the light strikes the trees in a certain way."

She battled breast cancer for several years, finally succumbing in 1980
with Melvyn at her side. "She was entranced always by the light," he
wrote upon her death. "In every house we ever occupied, she wanted
the windows to be wider. She thought no room could have too many
windows . . . She was always saying, 'Look at the light! Isn't it beautiful?' *She* was the light. And she was beautiful."

ACKNOWLEDGMENTS

Once again, I owe an enormous debt to literary agent extraordinaire and dear friend Gloria Loomis. She has unerringly navigated the turbulent waters of American publishing for me, always managing to find a perfect port in the storm. Her efforts this time were incomparable. I could not ask for a more insightful, informed, and creative partner than Peter Ginna. I feel fortunate and grateful to have him as my editor and to join his stable of writers. Also at Bloomsbury Press, Pete Beatty has been gracious, responsive, and efficient in shepherding this book toward publication, and copy editor Will Georgantas was characteristically impeccable.

I received two fellowships that contributed greatly to my research—one from the Hoover Institution at Stanford University and another from the LBJ Library. I wish to thank David Brady and Mandy MacCalla at Hoover, and Barbara Cline at the University of Texas.

I am always appreciative of the scholarship that precedes me, and in this case I am particularly beholden to Ingrid Scobie, Colleen M. O'Connor, and Greg Mitchell, whose trailblazing work on Helen Gahagan Douglas made my job far more manageable. Likewise, the many dedicated archivists, librarians, and researchers throughout the country amaze me with their thoroughness and generosity. Chief among those to whom I owe the deepest thanks are Mark Adams and Peggy Trujillo at the New Mexico State Library. Additionally, I wish to single out Mary Knill, Claudia Anderson, and Charlene McCauley at the LBJ Library in Austin, and Carolyn Hanneman at the Carl Albert Center at the University of Oklahoma.

To my colleagues—journalists, historians, investigators, lawyers, scholars, and activists—who selflessly made themselves, their ideas, and their files available, I thank you: Jack Clark, Gary Cohn, Ronnie Dugger, Jim Fitzpatrick, Dan Flores, Michael Green, Alonzo Hamby, James Houston, Kitty Kelley, Ryland Kelly, Don Lamm, Emily Loose, Dennis McBride, Dennis McDougal, Pat McGilligan, Ken Mate, Dan Moldea, Roger Morris, John Rubel, Mark Rudd, Gus Russo, Peter Dale Scott, Sam Smith, Anthony Summers and Robbyn Swan, David Thomson, Virginia Scharff, and Nicholas Von Hoffman. Many thanks especially to John Connolly of Actors' Equity for a thorough and thoughtful historic rendition of communism, progressivism, and unionism in the early California labor movement.

To Jeffrey Howell and Bill Press for putting me up in Austin; and to Tom and Anne Cori and Phyllis Schlafly for the most gracious hospitality and glimpse into how the other side sees it.

I am particularly indebted to friends and acquaintances of Helen Douglas who shared their memories of her: Gifford Phillips, Mercedes Eichholz, and Arthur Goldschmidt Jr.

Typically, I am overflowing with gratitude to my long-suffering friends who manage to cheerfully sustain me through the writing process of all of these books! Once again, to all the usual suspects— from the Martini Girls to the HBAGs to the River Rats to the Kettle-bellers to the Salonistas—I love you guys: Charmay Allred, Janeal Arison, Sandy Blakeslee, Maxine Champion, Frankie Sue Del Papa, Nancy Cook, Felice Gonzales, Joanna Hurley, Judy Illes, Terri Jerry, Dana Merrell, Lucy Moore, Julie Anne Overton, Marla Painter, and Ellen Reiben.

I especially want to thank Crosby Kemper, the book titan whose literary enthusiasm was an inspiration at a crucial moment; and Shaune Bazner, who set up a study for me on the fourth floor of the magical Palisades house where *Tosca* wafted out the window as I entered Helen's world.

I always save the best for last—my parents, my three sons, and their father. There is nothing in the world more important than family. Thank you for being mine.

Sally Denton
February 3, 2009

Notes

Abbreviations

ER   Eleanor Roosevelt
HGD   Helen Gahagan Douglas
MD   Melvyn Douglas
Douglas   *A Full Life* by Helen Gahagan Douglas
HGD Papers   Helen Gahagan Douglas Papers, Carl Albert Center, University of Oklahoma, Norman, Oklahoma.
OH   Helen Gahagan Douglas Oral History Project. Bancroft Library. University of California, Berkeley

Prologue

1 "Helen! You really must come": Douglas, 141.

1 "Like a swarm of invading locusts": Quoted in McWilliams, *Southern California Country*, 135.

2 "herded about like animals": John Steinbeck, "The Harvest Gypsies," *San Francisco News*, published in several parts between October 5 and October 12, 1936.

2 "listened in astonishment": Douglas, 141.

2 "I could not know it then": Douglas, 142.

3 "I have read a book recently": Quoted in Trodd, 97.

3 "faces stamped": Douglas, 143.

3 "I'm sorry but I simply can't": Steinbeck to Elizabeth Otis, March 7, 1938. Quoted in Grunwald and Adler.

3 "When you dig into a problem": Quoted in Mitchell, *Tricky Dick*, 22.

4 "The migrants were descended": Douglas, 143.

ONE: DIVA 1900–1930

5 "In every house": Douglas, x.

5 "the great moral upheaval": Unofficial Observer, 130.

6 "We were raised in acute awareness": Douglas, 18.

7 "She was one of those": Israel.

7 "Unlike many of his generation": Douglas, 5.

7 "Everything his mother did": Ibid.

7 "He picked my mother": Ibid., 4.

9 "Noisy, gregarious, affectionate": Ibid., 24.

9 "Lillian, do you see what the children are doing?": Ibid.

9 "white potato sprout": Ibid., 24.

10 "You must give up this notion": Ibid., 22.

10 "At the Gahagans' ": Ibid., 26.

10 "It's good to have a temper": Ibid., 27.

10 "He was an impressive man": Ibid., 3.

11 "In his mind": Ibid.

11 "When I began to read" . . . "Did I want to be just a breeding": Ibid., 7.

11 "To think was to be in control": Ibid.

12 "It brings me peace": Ibid., 34.

12 "It's a heartbreak to the wise": Ibid. HGD quotes a line from John Millington Synge's play *Deirdre of the Sorrows*.

13 "Don't make such a fuss": Ibid., 4.

13 "Her arrival dazzled": Ibid., 6.

14 "Have you stopped studying?" Ibid.

14 "Young, attractive girls": Ibid., 7.

14 "sank down and sobbed" . . . "If I defied my father": Ibid., 9.

15 "only for *boys*" . . . "They manage to get": Ibid., 10.

15 "the masculine routes of power": Horowitz, xviii.

15 "proved to be her ticket": Scobie, 21.

16 "ordered me to stop" . . . "blustering, rough-tongued": Douglas, 12.

16 "trivial" . . . "silly": Ibid., 13.

16 "I bravely told my parents": Ibid., 14.

17 "Father's bellow": Ibid., 3.

17 "Sign that, young lady": Ibid.

17 "her mobility and professional equality": Auster, 88.

17 "I felt like one of his prizefighters": Douglas, 15.

18 "If I didn't assert" . . . "The play would have to open": Ibid., 15.

18 "Keep her decent": Ibid., 16.

18 "new girl on the block": Scobie, 24.

18 "HELEN GAHAGAN BECOMES STAGE STAR" . . . "*Parents Opposed Career*" . . . "The first-nighters": *Brooklyn Daily Eagle* (September 22, 1922). See also Douglas, 16.

18 "Her father and I": Israel.

18 "the consummate actress": Douglas, 48.

18 "promiscuous lovemaking": Quoted in Scobie, 25.

19 "You know": Ibid.

19 "a real acting genius": Quoted in Douglas, 36.

19 "the most exciting and vibrant": Scobie, 25.

19 "Few, no matter how talented": Ibid., 28.

19 "I was determined": Douglas, 36.

20 "handsome, tall, slender" . . . "He . . . admires": Ibid., 37.

20 "Such a combination": *New York Evening Post* (January 25, 1925).

20 "an acting prodigy" . . . "a consuming love": The playwright and critic Colgate Baker, quoted in Douglas, 48.

20 "a beauty so compelling": O'Connor, "Through the Valley of Darkness," 18.

21 "That's irrelevant": Douglas, 17.

21 "[She] had a very drastic": Quoted in Scobie, *Center Stage*, 34.

21 "Much as she might have resisted": O'Connor, "Through the Valley of Darkness," 20.

21 "Like most stories about me": Douglas, 41.

22 "The most intrepid interviewers": Quoted in Douglas, 54.

22 "smitten with racing": Ibid., 39.

22 "You should be in bed, Helen": Ibid., 53.

23 "We must find you a *teacher*": Ibid., 54.

23 "Maestro Bamboschek tells me" . . . "Do you want to be a singer?" . . . "No" . . . "I trusted the authority" . . . "You are not a mezzo" . . . "sing single tones": Ibid., 55–56.

23 "My intensity led me": Ibid., 58.

25 "thunderstruck": Ibid., 63.

25 "devote herself to grand opera" . . . "Of course, the Metropolitan Opera": *Pittsburgh Post* (September 16, 1927).

26 "Go, then": Douglas, 63.

26 "I was enchanted" . . . "If I made a mess": Ibid., 67.

27 "Dear Helen" . . . "if it weren't": Correspondence between Power and Gahagan, Scobie, 49, 316 n. 13.

28 "America's foremost patron": *Time*, "Mr. Kahn & Mr. Gatti" (December 2, 1925).

28 "Don't be surprised" . . . "I have the pleasantest": Correspondence between Kahn and Gahagan, Scobie, 50, 316 n. 14.

28 "Despite the pain": Douglas, 69.

28 "for the American soprano": Ibid., 73.

29 "An extraordinary artist": *Salzburger Chronik* (October 19, 1929). Quoted in Douglas, 74.

29 "Stock prices have reached": Schlesinqer, *The Crisis of the Old Order*, viii.

Two: Activist 1931–1944

30 "fast-shrinking" . . . "frightful losses": Douglas, 65.

30 "I awaited his verdict": Ibid., 75.

31 "If you want to see Father" . . . "I have been waiting for you": Ibid., 78.

32 "monumentally silly" . . . "Mr. Belasco": Ibid., 79–80

32 "I make it a rule": *New York Herald Tribune* (April 5, 1931).

32 "when she is deflowered": Douglas, 82.

32 "He's a juvenile" . . . "If you still object": Ibid., 80.

32 "one hand poised": Douglas and Arthur, 79.

33 "He will do" . . . "That's the handsomest back" . . . "I was obsessed": Douglas, 80.

34 "fascinated and repelled": Douglas and Arthur, 8.

34 "Am I not the best caster": Douglas, 89.

34 "I'm a Jew": Ibid., 83.

35 "implied in popular tunes": Douglas and Arthur, 4.

35 "a yeasty place" . . . "got a first inkling": Ibid., 9.

35 "Shakespearean star": Ibid., 15.

35 "genuine native Americans" . . . "make plain" . . . "Christianized a community": Ibid., 28.

36 "if she could possibly be as dazzling": Ibid., 56.

36 "romantic and statuesque" . . . "everything" . . . "were ecstatically happy" . . .
"shunted from relative" . . . "This is obviously": Douglas and Arthur, 63–64. Rosalind Hightower would go on to marry the Louisiana novelist James B. Aswell Jr.
and become a prominent commercial illustrator.

36 "utterly fascinating": Douglas and Arthur, 59.

37 "he thrust an armful" . . . "We can't go through life": Douglas, 83.

37 "It was 1929": Sloat, 13.

38 "wild-eyed": Hofstadter, 383.

38 "The fundamental business": Quoted in Schlesinger, *The Age of Roosevelt: The
Crisis of the Old Order*, 158.

38 "Surely your administration": Hearst to Hoover, November 14, 1929. Quoted
in Grunwald and Adler, 188.

39 "If the crash of '29": Watkins, 249.

39 "Still . . . the dry horror": Ibid., 251.

39 "built-in economic stabilizers": Schlesinger, *The Age of Roosevelt: The Crisis of
the Old Order*, ix.

39 "What this country needs": Quoted in Smith, *The Shattered Dream*, 67.

40 "It was beautiful, Helen": Douglas, 85.

40 "Being single and occasionally engaged": Ibid., 91.

40 "To whom?": Ibid., 87.

41 "infinite capacity for kindness": Ibid., 105.

41 "The way you two play the love scene": Ibid., 89.

41 "It was love at first sight": Ibid., 90.

41 "Of course I'll be a good wife": Ibid., 91.

41 "I love you both": Quoted in Scobie, 68, 318 n. 10.

42 "madness" . . . "might wind up": Douglas, 88.

42 "The studio agents": Douglas and Arthur, 85.

43 "I was helplessly in love": Douglas, 89.

43 "I think that Helen": Quoted in Scobie, 70, 318 n. 15.

43 "I had tried to prepare myself" . . . "faced five years" . . . "where does one
live" . . . "There are only two places": Douglas, 94.

43 "I expected camels": Ibid., 95.

44 "a part of the country": Ibid., 98.

45 "angry stories": Ibid., 10.

45 "thousands of them": Quoted in Roger Morris, 538, and note, p. 926.

45 "I looked for signs" . . . "toughly administered dole": Douglas, 102–3.

46 "It came to me": Ibid., 105.

47 "Never have two people": Douglas and Arthur, 236.

47 "honeymoon cruise": O'Connor, "Through the Valley of Darkness," 22.

47 "Melvyn sensitized Helen": Scobie, 79.

48 "This is taking too long" . . . "We have a beautiful" . . . "were waiting" . . . "awful": Douglas, 115.

48 "[It] worries me": Quoted in Scobie, 82, 320 n. 4.

48 "I'd have twenty": Quoted in Scobie, 83, 320 n. 6.

49 "appalling" . . . "atrocious" . . . "I knew on the first day" . . . "detested having a makeup": Douglas, 120.

49 "It fell in the indeterminate": Ibid., 121.

49 "Each evening when the flower": MD to HGD, quoted in Scobie, 87, 320 n. 16.

50 "a balm" . . . "damaged self-esteem": Douglas, 123.

50 "white wool cape": Scobie, 89.

50 "Melvyn, a more deliberate actor": Douglas, 123.

51 "His enigmatic grin": This quote is from a Greta Garbo Web site: http://www .garboforever.com/Melvyn_Douglas.htm.

52 "the poorest Guild comedy": Douglas, 123.

52 "It was an expensive, romantic plan": Ibid., 126.

52 "Helen Gahagan Douglas . . . had not the slightest" . . . "Of course, Miss Gahagan": Roosevelt and Hickok, 47.

53 "Aryans such as we": Douglas, 131.

53 "Irish blood at the boiling point": Roosevelt and Hickok, 48.

54 "big enough for a camp of gypsies": Douglas, 139.

54 "She could do anything" . . . "Good-natured, bright" . . . "Helen, we have a beautiful little girl": Ibid., 137–38.

54 "The Birds were registered": Ibid., 135.

55 "I spoke the language": Ibid., 134.

55 "Previous to 1934" . . . "They churned out": Douglas and Arthur, 111.

56 "The anti-Sinclair crusade": Mitchell, *Tricky Dick*, xviii.

56 "the first serious movement": Quoted in Mitchell, *Campaign*, xiii.

56 "in which advertising men": Quoted in Mitchell, *Campaign*, xii.

56 "stirred up the moribund": Douglas, 136.

57 "What do you care": Israel.

58 "of ditchbank settlements": Douglas, 146.

58 "without doubt": Quoted in Douglas, 146.

58 "future plays will depend": Quoted in Hofstadter, 431.

58 "The New Deal will never be understood": Ibid.

58 "around him in his cabinet": Watkins, 2.

59 "a radical departure": Raymond Moley quoted in Terkel, 251.

59 "the responsibility of collecting": Douglas, 149.

60 "Unless democracy were renewed": Goodwin, *No Ordinary Time*, 10.

60 "We all remember the first time" . . . "Why did people like us": Arthur Gold-schmidt's eulogy at HGD's funeral, quoted in Douglas, 422–23.

61 "1. I loved you": HGD to MD, April 6, 1961. Quoted in Scobie, 123, 324 n. 44.

61 "There was an understanding" . . . "at once intimate": Douglas, 152.

61 "I suppose it is commonplace": Douglas and Arthur, 224.

62 "If it hadn't been for *that woman*": Israel.

62 "patronage system" . . . "same story" . . . "I was raised in a household": Douglas, 161.

63 "Oh, Mrs. Roosevelt" . . . "He seemed to accept" . . . "Please, don't go in there": Ibid., 154.

64 "the Communist party": Dick Meister, "The Legacy of John Steinbeck." Labornet News (2002). http://www.labornet.org/viewpoints/meister/jstein.htm

64 "I have never believed": Quoted in Douglas, 15.

THREE: CONGRESSWOMAN 1944–1950

65 "I *decided* I wanted": HGD, OH, vol. IV, 59.

65 "consider politics": Israel.

65 "fervent commitment": Scobie, 123.

66 "only a five-, six-months" . . . "Churchill was the best": Ickes, *Secret Diaries*, vol. 3, 175–76.

67 "OK, Helen": The account of the exchange between Helen Douglas and Franklin Roosevelt is quoted in Goodwin, *No Ordinary Time*, 39, and attributed to an interview between Goodwin and Billy Wilder. (See Goodwin, 644 n. 37.)

67 "very subdued" . . . "Surely, Mr. President" . . . "Don't tell me any more" . . . "were in France": Douglas, 170–71.

68 "The Japanese in California": *Washington Post* (February 15, 1942).

69 "distressed at the tide": Douglas, 179.

69 "Let 'em be pinched": Sportswriter Henry McLemore, quoted in Russo, 101.

69 "There is more potential danger": Testimony of Earl Warren before the U.S. House Committee Investigating National Defense, quoted in Russo, 102, 558 n. 36.

69 "the worst single wholesale": Burns, 216.

70 "The issue of the [N]isei's abandoned property" . . . "for speculators with deep pockets": Russo, 104–5.

70 "a withering attack" . . . "I want the members": Goodwin, *No Ordinary Time*, 324.

71 "Do we always have to have men": Quoted in Scobie, 132.

71 "[I]f we don't clean some": Quoted in Scobie, 133.

71 "at a special ceremony": Douglas, 182.

71 "I do not mind": Quoted in Scobie, 136, 326 n. 29.

72 "flung himself": Douglas, 185.

72 "left me with his savings": Ibid.

72 "a tiny dynamo": Ibid., 186.

73 "There is no leadership": HGD to MD, January 25, 1943, quoted in Scobie, 140, 327 n. 40.

73 "You're hooked" . . . "If you'll run in my place" . . . "I've sat in the gallery": Douglas, 186.

73 "Helen, don't you run": HGD Oral History, LBJ Library, 5.

73 "forefront of a new generation": Mitchell, *Tricky Dick*, 22.

74 "willing to compete": An address by Douglas in 1950, quoted in Mitchell, *Tricky Dick*, 70, 279 n.

74 "Certain people will heave bricks": Douglas and Arthur, 177.

74 "Helen, this is a call to duty": Thomas F. Ford to HGD, February 1, 1944. HGD Papers, box 163, folder 1.

75 "Every city has its boom": McWilliams, *Southern California Country*, 114.

75 "the White Spot" . . . "no crime, no corruption": McDougal, 105.

75 "L.A.'s moral fiber": Ibid.

75 "In the hands of an enterprising people": Dana, 237.

76 "Januslike, southern California": Roger Morris, 4.

76 "Supermob" . . . "a group of men" . . . "Kosher Nostra": Russo, xv, xvi.

77 "Hollywood was largely the invention": Tosches, 494.

77 "The Chicago group took over": Connie Carlson, quoted in Russo, 82.

77 a politician's "horror": "The Douglas Touch." *Fortnight* (January 21, 1959), 8.

77 "combustible mixture": O'Connor, 43.

78 "literally ran her campaign": Roosevelt and Hickok, 53.

79 "I saw before me": Douglas, 193.

79 "I just love the Negro people!" . . . "I knew": Ibid., 253.

79 "The sleeper in the campaign" . . . "I believed that the conservation": HGD Oral History, LBJ Library, 7.

80 "You are going to be": FDR to HGD, November 27, 1944. Quoted in Mitchell, *Tricky Dick*, 23.

80 "shrewish voice": *Los Angeles Examiner* (July 22, 1944).

80 "self-seeking, highly perfumed, smelly old girl": Harry Crowe, quoted in Mitchell, *Tricky Dick*, 4, 272 n.

80 "sufficiently odd": From HGD speech, "Women's Status in a Changing World," delivered February 20, 1950. HGD Papers, box 181.

80 "the bitch from California": Quoted in Roger Morris, 621.

81 "HELEN VS. CLARE": *Chicago Sun-Times* (July 16, 1944).

81 "How about a nation-wide": Quoted in O'Connor, 93.

81 "I'm not going to": *New York Daily News* (July 10, 1944).

81 "great respect for Mrs. Luce": *New York Post* (July 19, 1944).

81 "a strong wind of conservatism": Douglas, 197.

82 "The Democratic Party is the true conservative party": HGD speech to the 1944 Democratic National Convention. Quoted in Douglas, 197–98.

82 "alarmed by his deterioration" . . . "ferocious struggle": Janeway, 44.

82 "He just doesn't give a damn": Sherwood, 820.

83 "You tell the President": Rosenman, 466.

83 "rare loss of composure": O'Connor, "Through the Valley of Darkness," 94.

83 "Campaigning with the determination": Ibid., 96.

83 "My God, how out of touch": Douglas and Arthur, 143.

84 "The implication": Douglas, 198.

84 "Pretty Helen Gahagan": *Times-Herald* (January 29, 1941).

84 "turned around and looked at Helen": Chavoor, OH, vol. XI, 255.

84 "Congresswomen's ideas": HGD, quoted in Mitchell, *Tricky Dick*, 25, 274 n. 25.

84 "the gender": Sylvia Jukes Morris, 5.

84 "arch-liberal": Ibid., 194.

84 "I wanted to make an agreement": Shadegg, 123.

85 "The time has not yet come": Quoted in Sylvia Jukes Morris, 401.

85 "communist kikes": Michels, 258.

85 "splenetic chairman": Roger Morris, 388.

85 "An embarrassment even to his most": Ibid., 347.

86 "We're in a war": Douglas, 201.

86 "his long frame": Caro, 142. The affair between Helen Gahagan Douglas and Lyndon Johnson has been written about by Robert Caro in *Master of the Senate*, Michael Beschloss in *Taking Charge*, Joseph Califano in *The Triumph and Tragedy of Lyndon Johnson*, and Randall B. Woods in *LBJ*, and has been referred to by various other historians and Johnson insiders including Horace Busby Jr., Harry McPherson, and Jan Jarboe Russell. In a taped conversation between LBJ and HGD on January 1, 1964, in which President Johnson asked Douglas to travel to Liberia as his representative, their closeness is apparent. "Lady Bird was in the Oval Office at the time of the call," wrote Russell in her 1999 biography of Lady Bird. "She overheard him tell Douglas that he had given her a full four-day notice for the trip, which, Johnson said, was 'four days more notice than I usually give you.' The remark begged: notice for what?" (The transcript of the call can be found in Beschloss, 138.) Russell further reported an incident in which Douglas stayed overnight at the White House and Johnson provided her with a nightgown that belonged to Lady Bird.

Douglas's biographer, Ingrid Scobie, quoted a friend of LBJ as saying that the two "essentially 'lived together' for a period." (Scobie, 172.)

87 "how power and sex": Russell, 128.

87 "We were cut": HGD Oral History, LBJ Library, 11.

87 "open scandal": Pfiffner, 80.

87 "began arriving on Capitol Hill" . . . "openly holding hands": Caro, 141.

87 "night after night": Creekmore Faith, quoted in ibid., 145.

87 "Whatever the considerations": Ibid., 144.

88 "I told Lyndon": Quoted in Janeway, 103, 249 n. 33.

88 For Helen Douglas's account of her daily routine, see *Redbook* (February 1945), 60 ff.

88 "At home": *Rob Wagner's Script* (April 29, 1944).

88 "an unabashed New Deal liberal": Roger Morris, 540.

89 "above all else": HGD Oral History, LBJ Library, 13 ff.

89 "As in all congregations" . . . "His style was to vote": Douglas, 205.

90 "often overblown" . . . "There was always": HGD Oral History, LBJ Library, 13.

90 "a series of surrenders" . . . "It must be agreed": Goodwin, *No Ordinary Time*, 585.

90 "For the first time" . . . "Good-bye, Mr. President!": Douglas, 210.

91 "As word spread": Goodwin, *No Ordinary Time*, 605.

91 "huddled together in mutual grief" . . . "He had them scattered": Douglas, 211.

91 "The shock is terrific": Quoted in Scobie, 173, 335 n. 51.

92 "she dined": O'Connor, "Through the Valley of Darkness," 163.

92 "I can only say": Lorena Hickok to HGD, April 22, 1945. HGD Papers, box 212, folder 18.

92 "The prospect": Hamby, *Imperial Years*, 141.

92 "anything about what was going on" . . . "he had as background": Yergin, 70–72.

92 "Russia will emerge": OSS report (April 2, 1945) quoted in McCullough, 372.

93 "as soon as possible": Truman, *Memoirs*, vol. 1, *Years of Decision*, 85.

93 "within four months": Stimson, quoted in McCullough, 377, 1022 n. 377.

93 Regarding FDR's intention to use the atomic bomb, McCullough quotes a brief agreement Roosevelt signed with Churchill, stating, "It might perhaps, after mature consideration, be used against the Japanese, who should be warned that this bombardment will be repeated until they surrender" (McCullough, 379).

93 "The politicians do not appreciate": Isaacson, 483.

94 "We knew the world" . . . "A few people laughed": Oppenheimer, in a 1965 NBC television documentary. Quoted in Bird and Sherwin, 309.

94 "Now I am become death": Oppenheimer studied Sanskrit, and this quotation is a variation from the Bhagavad-Gita. Oppenheimer was vague about the exact reference he was using when naming the site "Trinity." The trinity in the Bhagavad-Gita is Brahma the creator, Vishnu the preserver, and Shiva the destroyer. The Donne poem to which Oppenheimer frequently referred is "Holy Sonnet 14":

> Batter my heart, three personed God; for, you
> As yet but knock, breathe, shine, and seek to mend;
> That I may rise, and stand, o'erthrow me, and bend
> Your force, to break, blow, burn, and make me new.

94 "I casually mentioned": Bird and Sherwin, *American Prometheus*, 314.

94 "Sixteen hours ago": President Truman's message released August 6, 1945. Presidential Papers, Harry S. Truman Library.

95 "Few of the celebrants" . . . "We shouldn't have": Douglas, 211.

95 "The scientific community": O'Connor, "Through the Valley of Darkness," 110.

95 "We are not only unable": Oppenheimer to Stimson, August 17, 1945. Quoted in Bird and Sherwin, 318, 647 n. 318.

96 "culmination of three centuries": Isador I. Rabi, quoted in Bird and Sherwin, 322.

96 "gentlemen don't read": Michael Warner, *The Office of Strategic Services: America's First Intelligence Agency* (Washington, D.C.: Center for the Study of Intelligence, United States Central Intelligence Agency, 2000).

96 "strongly worded statement": Bird and Sherwin, 324.

96 "Mr. President" . . . "Blood on his hands" . . . "want to see that son-of-a-bitch" . . . "cry-baby scientist": Ibid., 332, 649 n. 332.

97 "Long before Douglas came to Washington" . . . "This Black American–Red Russian": O'Connor, "Through the Valley of Darkness," 205–6.

98 "liberalism equaled socialism": Carter, 295.

98 "I was standing in the path of tanks": Douglas, 312.

99 "all-out, comprehensive" . . . "his domestic program": McCullough, 468.

99 "a shaky and inadequate": Douglas, 224.

100 "If I Were a Negro" . . . "quiet the righteous" . . . "no Negro problem": Douglas, "If I Were a Negro," 49–50.

100 "drove the Douglases": Brownstein, 57.

100 "a liberal is one": Kotsilibas-Davis and Loy, 206.

100 "unfinished business": *Congressional Record*. U.S. House of Representatives, 79th Congress, 2nd Session (August 2, 1947), 10771.

100 "were faced with portentous": Douglas, 214.

101 "release of atomic energy" . . . "We can't stand another global war": Harry S. Truman Presidential Papers (October 7, 1945), Harry S. Truman Library. Quoted in McCullough, 472, 1027 n. 472.

101 "As long as there will be man": Isaacson, 494.

101 "supranational": Isaacson, 489.

102 "I do not know": Ibid., 494.

102 "was still in a quandary": Kemper, 17.

102 "Unless Russia is faced": Truman to Byrnes, January 5, 1946. Quoted in McCullough, 480, 1028 n. 480.

103 "Russia to her rightful place" . . . "From Stettin in the Baltic": Quoted in McCullough, 489.

103 "call to war": Quoted in McCullough, 490.

103 "on a war program" . . . "One cannot legislate": Douglas, 219.

104 "Two of the people's": Newman and Miller, dedication.

104 "For Helen": Newman's personal inscription in HGD's first-edition copy of *The Control of Atomic Energy*. Douglas, 223.

104 "inappropriate" . . . "recommendation on political tactics": Oppenheimer telegram to HGD (November 21, 1945). HGD Papers, box 16, folder 1.

105 "back to the molten mass" . . . "givers of live": Quoted in Scobie, 186–87.

105 "Men haven't given up": Israel.

105 "the unnavigable sea": O'Connor, "Through the Valley of Darkness," 341.

105 "mental" . . . "Lots of people have": *How to Survive an Atomic Bomb*. Mitchell, *Tricky Dick*, 94.

105 "youthful looking" . . . "long bob": *Washington Post* (March 22, 1946).

106 "Senators and representatives": O'Connor, "Through the Valley of Darkness," 120.

106 "It is our task": Vandenberg and Morris, 224.

106 "a force of nature": Alis de Sola, "Helen Gahagan As I Knew Her." HGD Papers, box 203.

106 "three-hour verbal brawl": *San Francisco Chronicle* (February 28, 1946).

107 "You should tell your Jewish friends": *Congressional Record*. U.S. House of Representatives, 79th Congress, 2nd session (February 27, 1946), 1724.

107 "a U.S. government employee" . . . "*We* are made a laughing stock": Ibid.
107 "communist line" . . . "every inch" . . . "five feet six inches" . . . "I'll take the gentleman": *San Francisco Chronicle* (February 28, 1946).
107 "They whine about discrimination": *Congressional Record*. U.S. House of Representatives, 82nd Congress, 2nd Session (April 23, 1952), 4320.
108 "He has to answer you": The altercation between Rankin, Douglas, Johnson, and Rayburn has been reported numerous times. The dialogue in this narrative is drawn from vol. IV of OH, and from Douglas, 230 ff.
108 "Mr. Speaker": Douglas's Democratic Credo was read into the *Congressional Record* on March 26, 1946.
109 "Oil played a major role" . . . "appalled" . . . "He said the Jews": Douglas, 240.
109 "scattering good Democrats": Ibid., 244.
110 "threw everything they had" . . . "the heavyweight champion": Ibid., 242–43.
110 "Ironically, a factor": O'Connor, "Through the Valley of Darkness," 183.
110 "equal portions": Ibid., 188.
110 "Maybe we're just old fashioned": *Los Angeles Tribune* (March 30, 1946).
110 "secret trip to Moscow": Campaign flyer, quoted in O'Connor, "Through the Valley of Darkness," 188.
110 "This campaign is between": Frederick Roberts campaign material. HGD Papers, box 176, folder 6.
111 "I have long felt": HGD to the Lybecks, November 6, 1946. Quoted in O'Connor, "Through the Valley of Darkness," 201.
111 "Not only did Douglas beat back": O'Connor, "Through the Valley of Darkness," 195.
112 "You don't know what a relief": Quoted in Scobie, 196.
113 "For her": Douglas, *The Eleanor Roosevelt We Remember*, 30.
113 "the greatest engineering project": HGD, quoted in *Los Angeles Daily News* (October 29, 1946).
113 "A tall, well-tailored": *Brooklyn Eagle* (November 20, 1946).
113 "They send the stuff up": Quoted in Scobie, 198, 338 n.1.
114 "Mrs. R says": Ibid., 199, 339 n.4.
114 "Someday we may have": Douglas, 249.
114 "Throughout those long weeks": Baker, OH, vol. II, 484.
115 "at Lords and at the Oval": Whittaker, 11.
115 "carry on": Baker, OH, vol. II, 484.
116 "I have only one real concern": Quoted in Jones, 109.
116 "I did not know her" . . . "I went straight from the hall" . . . "What about stopping here" . . . "So after a little argument" . . . "As soon as we sat down" . . . "From that day" . . . "But all the time" . . . "You may draw your own" . . . "Gradually we found" . . . "immensely reluctant" . . . "I was bundled into": Baker, OH, vol. II, 180–83. Philip Noel-Baker's oral history interview was conducted by Amelia R. Fry on July 18, 1976, at the lakeside cottage on the Helen Gahagan and Melvyn Douglas compound at Fairlee, Vermont. Before the interview began, Helen prepared to leave the room and, turning to Noel-Baker, said laughingly: "Philip dear, you must be quite candid. This is for history, you know. You can say anything. I intend

to go upstairs and take a nap while you are recording." Ms. Fry noted that the Noel-Baker interview had a unique complexity. "However, under his reserve, under the perfection of his diction, was something more, a Philip Noel-Baker essence of sorts. It was communicated through a twinkle in his steady, bright eyes, as though whatever he said might have further meaning and his private game was to see who could catch it. A two-level conversation."

"When she sits on my bed and gives me tea in the morning I feel exactly as I felt in 1946," he recalled thirty years later. "Need I say more?"

While Noel-Baker's discussion of his relationship with Helen leaves little question as to the level of its intimacy, Helen was vigilantly circumspect about Noel-Baker in her autobiography. She merely referred to their decades-long correspondence, including two letters from Noel-Baker that were clearly affectionate, if not evidence of a romantic liaison.

117 "an era so distant": McCullough, 523.

118 "impact on American politics": Halberstam, *The Fifties*, 3.

118 "There have been only": Knebel and Wilson.

118 "It was a mean time": Ibid.

119 "For whatever reason": Douglas, 253.

119 "tiresome" . . . "not letting them think": Baker, OH, vol. II, 485.

120 "sent shock waves": Douglas, 254.

120 "Truman felt he faced": McCullough, 545.

120 "scare hell": Boyer, 102–3.

121 "A vague global policy": Lippmann quoted in Steele, 438–39.

121 "Sending arms" . . . "If we tried to frighten" . . . "should have been avoided": Douglas, 254.

121 "to the horror": Ibid., 261.

122 "saw too clearly" . . . "It began with weapons": Roger Morris, 541.

122 "the diabolic machinations" . . . "hoodwinked and duped": Quoted in Summers, *Official and Confidential,* 159–60.

122 "Is there any one area?": Roger Morris, 354.

122 "To kick off": Fariello, 255.

123 "The result was to be" . . . "the famous Hollywood Ten": Roger Morris, 354. The Hollywood Ten screenwriters were John Howard Lawson, Dalton Trumbo, Albert Maltz, Alvah Bessie, Samuel Ornitz, Herbert Biberman, Edward Dmytryk, Adrian Scott, Ring Lardner Jr., and Lester Cole.

123 "If the communists take over": Quoted in Douglas, 259.

123 "a handful of us" . . . "vanishing moderates": Douglas, 259–60.

123 "tragic farce": HGD Papers, box 81, folder 3.

123 "It is logical": Marshall speech, quoted in Mosley, 404–5.

124 "a model of economic" . . . "The answer" . . . "cooperated splendidly": Douglas, 265.

124 "Ironically, despite the hope": Ibid., 267.

125 "There was an embarrassed silence" . . . "They said good night" . . . "Mr. Secretary" . . . "conciliation and peaceful coexistence" . . . "manipulators": Ibid., 263–64.

125 "dangerous nonsense": Ibid., 273.

125 "good name" . . . "walked out in protest" . . . "a lost soul": Ibid., 263–64.

126 "We had a pleasant chat" . . . "ignorance of government": Ibid., 224.

126 "non-Communist liberal reponse": McCullough, 632.

126 "the Negroes don't cotton": Undated letter from Lybeck to HGD, quoted in O'Connor, "Through the Valley of Darkness," 332.

127 "I had disagreed": Douglas, 273.

127 "influential Democrats": Ibid., 274.

127 "I was generally astonished": Ibid.

127 "first genuine boom": Quoted in Scobie, 219.

128 "Can't the women of the country": Letter to Douglas from an unidentified woman, quoted in O'Connor, "Through the Valley of Darkness," 265.

128 "Congressmen were drooling": *Los Angeles Daily News* (May 9, 1947).

128 "Douglas is an experienced shopper": *San Francisco News* (April 29, 1948).

128 "unfurled with the grace" . . . "resurrect even just the shadow": O'Connor, "Through the Valley of Darkness," 334.

129 "All of the oratory": HGD, 1948 speech to the National Democratic Convention. Quoted in ibid., 335.

129 "To some degree": Douglas, 278.

129 "hatred of you": Lybeck to HGD, April 14, 1947. Quoted in O'Connor, "Through the Valley of Darkness," 312.

130 "I miss your intelligence": MD to HGD. Quoted in Scobie, 216.

130 "He had no yardstick": Douglas, 260.

131 "He had made the greatest": Ybarra, 435.

131 "superanimated whirlwind": "The Douglas Touch." *Fortnight* (January 21, 1959), 8.

131 "As a Congresswoman": O'Connor, "Through the Valley of Darkness," 6.

132 "I am getting": Chavoor quoted in Scobie, 224.

132 "in general, act like" . . . "G'night Senator": Lybeck to HGD, quoted in O'Connor, "Through the Valley of Darkness," 347.

132 "must have looked on Smith": Ibid., 349.

133 "communism upon the people" . . . "undesirables": U.S. Rep. Alfred Elliott, quoted in *Dinuba Sentinel* (April 10, 1947).

133 "elected by the little people": *Frontier* (February 15, 1950).

133 "with precisely opposite": Roger Morris, 544.

134 "would not hesitate to use": Ibid., 65.

134 "stood out from the beginning": Ibid., 117.

134 "rugged individualist" . . . "come up the hard way": Ibid., 223–24.

134 "He had wed a woman": Ibid., 229.

135 "young, brilliantly combative": Mitchell, *Campaign*, 155.

135 "some conservative ideas": Mitchell, *Tricky Dick*, 29.

135 "Dear Richard": HGD to Nixon, June 4, 1949. Quoted in ibid.

135 "95%": *San Diego Union* (March 26, 1950).

136 "This was the big leagues": Author's interview with Jack Clarke, March 18, 2008.

136 "I'd rather lose you": Lybeck to HGD, July 22, 1949. Quoted in Roger Morris, 545.

136 "If she makes up her mind": Quoted in Douglas, 286.

136 "stellar attraction on his own": Quoted in Scobie, 227.

137 "If Helen decides to run" . . . "hell living through the uncertainty": Chavoor to Lybeck, quoted in O'Connor, "Through the Valley of Darkness," 360.

137 "a scheme that seemed foolhardy": Douglas, 288.

137 "After all, Nixon will be running": Quoted in Watkins, 851.

137 "Mr. & Mrs. American Citizen" . . . "intensive study expedition": Douglas, 284.

138 "remove one of the most dedicated": Ibid., 286.

138 "Her entry": Nixon, *Six Crises*, 72.

FOUR: PINK LADY 1950

139 "right nice hair-do": *Los Angeles Daily News*, quoted in Mitchell, *Tricky Dick*, 143.

139 "hinting darkly at secret ties": Roger Morris, 579.

140 "set the record straight": Quoted in Douglas, 310.

140 "I failed to take his attacks" . . . "I just thought it was ridiculous": Douglas, 321.

141 "genocide machine": Bird and Sherwin, 419.

142 "As McCarthyism entered": Roger Morris, 503.

142 "was creating the hottest news" . . . "was to play a prominent role": Douglas, 279.

142 "The air was so charged": Block, 144.

142 "I know that it is rumored": Quoted in Scobie, 206.

143 "The Democratic Party has been captured": Roger Morris, 535.

143 "back-room strategists": Douglas, 293.

143 "That's all it took": Quoted in ibid., 296.

144 "Political power": McDougal, 192.

144 "slap her around a bit": *Los Angeles Times* (May 18, 1950).

144 "so-called Democrat": Quoted in Douglas, 297.

144 "If my entrance": Boddy to Downey, quoted in Roger Morris, 554.

144 "In short": O'Connor, "Through the Valley of Darkness," 363.

144 "revenge": Douglas, 298.

145 "sound liberals" . . . "on his team": *Los Angeles Daily News* (May 18, 1950).

145 "comfort to the Soviet tyranny": Downey, quoted in Douglas, 300.

145 "Richard Nixon greeted": Roger Morris, 553.

145 "a crippling blow": Douglas, 298.

145 "one of California's": *San Diego Union* (April 2, 1950).

145 "afloat with $250,000 options": Douglas, 298.

146 "softly suffused with pink": Hearst quoted in Mitchell, *Tricky Dick*, 106, 284 n.

146 "We are going to win this fight": HGD to Amerigo Bozzani, October 14, 1949. Quoted in Scobie, 229, 343 n. 15.

146 "I'm scared to death": Tipton quoted in Scobie, 232.

146 "the hardest thing about Helen": Ed Lybeck quoted in Scobie, 155.

147 "The whole GOP campaign": Quoted in Roger Morris, 555.

147 "As One Democrat to Another" . . . "Is Helen Douglas a Democrat?" . . . "the man who puts country": Douglas, 301.

147 "The car will stop": Quoted in Mitchell, *Tricky Dick*, 51.

148 "He gave a magnificent speech": Roger Morris, 556–57.

148 "godless would-be 'supermen'" *Los Angeles Herald Examiner* (April 17, 1950).

148 "stream of treason": Nixon, *Six Crises*, 69.

148 "wearing the satisfied mien": Roger Morris, 499.

148 "There's no use trying": Quoted in Ibid., 557.

148 "ally of Communist Partyliner": *Santa Monica Evening Outlook* (May 18, 1950).

148 "traveled the 'pink fringe'": *Santa Ana Register* (May 19, 1950).

148 "mood of pure hatred": Douglas, 301.

149 "heretofore copious" . . . "Last year she was all over": O'Connor, "Through the Valley of Darkness," 374–75.

149 "pipsqueak" . . . "peewee": Douglas, quoted in Roger Morris, 561.

149 "scarcely aware" . . . "I was too busy": Douglas, 297.

149 "Anti-Communist fervor": Pepper, 200.

150 "conditioned on a slight reversal": Letter from HGD to ER, March 10, 1950. Quoted in Mitchell, *Tricky Dick*, 33.

150 "I am convinced": Scobie, 251.

150 "It gives me the greatest": Truman to HGD, June 8, 1950. HGD Papers, box 173, folder 7.

151 "What my campaign now needed": Douglas, 302.

151 "For a shocking while" . . . "it appeared": Ibid.

151 "The natural parentage": Russo, 64.

152 "the most important contact": Quoted in Tosches, 498.

152 "In the land of dreams": Tosches, 498.

152 "The Democrats' Man of Mystery" . . . "Within seven years": Velie, "Paul Ziffren," 111–12.

152 "Paul Ziffren raised money": Douglas, 223.

153 "Chicago underworld cash": Velie, "Paul Ziffren," 113.

153 "an insider gravy train": For fascinating details about Ziffren and the LAPD investigation of the Hayward Hotel, see Russo, 84 ff. As Russo writes: "What most disturbed investigators was the appearance of assistance coming from Ziffren's closest friend, David Bazelon, by then a high-ranking member of the Truman administration—who just happened to control millions of dollars' worth of recently seized real estate that was in the need of new owners" (Russo, 90).

153 "of Japanese ancestry": Confidential memorandum from January 16, 1950, meeting attended by HGD and several California activists. HGD Papers, box 87, folder 7.

154 "soft-spoken civic leader" . . . "hardworking patriot": *Los Angeles Times*, April 4, 1991. Paul Ziffren would be a kingmaker in the California Democratic Party for forty years after the Douglas-Nixon campaign. He would be responsible for bringing the historic 1960 Democratic Convention to Los Angeles—which nominated JFK—as well as the 1984 Olympics.

154 "Isn't it interesting": Connie Carlson, quoted in Russo, 511.

154 "I got a call" . . . "the front man": Author's interview with Gifford Phillips, November 6, 2007.

155 "It didn't ring true": Velie, "Paul Ziffren," 115.

155 "mob clients" . . . "the movie people": Author's interview with Gifford Phillips, November 6, 2007.

155 "When I tried to determine": Velie, "Paul Ziffren," 115.

155 "Chotiner and Ziffren" . . . "They sold her down the river": Author's interview with Jack Clarke, March 18, 2008.

155 "Helen . . . is still a beauty": (Hollywood) *Sunday News* (June 4, 1950).

155 "The panic was most acute": Douglas, 302.

156 "linking Congresswoman": "Drew Pearson's Washington Merry-Go-Round," *Washington Post* (June 8, 1950).

156 "Machiavelli of California politics": Brodie, 175.

156 "a man with kindred tastes": Ibid., 176.

156 "hit 'em, hit 'em": Author's interview with Anthony Summers, January 22, 2008.

156 "Show me a good loser": Nixon's football coach, Wallace "Chief" Newman, quoted in Mitchell, *Tricky Dick*, 41.

157 "ungallant": Nixon, *Six Crises*, 75.

157 "a total scorn": James Bassett quoted in Brodie, 235.

157 "who could hold her own": Brodie, 238.

157 "No club in America" . . . "Not only was Nixon": Ibid., 233–34.

157 "the man's world" . . . "was a silent patriot": Quoted in ibid., 235.

158 "hair was an absolute mess": The San Fernando incident is described in Mitchell, *Tricky Dick*, 35–36.

158 "blushing complexion" . . . "bear down" . . . "shove the 'Pink Lady'" . . . "expects to devote": Republican campaign literature, quoted in Mitchell, *Tricky Dick*, 154.

158 "would naturally like to support": Mrs. Harry Goetz, quoted in *Los Angeles Times* (September 20, 1950).

158 "Of all the contrasts": Mitchell, *Tricky Dick*, 157.

159 "The Korean War came": Roger Morris, 572.

159 "I was asked": Drew Pearson and Jack Anderson, "A Note on Mr. Nixon."

160 "She always had all the money": Author's interview with Jack Clarke, March 18, 2008.

160 "Neighbors informed on neighbors": Fariello, 25.

160 "His is the most devious": Douglas, 303.

161 "You know what I'm going to do": Thayers, OH, vol. II, 318.

161 "One by one" . . . "He'll beat your brains" . . . "How does it feel": Douglas, 304–5.

161 "untiring service": Roger Morris, 579.

161 "I believed the worst was over": Douglas, 308.

161 "If Vito Marcantonio": Mankiewicz, 50.

162 "During five years" . . . "a red-hot broadside": The original press release is in "Nixon Campaign File" in HGD papers. Also published in the *Los Angeles Times* (August 30, 1950).

162 "it just seemed to appeal": Chotiner, "Fundamentals of Campaign Organization." Lecture delivered at Republican National Committee Campaign School, Washington, D.C., September 7–10, 1955.

162 "All we added": Nixon, *Six Crises*, 74.

162 "we didn't get Helen Douglas": Quoted in Summers, *Arrogance of Power*, 117.

162 "Helen Gahagan Douglas was one of": Oral history interview with Dr. Shaw Livermore, conducted by James R. Fuchs, March 1, 1974, Harry S. Truman Library.

162 "smearing distortion": Klein, 79.

163 "I don't know to this day": Douglas, 311.

163 "a supporter of the socialist program": Ibid., 312.

163 "I don't know why I didn't": Ibid., 310.

163 "an emotional artist": *Los Angeles Times* (September 10, 1950).

163 "The effect of the 1950 campaign": Brodie, 244.

164 "Richard Nixon never said openly": Douglas, 317.

164 "a political madman": Roger Morris, 571.

164 "the national hero": Douglas, 327.

164 "political has-beens": McWilliams, "Bungling in California."

164 "which was being waved": Douglas, 316.

164 I HAVE RUN INTO: Ibid., 315.

165 "She has convictions": Watkins, 851–52.

165 "mostly trying to maintain": Author's interview with Alonzo L. Hamby, January 15, 2008.

165 "I hope everything": Truman to Douglas, September 11, 1950. HGD Papers, Harry S. Truman Library, box 63, folder A.

165 "one of the worst": Quoted in Mitchell, *Tricky Dick*, 162.

165 "They have lost all proportion": Quoted in Mitchell, *Tricky Dick*, 226.

165 "like many Democratic politicos": Author's interview with Alonzo L. Hamby, December 15, 2007.

165 "was a cultural traditionalist" . . . "cynical about starry-eyed": Author's interview with Alonzo L. Hamby, January 15, 2008.

165 "Perhaps I shouldn't": Douglas, 316.

166 "came back to haunt him" . . . "against Helen": O'Neill, 81.

166 "feminine necessities" . . . "A man goes": Mitchell, *Tricky Dick*, 5.

166 "Nixon and Chotiner had woven": Douglas, 332.

166 "Democrats, Catholics": Ibid., 321.

166 "torn the community apart": Ibid., 323.

167 "The question of naming names" . . . "As the Cold War": Navasky, 110–111.

168 "I hope you beat the bitch": Klein, 80.

168 VOTE FOR HELEN: Roger Morris, 607.

168 "one of the most skilled": *Washington Post* (October 28, 1950).

168 "a great disaster": Baker, OH, vol. II, 490.

168 "After all, it's your job": Quoted in Scobie, 273.

168 "I had not intended": MD radio speech, November 6, 1950. HGD Papers, box 204.

170 "they were about to be hurled" . . . "uncertainty, danger": Roger Morris, 611.

171 "There was the United States": Douglas, 318.

171 "The worst moment": Ibid., 334.

171 "a desolate scene": Ibid., 335.

171 "Oh, Mrs. Douglas": HGD, OH, vol. XI, 325–326.

171 "The Cold War": Halberstam, *Powers That Be,* 370.

172 "should receive nothing": "Newscaster Tells of Order to 'Slant' "; *New York Times* (March 15, 1950).

172 "Mrs. Douglas had been crucified": Manchester, 759.

173 "had gained control": Art White, *A Benign Machiavelli of the West,* unpublished manuscript, quoted in Russo, 114.

173 "The trio of Korshak": Tosches, 521.

173 "They were never going to": Author's interview with Jack Clarke, March 18, 2008.

173 "GOP schools": Brodie, 176.

173 "Discredit your opponent": Chotiner quoted in Brodie, 176–177.

174 "His enemies": Spaulding, 280.

174 "I'm sorry about that episode": Costello, 74. See also Roger Morris, 617 ff.

174 "The impression": Roger Morris, 617, 937 n.

174 "There's not much to say": Douglas, 341.

FIVE: HUMANITARIAN 1951–1980

176 "I have always thought": Douglas and Arthur, 179.

"I suppose it is commonplace": Ibid., 224.

176 "They were de facto": Author's interview with Gifford Phillips, November 6, 2007.

176 "the critics were kind" . . . "it was not possible": Douglas, 358.

176 "There are things more precious": Stevenson quoted in Kotsilibas-Davis and Loy, 281.

177 "This was the fate of man" . . . "This business of you" . . . "You say when questioned" . . . "I keep asking myself" . . . "emotionally as well as physically": MD to HGD, and HGD to MD, quoted in Scobie, 292–293.

179 "Happy New Year, sweetheart" . . . "I'm cutting down the military": LBJ to HGD, quoted in Beschloss, 137. The intimate tone of this taped conversation is unmistakable.

180 "He had supplied her": Beschloss, 268 n.6.

180 "her husband's flaunting": Woods, 481.

180 "So at breakfast": Beschloss, 268 n. 6.

180 "Dear Jack Valenti": HGD to Jack Valenti, April 1964. HGD Files, LBJ Presidential Library.

180 "Dear Bill Moyer[s]": HGD to Bill Moyers, January 1, 1964. HGD Files, LBJ Presidential Library.

180 "Do you have any objections?": HGD to LBJ, January 4, 1964. HGD Files, LBJ Presidential Library.

181 "I left New York": Noel-Baker to HGD, quoted in Scobie, 291.

181 "While she was with me": Philip Noel-Baker, OH, vol. II, 493.

181 "At time, history and fate": LBJ speech to a joint session of Congress, March 15, 1965.

181 "one of the epic orations": Philip Noel-Baker, OH, vol. II, 493.

182 "Vietnam is far away": LBJ speech, April 7, 1965.

182 "Lyndon has made the speech" . . . "Helen and I were both wrong": Philip Noel-Baker, OH, vol. II, 493.

182 "was against everything" . . . "a stump in the way of the plow" . . . "was not indifferent" . . . "Great White Father" . . . "rationalize the suffering" . . . "he would make things right" . . . "cleaning up the military" . . . "Oh, Lyndon": HGD Files, LBJ Presidential Library.

183 "I didn't try to contact": Douglas, 388.

183 "Khrushchev is an old man": Ibid., 386.

183 "It was no use": Ibid., 388.

184 "struck me as sad": Ibid., 389.

EPILOGUE

185 "She was a light": Quoted in Scobie, xv.

185 "He is way beyond": Dean interview with Strobe Talbott in *Salon*, March 31, 2004. "It appears the Watergate prosecutors were interested in Rove's activities in 1972," Dean told an interviewer thirty years later, "but because they had bigger fish to fry they did not aggressively investigate him." Chotiner's protégé at the time was Lee Atwater, who engineered President George H. W. Bush's victory in 1988 with the notorious "Willie Horton" ad against Michael Dukakis. "Atwater made dirty politics into an art form," according to Dean. Chotiner was a Nixon operative from the 1940s until his death in 1974 following a mysterious car accident outside the home of one of Nixon's rivals, Democratic Senator Edward Kennedy.

186 "I raised the matter": Douglas, 398–99.

186 "I threw myself": Ibid., 401.

186 "I don't feel the need": Israel.

186 "People rather expected": Quoted in Douglas, 403.

187 "There are more women": Israel.

187 "Women themselves fail women": Ibid.

187 "Since government is only housekeeping": Scobie, 209.

187 "I was not one of those 200,000": Douglas, 233.

187 "as smart as she is beautiful": Quoted in Mitchell, *Tricky Dick*. xviii.

188 "MUTED TONES OF QUIET AUTHORITY" . . . "tool for playing with the boys": *Washington Post* (November 10, 2006).

188 "Will this country want to": *Rush Limbaugh Show*, December 17, 2007.

188 "babe" . . . "doesn't have to wear": *Rush Limbaugh Show*, August 29, 2008.

188 "plastered on suggestive": "Charges of Sexism, Racism, Fly in Presidential Race." Julie Carr Smith, Associated Press (September 24, 2008).

188 "Everyone is treating Sarah": http://gawker.com/5055436/how-we-all-got-permission-to-be-sexist-about-sarah-palin.

189 "I feel sure that at some time": Philip Noel-Baker, OH, vol. II, 490.

189 "It's you who should be running": Ibid.

189 "as individuals, not as women": HGD speech to the Business and Professional Women's Club of Fresno, February 20, 1950. Quoted in Mitchell, *Tricky Dick*, 70.

190 "I cried when I was moved": Douglas and Arthur, 224.

190 "I get great delight": Israel.

190 "She was entranced always": MD introduction, in Douglas, x.

BIBLIOGRAPHY

BOOKS

Abell, Tyler, ed. *Drew Pearson's Diaries: 1949–1959.* New York: Henry Holt, 1974.

Acheson, Dean. *Present at the Creation.* New York: Norton, 1969.

Ackerman, Kenneth D. *Young J. Edgar Hoover, the Red Scare, and the Assault on Civil Liberties.* New York: Carroll & Graf, 2007.

Alpern, Sara, et al., eds. *The Challenge of Feminist Biography: Writing the Lives of Modern American Women.* Urbana: University of Illinois Press, 1992.

Barnard, Hollinger, ed. *Outside the Magic Circle: The Autobiography of Virginia Foster Durr.* Tuscaloosa: University of Alabama Press, 1985.

Bernstein, Walter. *Inside Out: A Memoir of the Blacklist.* New York: Alfred A. Knopf, 1996.

Beschloss, Michael R. *Taking Charge: The Johnson White House Tapes, 1963–1964.* New York: Simon & Schuster, 1997.

Bird, Kai, and Martin J. Sherwin. *American Prometheus: The Triumph and Tragedy of J. Robert Oppenheimer.* New York: Vintage, 2006.

Bird, Kai, and Lawrence Lifschultz, eds. *Hiroshima's Shadow.* Stony Creek, Connecticut: The Pamphleteer's Press, 1998.

Black, Conrad. *Franklin Delano Roosevelt.* New York: Public Affairs, 2003.

Block, Herb. *The Herblock Book.* Boston: Beacon, 1952.

Boyer, Paul. *By the Bomb's Early Light: American Thought and Culture at the Dawn of the Atomic Age.* New York: Pantheon, 1985.

Brodie, Fawn M. *Richard Nixon: The Shaping of His Character.* New York: W.W. Norton, 1981.

Brown, Anthony Cave. *Wild Bill Donovan: The Last Hero.* New York: Times Books, 1982.

Brownstein, Ronald. *The Power and the Glitter: The Hollywood-Washington Connection.* New York: Pantheon Books, 1990.

Burns, James MacGregor. *Roosevelt: Soldier of Freedom*. New York: Harcourt Brace Jovanovich, 1970.

Califano, Joseph A. Jr. *The Triumph and Tragedy of Lyndon Johnson: The White House Years*. New York: Simon & Schuster, 1991.

Caro, Robert A. *Master of the Senate: The Years of Lyndon Johnson*. New York: Alfred A. Knopf, 2002.

Carr, Robert. *The House Committee on Un-American Activities, 1944–1950*. New York: Octagon Books, 1979.

Carter, Dan T. *The Politics of Rage: George Wallace, the Origins of the New Conservatism, and the Transformation of American Politics*. New York: Simon & Schuster, 1995.

Ceplair, Larry, and Steven Englund. *The Inquisition in Hollywood: Politics in the Film Community, 1930–1960*. Garden City, New York: Anchor Press/Doubleday, 1980.

Cirincione, Joseph. *Bomb Scare: The History and Future of Nuclear Weapons*. New York: Columbia University Press, 2007.

Cohen, Mickey. *Mickey Cohen: In My Own Words: The Underworld Autobiography of Michael Mickey Cohen as told to John Peer Nugent*. Englewood Cliffs, New Jersey: Prentice-Hall, Inc., 1975.

Cooke, Alistair. *A Generation on Trial*. New York: Alfred A. Knopf, 1952.

Cook, Blanche Wiesen. *Eleanor Roosevelt*. Vol. 2, *1933–1938*. New York: Viking, 1999.

Costello, William. *The Facts About Nixon: An Unauthorized Biography*. New York: Viking, 1960.

Dana, Richard H. *Two Years Before the Mast: A Personal Narrative of Life at Sea* (reprint) 1887; New York: Viking Penguin, 1981.

Dean, John W. *Worse Than Watergate: The Secret Presidency of George W. Bush*. Boston: Little, Brown, 2004.

Demaris, Ovid. *Captive City: Chicago in Chains*. New York: Lyle Stuart, 1969.

Donner, Frank J. *The Age of Surveillance: The Aims and Methods of America's Political Intelligence System*. New York: Alfred A. Knopf, 1980.

Douglas, Helen Gahagan. *The Eleanor Roosevelt We Remember*. New York: Hill and Wang, 1963.

———. *A Full Life*. New York: Doubleday, 1982.

Douglas, Melvyn, and Tom Arthur. *See You at the Movies: The Autobiography of Melvyn Douglas*. Lanham, Maryland: University Press of America, 1986.

Dunne, Philip. *Take Two: A Life in Movies and Politics*. New York: McGraw-Hill, 1980.

Elms, Alan C. *Personality in Politics*. New York: Harcourt Brace Jovanovich, 1999.

Faber, Doris. *The Life of Lorena Hickok, E.R.'s Friend*. New York: William Morrow, 1980.

Fariello, Griffin. *Red Scare: Memories of the American Inquisition*. New York: W.W. Norton, 1995.

Finan, Christopher M. *From the Palmer Raids to the Patriot Act: A History of the Fight for Free Speech in America*. Boston: Beacon Press, 2007.

Gentry, Curt. *J. Edgar Hoover: The Man and the Secrets*. New York: W. W. Norton, 1991.

Goodwin, Doris Kearns. *Lyndon Johnson and the American Dream*. New York: Harper and Row, 1976.

———. *No Ordinary Time: Franklin & Eleanor Roosevelt: The Home Front in World War II*. New York: Touchstone, 1994.

Gottlieb, Robert, and Irene Wolt. *Thinking Big: The Story of the* Los Angeles Times, *Its Publishers, and Their Influence on Southern California*. New York: G.P. Putnam's Sons, 1977.

Grodzins, Morton, and Eugene Rabinowitch. *The Atomic Age: Scientists in National and World Affairs*. New York: Simon & Schuster, 1963.

Grunwald, Lisa, and Stephen J. Adler. *Letters of the Century: America 1900–1999*. New York: Dial Press, 1999.

Gunther, John. *Inside USA*. London: Hamish Hamilton, 1947.

Halberstam, David. *The Best and the Brightest*. New York: Random House, 1969.

———. *The Fifties*. New York: Laurel, 1979.

———. *The Powers That Be*. New York: Laurel, 1979.

Hamby, Alonzo L. *Beyond the New Deal: Harry S. Truman and American Liberalism*. New York: Columbia University Press, 1973.

———. *The Imperial Years: The United States Since 1939*. New York: Weybright and Talley, 1976.

Hartmann, Susan M. *Truman and the 80th Congress*. Columbia: University of Missouri Press, 1971.

Hellman, Lillian. *Scoundrel Time*. Boston: Little, Brown, 1976.

Hofstadter, Richard. *The American Political Tradition and the Men Who Made It*. New York: Vintage, 1989.

Horowitz, Helen Lefkowitz. *Alma Mater: Design and Experience in the Women's Colleges from Their Nineteenth-Century Beginnings to the 1930s*. New York: Alfred A. Knopf, 1984.

Houston, Jeanne Wakatsuki, and James D. Houston. *Farewell to Manzanar*. New York: Bantam Books, 1973.

Ickes, Harold L. *The Secret Diaries of Harold L. Ickes*, Vol. III, *The Lowering Clouds*. New York: Simon & Schuster, 1954.

Isaacson, Walter. *Einstein: His Life and Universe*. New York: Simon & Schuster, 2007.

Isaacson, Walter, and Evan Thomas. *The Wise Men: Six Friends and the World They Made. Acheson, Bohlen, Harriman, Kennan, Lovett, McCloy*. New York: Simon & Schuster, 1986.

Janeway, Michael. *The Fall of the House of Roosevelt: Brokers of Ideas and Power from FDR to LBJ*. New York: Columbia University Press, 2004.

Jones, Mervyn. *A Radical Life: The Biography of Megan Lloyd George, 1902–66*. London: Hutchinson, 1991.

Kaplan, Fred. *The Wizards of Armageddon*. Palo Alto, California: Stanford University Press, 1983.

Kemper, R. Crosby III, ed. *Winston Churchill: Resolution, Defiance, Magnanimity, Good Will*. Columbia and London: University of Missouri Press, 1996.

Kennedy, David M. *Freedom from Fear: The American People in Depression and War, 1929–1945*. New York and Oxford: Oxford University Press, 1999.

Klein, Herbert. *Making It Perfectly Clear*. Garden City, New York: Doubleday, 1980.

Knight, Amy. *How the Cold War Began: The Igor Gouzenko Affair and the Hunt for Soviet Spies*. New York: Carroll & Graf, 2005.

Kotsilibas-Davis, James, and Myrna Loy. *Myrna Loy: Being and Becoming*. New York: Alfred A. Knopf, 1987.

Lanouette, William, with Bela Silard. *Genius in the Shadows: A Biography of Leo Szilard*. New York: Charles Scribner's Sons, 1992.

Leuchtenburg, William E. *Franklin D. Roosevelt and the New Deal, 1932–1940*. New York: Harper Torchbooks, 1963.

Manchester, William. *The Glory and the Dream: A Narrative History of America, 1932–1972*. New York: Little, Brown, 1973.

Mankiewicz, Frank. *Perfectly Clear: Nixon from Whittier to Watergate*. New York: Quadrangle Books, 1973.

Mazo, Earl. *Richard Nixon: A Political and Personal Portrait*. New York: Harper, 1959.

McCullough, David. *Truman*. New York: Simon & Schuster, 1992.

McDougal, Dennis. *Privileged Son: Otis Chandler and the Rise and Fall of the L.A. Times Dynasty*. New York: Perseus Publishing, 2001.

McFarland, Keith D., and David L. Roll. *Louis Johnson and the Arming of America: The Roosevelt and Truman Years*. Bloomington: Indiana University Press, 2005.

McKeever, Porter. *Adlai Stevenson: His Life and Legacy*. New York: William Morrow, 1989.

McMillan, Priscilla J. *The Ruin of J. Robert Oppenheimer and the Birth of the Modern Arms Race*. New York: Viking, 2005.

McWilliams, Carey. *Brothers Under the Skin*. Boston: Little, Brown, 1943.

———. *Prejudice: Japanese Americans, Symbol of Racial Intolerance*. Boston: Little, Brown, 1944.

———. *Southern California Country: An Island on the Land*. New York: Duell, Sloan & Pearce, 1946.

Michels, Tony. *A Fire in Their Hearts: Yiddish Socialists in New York*. Cambridge, Massachusetts: Harvard University Press, 2005.

Mitchell, Greg. *The Campaign of the Century: Upton Sinclair's Race for Governor of California and the Birth of Media Politics*. New York: Random House, 1992.

———. *Tricky Dick and the Pink Lady: Richard Nixon vs. Helen Gahagan Douglas— Sexual Politics and the Red Scare, 1950*. New York: Random House, 1998.

Moley, Raymond. *After Seven Years*. Lincoln: University of Nebraska, 1967.

Morris, Roger. *Richard Milhous Nixon*. New York: Henry Holt, 1990.

Morris, Sylvia Jukes. *Rage for Fame: The Ascent of Clare Boothe Luce*. New York: Random House, 1977.

Mosley, Leonard. *Marshall: Hero for Our Times*. New York: Hearst, 1982.

Navasky, Victor S. *Naming Names*. New York: Viking, 1980.

Newman, James R. and Byron S. Miller. *The Control of Atomic Energy: A Study of Its Social, Economic and Political Implications*. New York: Whittlesey House, 1948.

Nixon, Richard Milhous. *RN: The Memoirs of Richard Nixon*. New York: Grosset and Dunlap, 1978.

———. *Six Crises*. Garden City, New York: Doubleday, 1962.

Noel-Baker, Philip. *The Arms Race: A Programme for World Disarmament.* New York: Oceana Publications, 1958.

O'Neill, Tip, with William Novak. *Man of the House: The Life and Political Memoirs of Speaker Tip O'Neill.* New York: Random House, 1987.

Oshinsky, David M. *A Conspiracy So Immense: The World of Joe McCarthy.* Oxford: Oxford University Press, 2005.

Pachter, Marc, ed. *Telling Lives: The Biographer's Art.* Washington, D.C.: New Republic Books, 1979.

Pepper, Claude Denson, with Hays Gorey. *Pepper: Eyewitness to a Century.* New York: Harcourt Brace Jovanovich, 1987.

Pfiffner, James P. *The Character Factor: How We Judge America's Presidents.* College Station: Texas A&M University Press, 2004.

Rarick, Ethan. *California Rising: The Life and Times of Pat Brown.* Berkeley: University of California Press, 2005.

Rhodes, Richard. *Arsenals of Folly: The Making of the Nuclear Arms Race.* New York: Alfred A. Knopf, 2007.

———. *The Making of the Atomic Bomb.* New York: Simon & Schuster, 1986.

Roosevelt, Eleanor, and Lorena A. Hickok. *Ladies of Courage.* New York: G.P. Putnam's Sons, 1954.

Rosenman, Samuel I. *Working with Roosevelt.* New York: Harper, 1952.

Russell, Jan Jarboe. *Lady Bird: A Biography of Mrs. Johnson.* New York: Scribner, 1999.

Russo, Gus. *Supermob: How Sidney Korshak and His Criminal Associates Became America's Hidden Power Brokers.* New York: Bloomsbury, 2006.

Schlesinger, Arthur M. Jr. *The Age of Roosevelt: The Coming of the New Deal.* Boston: Houghton Mifflin, 1959.

———. *The Age of Roosevelt: The Crisis of the Old Order.* Boston: First Mariner Books, 2003.

———. *The Age of Roosevelt: The Politics of Upheaval.* Boston: Houghton Mifflin, 1960.

Scobie, Ingrid Winther. *Center Stage: Helen Gahagan Douglas, A Life.* New York: Oxford University Press, 1992.

Shadegg, Stephen C. *Clare Boothe Luce: A Biography.* New York: Simon & Schuster, 1970.

Sheed, Wilfrid. *Clare Boothe Luce.* New York: E.P. Dutton, 1982.

Sherwood, Robert E. *Roosevelt and Hopkins: An Intimate History.* New York: Harper, 1948.

Shevky, Eshref, and Molly Lewin. *Your Neighborhood: A Social Profile of Los Angeles.* Los Angeles: The Haynes Foundation, 1949.

Sime, Ruth Lewin. *Lise Meitner: A Life in Physics.* Berkeley: University of California Press, 1996.

Sloat, Warren. *1929: America Before the Crash.* New York: Macmillan Publishing Co., 1979.

Smith, Jean Edward. *FDR.* New York: Random House, 2007.

Spaulding, Henry D. *The Nixon Nobody Knows.* Middle Village, New York: Jonathan David Publishers, 1972.

Steel, Ronald. *Walter Lippmann and the American Century*. Boston: Atlantic Monthly Press, 1980.

Steinberg, Alfred. *Sam Rayburn: A Biography*. New York: Hawthorne Books, 1975.

Summers, Anthony, with Robbyn Swan. *The Arrogance of Power: The Secret World of Richard Nixon*. New York: Viking, 2000.

———. *Official and Confidential: The Secret Life of J. Edgar Hoover*. New York: G.P. Putnam's, 1993.

Talbert, Roy Jr. *Negative Intelligence. The Army and the American Left, 1917–1941*. Jackson: University Press of Mississippi, 1991.

Taylor, John Russell. *Strangers in Paradise: The Hollywood Émigrés, 1933–1950*. New York: Holt, Rinehart and Winston, 1983.

Terkel, Studs. *Hard Times: An Oral History of the Great Depresssion*. New York: Pantheon Books, 1970.

Thomson, David. *The Whole Equation: A History of Hollywood*. New York: Alfred A. Knopf, 2004.

Tosches, Nick. *The Nick Tosches Reader*. New York: Da Capo Press, 2000.

Trodd, Zoe, ed. *American Protest Literature*. Cambridge, Massachusetts: The Belknap Press, 2006.

Truman, Harry S. *Memoirs,* 2 vols. Garden City, New York: Doubleday, 1955.

Unofficial Observer. *The New Dealers*. New York: Simon & Schuster, 1934.

Vandenberg, Arthur H. Jr., and Joe Alex Morris, eds. *The Private Papers of Senator Vandenberg*. Boston: Houghton Mifflin, 1952.

Voorhis, Jerry. *The Strange Case of Richard Milhous Nixon*. Middlebury, Vermont: Paul S. Eriksson, 1972.

Ware, Susan. *Partner and I: Molly Dewson, Feminism, and New Deal Politics*. New Haven and London: Yale University Press, 1987.

Watkins, T. H. *Righteous Pilgrim: The Life and Times of Harold L. Ickes, 1874–1952*. New York: Henry Holt, 1990.

Whittaker, David J. *Fighter for Peace: Philip Noel-Baker, 1889–1982*. York, England: William Sessions Limited, 1989.

Wittner, Lawrence S. *Cold War America: From Hiroshima to Watergate*. New York: Holt, Rinehart & Winston, 1978.

Woods, Randall B. *LBJ: Architect of American Ambition*. New York: Free Press, 2006.

Ybarra, Michael J. *Washington Gone Crazy: Senator Pat McCarran and the Great American Communist Hunt*. Hanover, New Hampshire: Steerforth Press, 2004.

Yergin, Daniel. *Shattered Peace: The Origins of the Cold War and the National Security State*. Boston: Houghton Mifflin, 1978.

York, Herbert F. *Making Weapons, Talking Peace. A Physicist's Odyssey from Hiroshima to Geneva*. New York: Basic Books, 1987.

PERIODICALS

Bird, Kai, and Svetlana Chervonnaya. "The Mystery of Ales: Who Was Wilder Foote?" *American Scholar* (Summer 2007).

Bourne, Tom. "Nixon's First Victim." *Reader: Los Angeles's Free Weekly* (January 9, 1981).

Cannon, Lou. "The California Smear." *Washington Post* (May 20, 1973).

———. "The Forces That Forged the Future." *Washington Post* (August 9, 1974).

Culligan, Glendy. "Ladies in Politics Hoe a Rough Row." *Washington Post* (May 30, 1954).

Douglas, Helen Gahagan. "If I Were a Negro." *Negro Digest* (October 1943).

Dubose, Louis. "Bush's Hit Man." *Nation* (March 5, 2001).

Engel, Arthur A. "Paul Ziffren: California's Cure for Tired Democratic Blood." *Harper's* (September 1959).

Epstein, Jason. "Hurry Up Please It's Time." *New York Review of Books* (March 15, 2007).

Falk, Richard, et al. "Gone Nuclear: How the World Lost Its Way." *Nation* (October 10, 2006).

Hamby, Alonzo L. "1948 Democratic Convention: The South Secedes Again." *Smithsonian* (August 2008).

Hitt, Jack. "Harpy, Hero, Heretic: Hillary." *Mother Jones* (January/February 2007).

Israel, Lee. "Helen Gahagan Douglas: The First to Know the Real Nixon." *Ms.* (October 1973).

Kerby, Phil. "California: The Politics of Confusion." *Frontier* (October 1962).

Kessel, John H. "The Character Factor: How We Judge America's Presidents." *Presidential Studies Quarterly*, 31, no. 4 (December 2004).

Knebel, Fletcher, and Jack Wilson. "The Scandalous Years." *Look* (May 22, 1951).

Lowry, Margaret M.S. "Pretty and Therefore 'Pink.'" *Rhetoric Review* 22, no. 3 (2003).

MacDonald, Dwight. "Henry Wallace." *Politics* (May–June 1947).

McWilliams, Carey. "Bungling in California." *New Republic* (November 4, 1950).

O'Connor, Colleen M. "Imagine the Unimaginable: Helen Gahagan Douglas, Women, and the Bomb." In the anthology *Women in the Life of Southern California*, ed. Doyee B. Nunis, Jr. Los Angeles: Historical Society of Southern California, 1996.

Pearson, Drew, and Jack Anderson, "A Note on Mr. Nixon."

Velie, Lester. "The Capone Gang Muscles into Big-Time Politics." *Collier's* (September 30, 1950).

———. "The Secret Boss of California." *Collier's* (August 13, 1949).

———. "Paul Ziffren: The Democrats' Man of Mystery." *Reader's Digest* (July 1960).

"The Douglas Touch." *Fortnight* (January 21, 1949).

GOVERNMENT DOCUMENTS

U.S. Senate, Special Committee to Investigate Organized Crime in Interstate Commerce. *Kefauver Committee Interim Report #2*. 82nd Congress, 1st session, 1951 (February 28, 1951).

THESES

Arthur, Thomas H. "The Political Career of an Actor: Melvyn Douglas and the New Deal." Ph.D. dissertation, Indiana University, 1973.

Auster, Albert. "Chamber of Diamonds and Delight: Actresses, Suffragists and Feminists in the American Theatre, 1890–1920." Ph.D. dissertation, State University of New York, Stonybrook, 1981.

O'Connor, Colleen M. "Through the Valley of Darkness: Helen Gahagan Douglas' Congressional Years." Ph.D. dissertation, University of California, San Diego, 1982.

MANUSCRIPT COLLECTIONS

LBJ Library, Austin, Texas

Baker, Robert G. "Bobby." Interview by Michael L. Gillette, October 11, 1984. Part of the University of Texas Oral History Project.

Carpenter, Elizabeth. Oral history interviews, December 3, 1968; April 4, 1969; May 15, 1969; August 27, 1969; and February 2, 1971.

Douglas, Helen Gahagan. Interview by Joe B. Frantz, November 10, 1969.

Goldschmidt, Elizabeth Wickenden. Interview by Michael L. Gillette, November 6, 1974.

Macy, John. Office files.

Pearson, Drew. Personal papers.

Peterson, Esther. Interview by Michael L. Gillette, October 29, 1974; and by Paige Mulholland, November 25, 1968.

Reedy, George. Interview by Michael L. Gillette, June 7, 1975. Part of the University of Texas Oral History Project.

Valenti, Jack. Interview by T. H. Baker, July 12, 1972. Part of the University of Texas Oral History Project.

Harry Truman Library, Independence, Missouri

Livermore, Dr. Shaw. Oral history interview, March 4, 1974.

Special Collections, Stanford University
Libraries John Steinbeck Collections

Special Collections Library, University
of California at Los Angeles

"Present Situation in the Fourteenth Congressional District." Lybeck Papers, Collection 901.

University of California, Berkeley, Helen Gahagan Douglas Project:
An Oral History Conducted by the Regional
Oral History Office, the Bancroft Library

Interviews with the following people are included in the Helen Gahagan Douglas component of the California Women Political Leaders Oral History Project:

Juanita Terry Barbee, Albert Cahn, Evelyn Chavoor, Alis De Sola, India Edwards, Arthur Goldschmidt, Elizabeth Wickenden Goldschmidt, Kenneth Harding, Chester A. Holifield, Helen O. Lustig, Philip Noel-Baker, and Walter R. Pick. While housed at the Bancroft Library at the University of California, Berkeley, these oral histories are shared with Columbia University, the UCLA Research Library, and many other facilities. The project consists of a series of tape-recorded memoirs, which were conducted by Amelia R. Fry, Miriam Stein, Gabrielle Morris, Malca Chall, Fern Ingersoll, and Ingrid Scobie.

INDEX

A NOTE ON THE AUTHOR

Sally Denton is the author of *Passion and Principle, Faith and Betrayal, American Massacre, The Bluegrass Conspiracy,* and, with Roger Morris, *The Money and the Power.* She has been the recipient of a Guggenheim Fellowship, two Western Heritage awards, a Lannan Literary Grant, and has been inducted into the Nevada Writers Hall of Fame. Her award-winning investigative reporting has appeared in the *New York Times,* the *Washington Post,* and *American Heritage.* She lives with her three sons in Santa Fe, New Mexico.